ART OF BEING TUAREG

ART OF BEING TUAREG

Sahara Nomads in a Modern World

Edited by Thomas K. Seligman and Kristyne Loughran

with essays contributed by

Edmond Bernus
François Borel
Jean-Yves Brizot
Gian Carlo Castelli Gattinara
Mohamed ag Ewangaye
Kristyne Loughran
Susan Rasmussen
Thomas K. Seligman

IRIS & B. GERALD CANTOR CENTER FOR VISUAL ARTS AT STANFORD UNIVERSITY
UCLA FOWLER MUSEUM OF CULTURAL HISTORY

LOS ANGELES

Funding for this publication and the accompanying exhibition has been provided by

C. Diane Christensen
Karen Christensen

CANTOR ARTS CENTER
Halperin Director's Discretionary Fund
Phyllis C. Wattis Program Fund

UCLA FOWLER MUSEUM
Shirley and Ralph Shapiro Director's Discretionary Fund
Manus, the support group of the Fowler Museum
Yvonne Lenart Public Programs Fund

Art of Being Tuareg: Sahara Nomads in a Modern World is published in conjunction with an exhibition of the same name organized by the Iris & B. Gerald Cantor Center for Visual Arts at Stanford University and the UCLA Fowler Museum of Cultural History, part of UCLA's School of the Arts and Architecture.

Lynne Kostman, *Managing Editor*
Danny Brauer, *Designer and Production Manager*
Gassia Armenian, *Editorial Assistant*
Don Cole, *Photographer*, UCLA Fowler Museum of Cultural History
M. Lee Fatherree, *Photographer*, Iris & B. Gerald Cantor Center
    for Visual Arts and private collection materials
Alain Germond, *Photographer*, Musée d'ethnographie, Neuchâtel
Staff photographers, Musée du Quai Branly, Paris
David L. Fuller, *Cartographer*

Requests for permission to reproduce material from this volume should be sent to:
Publications Department
UCLA Fowler Museum of Cultural History
Box 951549
Los Angeles, California 90095-1549

Printed and bound in Hong Kong by South Sea International Press, Ltd.

Vintage photographs (figs. 1.10, 1.11, A.1, 2.4, 2.18, 3.2, 3.6, 4.13, 5.6, 6.11, 6.15, 7.3) were supplied by the former Musée de l'homme, Paris, now incorporated into the Musée du Quai Branly. Inquiries concerning these photographs should be directed to the Photothèque, Musée du Quai Branly, Paris.

Library of Congress Cataloging-in-Publication Data

Art of being Tuareg : Sahara nomads in a modern world / Thomas K. Seligman and Kristyne Loughran, editors ; with essays contributed by Edmond Bernus ... [et al.].
    p. cm.
    "Published in conjunction with an exhibition of the same name organized by the Iris & B. Gerald Cantor Center for Visual Arts at Stanford University and the UCLA Fowler Museum of Cultural History, part of UCLA's School of the Arts and Architecture."
    Includes bibliographical references and index.
    ISBN-13: 978-0-9748729-4-0 (soft cover)
    ISBN-10: 0-9748729-4-6 (soft cover)
    ISBN-13: 978-0-9748729-6-4 (hard cover)
    ISBN-10: 0-9748729-6-2 (hard cover)
1. Art, Tuareg—Exhibitions. 2. Tuaregs—Material culture—Exhibitions. 3. Tuaregs—Social life and customs—Exhibitions. 4. Iris & B. Gerald Cantor Center for Visual Arts at Stanford University—Exhibitions. 5. University of California, Los Angeles. Fowler Museum of Cultural History—Exhibitions. I. Seligman, Thomas K. II. Loughran, Kristyne. III. Bernus, Edmond. IV. Iris & B. Gerald Cantor Center for Visual Arts at Stanford University. V. University of California, Los Angeles. Fowler Museum of Cultural History.
    DT346.T7A78 2006
    966'.004933007479494—dc22

                                                    2005028611

Front cover, top–fig. 1.12; front cover, bottom–Truck crossing the Tenere Desert, Niger, photograph by Thomas K. Seligman, 2001; back cover–fig. 7.29; p. 1–fig. G.1; pp. 2–3–Anakou Dunes, Tenere Desert, Niger, photograph by Thomas K. Seligman, 2001; p. 4–Tuareg man on camel, Talak, Niger, photograph by Thomas K. Seligman, 2001; p. 5–fig. G.8; p. 7–detail of fig. 6.20; p. 8–detail of fig. D.4; pp. 16–17–View of Ahaggar near Tamanrasset, Algeria, photograph by Thomas K. Seligman, 1984; pp. 270–71–Camel caravan in the Tenere Desert en route to Bilma, Niger, photograph by Thomas K. Seligman, 2001; p. 292–Tuareg guide in Tassili-n-Ajjer region, Algeria, photograph by Thomas K. Seligman, 1984.

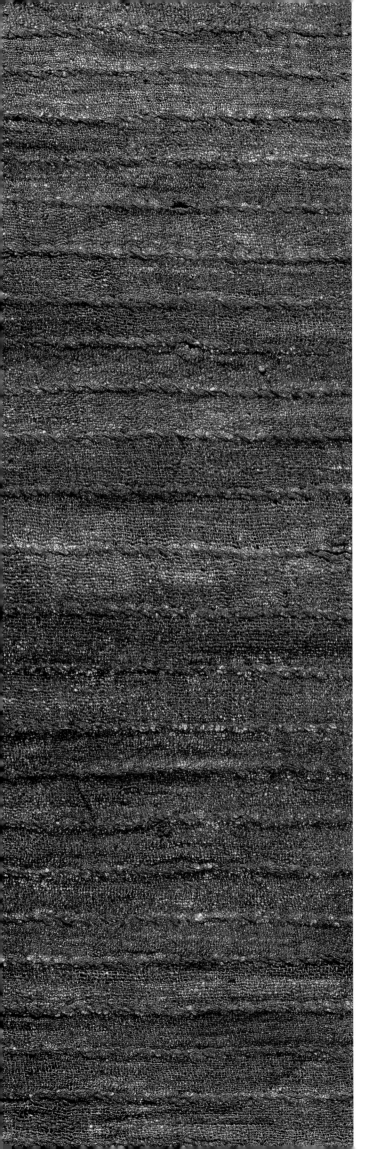

*This volume is dedicated
to the Tuareg people
and to their true friend
Professor Edmond Bernus (1929-2004),
our comrade and colleague.*

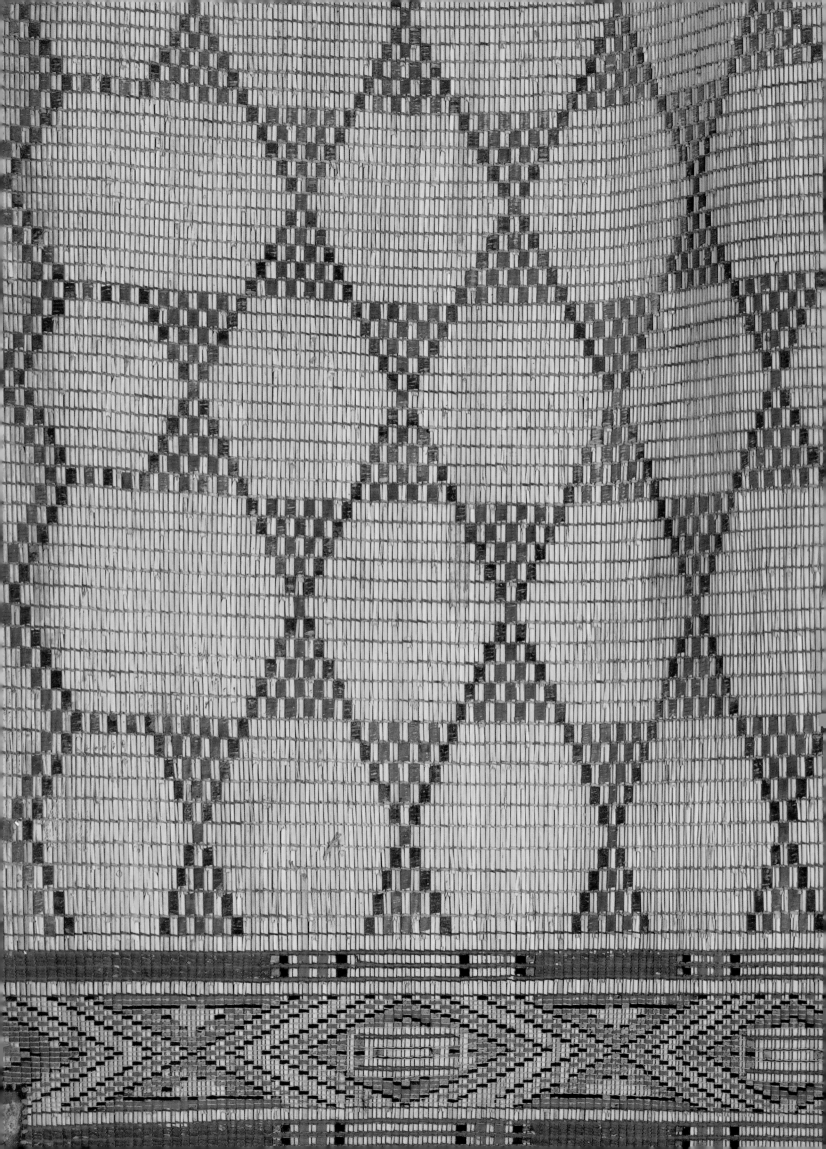

CONTENTS

FOREWORD

Art of Being Tuareg: Sahara Nomads in a Modern World is the result of three decades of research and collaboration on the part of American, European, and Tuareg scholars and institutions. It is the first major scholarly work published in English to focus on the Tuareg peoples of Niger, Mali, Burkina Faso, Algeria, and Libya and the aesthetic dimensions of their lives. Indeed, it is one of only a handful of books on any aspect of Tuareg culture available in English. The exhibition that accompanies this volume is, moreover, the first on Tuareg art to be presented in the United States. As such, both the exhibition and publication help fulfill the missions of our respective museums to bring the artistic richness and cultural vibrancy of the world's diverse peoples to our constituencies: students, scholars, colleagues, members, and visitors.

This project also seeks to add nuance and depth to the understanding and appreciation of the Tuareg and their arts. The Tuareg have been significantly stereotyped in the West—seen as romantic desert-dwelling warriors and nomads, or even as "bandits" resisting the central authority of the governments of the countries in which they live. In the context of contemporary global politics, the Tuareg, many of whom are practicing Muslims, have been viewed with suspicion and sometimes considered potential foes of the West. All such generalizations about *who* the Tuareg are or were ignore the complexities of their history and fail to acknowledge their resilience and responsiveness to dramatically changing circumstances, especially their late twentieth-century adaptation to modern life. In fact, their strong sense of "being" Tuareg has allowed many of them to thrive within their own society, their national contexts, and the world at large. However misunderstood the Tuareg may be as a people, their art has long been widely admired and sought after globally. This publication and accompanying exhibition present a comprehensive view of what it is to be Tuareg and explore in depth the remarkable arts that remain dynamic markers of the strength and perseverance of this highly inventive people.

Art of Being Tuareg is the first partnership between the Iris & B. Gerald Cantor Center for Visual Arts at Stanford University and the UCLA Fowler Museum of Cultural History. We have joined our museum staffs, a long list of international scholars, colleagues at other museums, and our generous supporters in a wonderful collaboration with Tuareg people and culture, and we are all richer for the experience. We wish to thank all of the staff members of our respective museums (listed at the back of this volume) but most especially, at the Cantor Arts Center: Bernard Barryte, Katie Clifford, Mona Duggan, Alice Egbert, Jeff Fairbairn, Anna Koster, Susan Roberts Manganelli, Sarah Miller, Alison Roth, and Lauren Silver; and at the UCLA Fowler Museum: Stacey Ravel Abarbanel, David Blair, Lynne Brodhead Clark, Jo Hill, Sarah Kennington, Fran Krystock, David Mayo, Betsy Quick, Rachel Raynor, and Polly Nooter Roberts.

The essays in this publication were written by many of today's most accomplished scholars of Tuareg art and society. Each author has been exceptionally responsive and cooperative, and all have contributed to the collective richness of this volume. We thank them all. Rose Vekony translated four of the essays from French and has kept their content layered and highly readable. We are grateful to the Fowler's publication team for their work with the editors in producing this volume: Managing Editor Lynne Kostman for her sensitive and rigorous editing and Director of Publications Danny Brauer for his handsome and visually exciting design. The beautiful object photography was done by Don Cole (UCLA Fowler Museum), M. Lee Fatherree (Cantor Arts Center and private collection materials), Alain Germond (Musée d'ethnographie, Neuchâtel), and various staff photographers of the Musée du Quai Branly.

The exhibition has drawn on the collections of several major museums in addition to the Fowler and the Cantor. We are grateful for the superb support of our lenders from the Musée du Quai Branly in Paris, directed by Stéphane Martin, and the Musée d'ethnographie in Neuchâtel, directed by Jacques Hainard. Curators Germain Viatte and Marie-France Vivier in Paris and François Borel in Neuchâtel provided invaluable assistance and collegiality. We are also grateful to Marjolaine Pierrot and Ménéhould de Bazelaire du Chatelle for providing the loans from Hermès.

We are delighted to have the National Museum of African Art, Smithsonian Institution, Washington, D.C., as a partner in the exhibition's tour and thank its director Sharon Patton, the board of trustees, and staff for their participation and cooperation.

Finally, several individuals have made this project possible through their generous financial support. Assistance to the Cantor Arts Center was given through the Halperin Director's Discretionary Fund and the Phyllis C. Wattis Program Fund. Assistance to the Fowler Museum was provided through the Shirley and Ralph Shapiro Director's Discretionary Fund, Manus, the support group of the Fowler Museum, and the Yvonne Lenart Public Programs Fund. Friends of both museums, Diane and Karen Christensen, provided major funding, insuring the full realization of this book and the accompanying exhibition.

To our many colleagues, friends, supporters, and, most of all, to the Tuareg people, thank you for the opportunity to present the *Art of Being Tuareg*.

Thomas K. Seligman *John & Jill Freidenrich Director, Cantor Arts Center*
Marla C. Berns *Director, UCLA Fowler Museum*

PREFACE

Art, gestures, and postures are all intended to express qualities of elegance, arrogance, refinement and strength…many Tuareg, both in Ahaggar and Air wear Islamic amulets, which are believed to make the wearer look great and important. "Prestige" is constantly in the mind of the Tuareg who are highly sophisticated.

NICOLAISEN AND NICOLAISEN (1997, 52)

The "art" of being Tuareg has fascinated travelers and scholars alike throughout recorded history. The elegance and beauty of the Tuareg peoples, their dress and exquisite ornament, their large white riding camels, their refined song, speech, and dance—all have been subjects of rhapsodic descriptions and all suggest a Tuareg "mystique," an existence made "art" and carried out in one of the harshest environments in the world. The essays that follow examine this "mystique," or identity, as it as been constructed by the Tuareg themselves and by observers of the Tuareg. This volume is unique in its focus on the evolution of a Tuareg ethos through time and the consideration of how "modernity" has impacted the process of Tuareg self-invention. Special attention has been given to the *inadan* (smiths and artists) and how their role within the larger Tuareg social structure has changed with the development of a new clientele and the necessity of working in a cash economy.

We are fortunate to be able to include essays on various aspects of Tuareg life and culture from contributors based on three continents and representing a number of specialties, including anthropology, ethnomusicology, political science, art history, and jewelry design. The initial chapter by Thomas Seligman provides a brief introduction to the Tuareg, their history, and the environment in which they live. In chapter 2 Gian Carlo Castelli Gattinara draws upon five years spent living among the Tuareg to analyze the role that their pervasive oral poetry plays in reflecting and preserving cultural values while simultaneously addressing new political and social realities. Tuareg intellectual and political activist Mohamed ag Ewangaye then considers Tuareg identity from the standpoint of the *inadan*. In the course of elucidating long-standing Western misperceptions, Ewangaye examines and demystifies Tuareg aesthetics and points up the creativity and flexibility that have brought relative success to the *inadan* in changing economic circumstances. In the fourth chapter the late Edmond Bernus explores the spectrum of roles played in the past by the *inadan* and the complex relationships that this unique group—at once reviled and cherished—maintain with the larger Tuareg population. In the fifth chapter, François Borel provides an overview of Tuareg music, considering instruments, song types, performance contexts, and vocal styles, as well as factors— political and otherwise—that have prompted the adoption of new musical genres.

Susan Rasmussen addresses issues of dress in chapter 6, demonstrating how Tuareg clothing may be "read" to reveal highly charged messages relating to gender, identity, social distinctions, stages of the life cycle, and the transformation of cultural values over time. Like dress, jewelry may also prove a powerful communicator, and in chapter 7 Kristyne Loughran explores the complex stances that Tuareg women maintain toward objects of personal adornment. Examining jewelry types that have prevailed over time, Loughran considers as well the importance of fashion and the changing preferences that have resulted in part from the increased ability of Tuareg women to purchase their own ornaments. In chapter 8 Thomas Seligman draws upon his thirty-year-long association with *inadan* Saidi Oumba and Andi Ouhoulou and their extended family to illuminate developments in the practice of jewelry making; patterns of teaching and transmission of knowledge; and changing attitudes and economies and their impact on Tuareg artisans over several generations.

A specific—and undoubtedly the most well known—jewelry type, the cross of Agadez, forms the focus of the next chapter, co-authored by Loughran and Seligman. Together they examine competing theories regarding the origin of this cross type and consider its widening circle of influence from a Tuareg to an African and, finally, to a global symbol. The final chapter by Jean-Yves Brizot is a poetic appreciation of the mystery surrounding the forge, an ode to those who use fire to transform metal into art of enduring beauty.

In between the chapters, photo essays on subjects as diverse as Tifinar (the Tuareg writing system), the drinking of tea, the tent, and beautification and grooming serve as a visual introduction to the wealth and refinement of Tuareg art and material culture. It is our sincere hope that the essays and accompanying photographs in this volume will encourage further study of and appreciation for the Tuareg and their lived art.

Thomas K. Seligman
Kristyne Loughran

ACKNOWLEDGMENTS

During the past three decades spent conducting research, carrying out fieldwork, and developing this volume and the accompanying exhibition, we and our contributing authors have been assisted in myriad ways. In the course of our long involvement with Tuareg populations in Niger, Mali, Algeria, Europe, and America, literally hundreds of people have been more than generous with their knowledge, insights, and wisdom and have demonstrated unbelievable kindness in their respective campsites, homes, museums, ministries, and universities. To all who have so freely given of their time and expertise, we express our deepest gratitude.

Many Tuareg friends and their extended families have been patient beyond belief, tolerating our ignorance, questions, cameras and videos, and often-intrusive Western ways. We especially wish to acknowledge El Hadj Saidi Oumba and Hadja Andi Ouhoulou, Moussa Albaka, Rhissa ag Boula, Mohamed ag Ewangaye, Moussa Haidrara, Elhadji Koumama, and Agak Mohamed. Their wisdom and kind assistance have only served to enhance the great respect in which we hold the Tuareg people. In addition to our authors, fellow Africanists and scholars Marla C. Berns, Manuel Jordán Pérez, Labelle Prussin, Mary Nooter Roberts, and Doran H. Ross have also actively assisted us in our work, providing vital insights and inspiration.

The length and complexity of a project such as this necessitate the support of many people with research, translation, the arranging for the borrowing, proper transport, and careful handling of works of art, photography, transcription, and administration of all these tasks. Among the many who aided us in these domains, we would like to single out for special recognition Jean-Yves Brizot, Claude and Katya Chelli, Odile Dayak, Jen Burt Davis, Ann Elston, Marc Leo Felix, Charles L. Frankel, Franceline Franquet, James L. Gibbs Jr., Jean-Pierre Herrero, Larry Lossing, Alison Mezey, Alison Roth, and Ellen Hvatum Werner. We are profoundly grateful for their support.

Finally we wish to thank our families, parents, spouses, and children for their love and for caring for us during long periods of fieldwork, collection research, and the preparation of this publication and exhibition. Without their devotion and interest, we might never have been able to realize this project.

Kristyne Loughran
Thomas K. Seligman

NOTES TO THE READER

Over the years scholars from various countries have recorded Tamasheq, the language of the Tuareg, using a variety of systems of orthography. As the contributors to this volume wrote their essays in English, French, and Italian, they rendered the Tamasheq into their respective languages in a variety of ways. In order to assure the readability of this volume, we have standardized the spelling of Tamasheq words across the essays, eliminating diacritical marks as far as possible. In the case of chapter 2, however, we have retained Gian Carlo Castelli Gattinara's original transcriptions of Tuareg verse. We hope that although our system is basic—and in some cases may be wanting in terms of precision or consistency—it will nonetheless be helpful to the general reader.

The Tuareg are organized in politically autonomous federations, which may be broadly divided into northern and southern groups. The names of these federations often refer to the regions from which they originate (Nicolaisen 1963, 7). The location of Tuareg groups in relation to the geographical sources for their names indicate a slow migration from northern to southern areas, although political allegiances are also known to change over time. The principal Tuareg federations are represented on the map on page 24. The federations include subgroups, which are often divided into smaller groups. The following is a listing of the principal federations and those of their sub-groups that are mentioned in this volume.

The Kel Ahaggar and the Kel Ajjer are northern federations. The Kel Ahaggar inhabit the Ahaggar Mountains and neighboring areas of southern Algeria. Some also live in the Tamesna plains of Niger. The Kel Ahaggar include the Taitok and the Kel Rela drum groups (the Dag Rali being a Kel Rela vassal group). The Kel Ajjer live in the Tassili-n-Ajjer Mountains and extend into southeastern Libya.

The numerous southern Tuareg groups include the Kel Adrar, the Kel Aïr, the Iwellemmeden, the Kel Geres, the Tuareg of Damergou and of Gourma, and the Oudalen Tuareg. The Kel Adrar inhabit the Adrar des Ifoghas region. The Kel Aïr live in the Aïr Mountains, as well as the areas to the west and southwest, and are subdivided into the Kel Ewey (the plains north of Agadez), the Kel Ferwan (Aïr Mountains and around Agadez), the Kel Fadey (east and northeast of In Gall), and the Kel Tamat. The Kel Geres and the Intesan inhabit the Tessaoua region.

The Iwellemmeden federation is divided into eastern and western groups. The Iwellemmeden Kel Denneg (east) inhabit the plains of the Tahoua region. The Kel Denneg drum group includes the Kel Nan, the Kel Aghlal, and the Tellemidez. The Tuareg of Damergou include the Kel Icheriffen. The Iwellemmeden Kel Ataram drum group inhabits the area between the Malian border and the Menaka region along the Niger River.

Federations of southwestern Tuareg are the Kel Tademaket, the Oudalen Tuareg and the Kel es Suq (a religious group). The Kel Tademaket live in the territory around Timbuktu in Mali. They once controlled Timbuktu and include the Kel Intesser and the Tenguerendieff.

K.L.

1

AN INTRODUCTION TO THE TUAREG

Thomas K. Seligman

The numerous beautiful paintings and engravings found on rock formations in the central Sahara attest to the fact that it was once a vast and fertile plain (figs. 1.2–1.4).[1] Giraffes, elephants, antelope, and human beings—sometimes garbed in ritual dress (fig. 1.6) and often accompanied by large herds of cattle—figure in these striking depictions, as do mythical beings. The oldest of these paintings are thought to have been made nearly eight thousand years ago by pastoral proto-Berber peoples inhabiting the then-grassy plains of north central Africa. Sometime during the first millennium BCE, paintings and engravings begin to show camels (fig. 1.5), two-wheeled horse-drawn chariots in a Carthaginian style, and Tifinar, the writing system of the Tuareg (fig. 1.7), a seminomadic pastoralist people of North African Berber origin.

Ecological and archaeological evidence suggests that around 2500 BCE the Sahara underwent a major climatic shift that resulted in the formation of the vast desert we know today. To avoid drought, the pastoral inhabitants of the region had to move north or south in search of food for their animals or try to eke out an existence in the few oases that retained a permanent water supply. Traversing the desert only became possible with the introduction of the camel into North Africa and the Sahara, which probably occurred during the first millennium BCE. Ideally suited for desert travel, the camel allowed northern Berber peoples to penetrate and cross the Sahara for trade.

Over many centuries, different groups of Berber-speaking peoples have lived in the northern and central areas of the Sahara capable of supporting animal husbandry. Most Tuareg oral histories suggest that their ancestors came from the north, probably from the region of present-day eastern Algeria and western Libya.[2] It is likely that early Berber pastoral goat herders, who had intermarried with peoples originally from south of the Sahara, were conquered by more recently arrived North African Berber camel riders. These more recent Berbers in turn mixed with the earlier inhabitants and are the Tuareg of today.

Their unique form of dress, refined aesthetic sense, pride, and skill in negotiating the desert landscape have long attracted attention to the Tuareg. Early Arabic texts mention them, including those by Ibn Hawkal in the tenth century, El Bekri in the eleventh century, and, more extensively, Ibn Batutah and Ibn Khaldun in the fourteenth century and Leo Africanus in the sixteenth century. These travelers crossed the Sahara following well-established caravan routes, which had also facilitated the introduction of Islam into the region beginning in the seventh century. Islamic penetration intensified with the invasion across North Africa of nomadic Bedouins from central Arabia in the eleventh century—known as the Hilalian invasion—which drove many pastoral nomads

1.1

Bag (*taseihat*)

Tuareg, Kel Icheriffen
Gao, Mali
Leather, pigment
88 x 81 cm
Musée d'ethnographie, Neuchâtel
48.3.2

Great value and prestige are attached to leather bags. They are used to hold clothing, personal belongings, household items, and foodstuffs such as tea and milk. Some bags are specifically designed as saddlebags, used during migration. Bag shapes are rectangular, square, conical, oval, or elongated. Some have closure flaps, and others simply have a long neck, which gets folded over and tied or secured with an ornamented metal lock. Almost all bags are decorated with colorful fringes, which have impressed, stitched, or excised motifs. Sometimes pendants and tassels are added for extra visual impact. The most consistent designs are diamonds, triangles, dots, zigzag lines, and cross shapes.

Women, who spend many months working on a single item, mostly make bags with goatskins. This particular type of bag is used by women as a saddlebag. The suspension rings attach the bag to the saddle. It is decorated with appliquéd strips of leather and embellished with geometric embroidery designs and many fringes and pendant shapes.

1.2

Petroglyph with elephant and other quadrupeds, circa 2000 BCE.

Photograph by Thomas K. Seligman, Anakome, Niger, 2001.

1.3

Painting with human figures, Bovidian period (4000–2000 BCE).

Photograph by Thomas K. Seligman, Tassili-n-Ajjer, Sefar, Algeria, 1984.

SELIGMAN

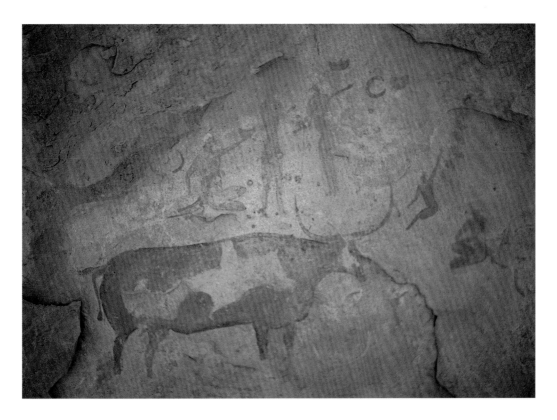

1.4
Painting with cattle and humans,
Bovidian period (4000–2000 BCE).

Photograph by Thomas K. Seligman,
Tassili-n-Ajjer, In Itinen, Algeria, 1984.

1.5
Painting with camels and humans,
Camel period (400 BCE–400 CE).

Photograph by Thomas K. Seligman,
Tassili-n-Ajjer, In Itinen, Algeria, 1984.

Petroglyph with figures, possibly humans in ritual dress or mythical beings, circa 2000 BCE.

Photograph by Thomas K. Seligman, Tirghimisse, Niger, 2001.

1.7

Petroglyph with Tifinar, circa 500 BCE.

Photograph by Jean-Yves Brizot, Aïr, Niger, circa 1995.

further south into the Sahara or beyond. The spread of Islam was pronounced throughout the Sahara and western Sudan and had considerable influence on the Tuareg as well.

In the nineteenth century European explorers often employed the Tuareg as desert guides. Some of these visitors, notably Heinrich Barth and Henri Duveyrier, stayed among the Tuareg and wrote fascinating accounts of their experiences. During the rush to colonize Africa in the early twentieth century, European, and particularly French, interest in the region intensified. The French invaded Tuareg areas in Algeria and tried to dominate the Tuareg and the other nomadic peoples of the Sahara. The Tuareg managed to resist the French for two decades, often using their mastery of the desert environment to defeat their invaders militarily. Although the French ultimately prevailed, their control of the Tuareg region was always tenuous—punctuated by numerous uprisings and rebellions. The French West African colonies gained their independence in the 1950s and 1960s, and today the independent nations of Algeria, Niger, and Mali are home to the largest concentration of Tuareg (fig. 1.8). Their entire population worldwide is estimated at between 1.5 and 2 million (Keenan 2004, 68).

The Tuareg are a loose confederation of groups of pastoral nomads, settled agriculturists, and, today, city dwellers, who speak a Berber language known as Tamasheq in the northern region and Tamachek in the more populous southern region. They refer to themselves as Kel Tamasheq or Kel Tamachek (people who speak Tamasheq/Tamachek) and sometimes as Kel Tagulmust (men who wear the veil). According to Nicolaisen (1963; 1997), the four main groups of Tuareg are the Ahaggar, Ajjer, Adrar, and Aïr (see map, fig. 1.9). While there is considerable variation among these groups, social strata (often referred to as "castes" in the literature) exist within all of them with powerful nobles (*imajeren* or *ihaggaren*) assuming leadership. Nobles are the descendants of the camel breeders who dominated the vassal groups of goat breeders known as *imrad*. Controlling the caravan trade routes, nobles undertook raids for camels and sometimes enslaved peoples from the south, who were then known as *iklan*. Other sub-Saharan peoples (*izeggaren*), who were settled agriculturists, gave part of their crops to the nobles in return for protection. Two other social groups had special relationships to the nobles,

1.8

Tuareg and camel.

Photograph by Thomas K. Seligman, Aïr, Niger, 1988.

as well as to other Tuareg. The first was composed of Islamic teachers (*ineslemen*), who achieved their status through training and religious practice. The second was constituted of artists or smiths, known as *inadan* (sing., *enad*), who form a major focus of this volume and the exhibition that accompanies it.

There are several accounts of the origins of the *inadan*, but it is likely that they are, in part, descendants of Jews who were forced out of southern Morocco in the fourteenth and fifteenth centuries and followed long-established trans-Saharan trade routes to the region of the Tuareg. Some *inadan* even today claim Lord Dauda (David) as their patron saint. They have a complex and ambiguous relationship to the larger group and are often not considered "true" Tuareg, as their social origins were from outside the culture. They are essential to the Tuareg for they make all weapons, tools, leather objects, jewelry, and camel saddles. Their fellow-Tuareg, however, regard them with some suspicion or apprehension because of their ability to make objects from the mysterious interaction of fire and metal; their secret language (Tenet); their capacity to engage the world of spirits with a mystic power known as *ettama* or *tezma;* their role as confidants and ambassadors operating between Tuareg families and groups; and their lack of social reserve, a trait highly valued by noble Tuareg.

The Tuareg do not form a cohesive whole, and they have a long history of intergroup conflict. Beyond the extended family of nobles, vassals, and the enslaved, the local unit of authority is the drum group (*ettebel*), which is sometimes named after the dominant noble within it. The nobles have political authority but are also highly dependent on vassals and slaves for the production of food and the tending of herds of goats, camels, donkeys, and cattle (in the southern region). Conversely, the nobles are obliged to protect their vassals and those who are enslaved. Historically several drum groups have joined together for trade caravans, for raiding other Tuareg or neighboring peoples, and for defense—particularly against the French colonists and, more recently, the central governments of Niger and Mali. These temporary confederations have tended to shift frequently, however, as the Tuareg prefer the relative independence and freedom of the extended family and drum group (fig. 1.10).

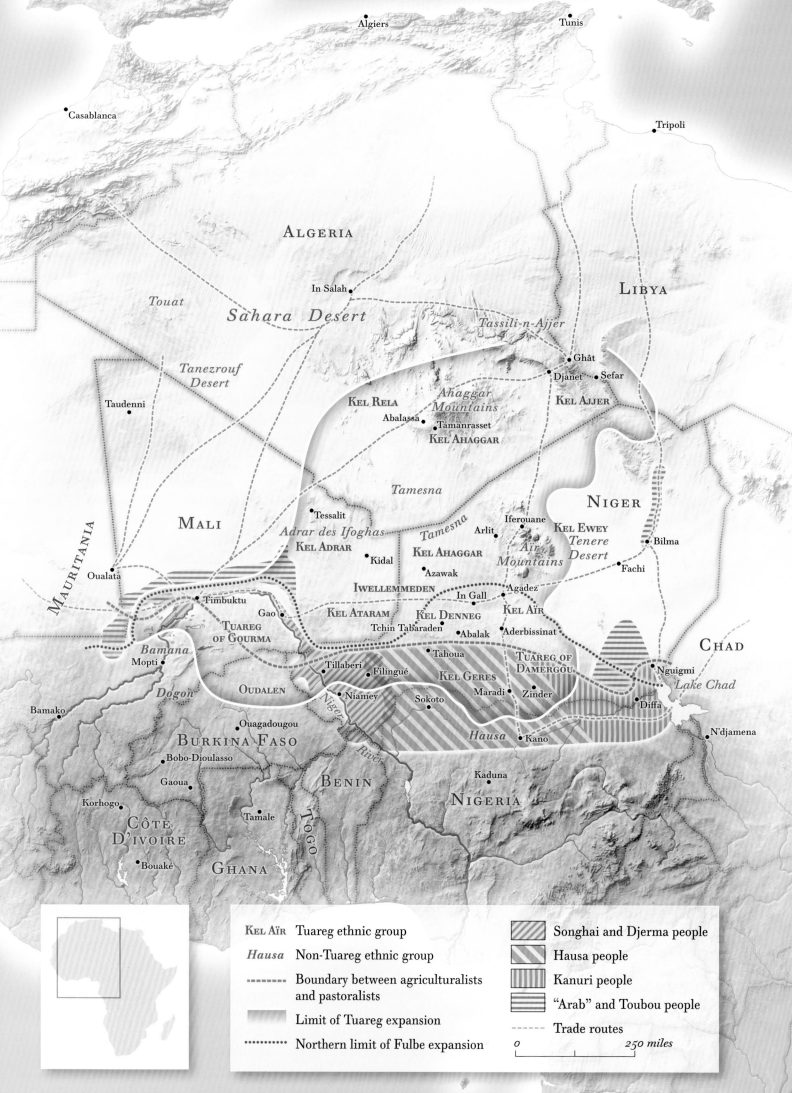

Algiers •   • Tunis

• Tripoli

• Casablanca

ALGERIA

In Salah •

Touat

Sahara Desert

Tanezrouf Desert

Tassili-n-Ajjer

LIBYA

Ghât •
Djanet •   • Sefar

• Taudenni

KEL RELA

Ahaggar Mountains

KEL AJJER

Abalassa •
   • Tamanrasset
KEL AHAGGAR

Tamesna

NIGER

MALI

Tessalit •

Adrar des Ifoghas
KEL ADRAR

Tamesna

Arlit •
  Iferouane •

KEL EWEY
Tenere Desert

• Bilma

MAURITANIA

Kidal •
   KEL AHAGGAR
Azawak •

Aïr Mountains

Fachi •

• Oualata

IWELLEMMEDEN

In Gall •
  • Agadez

Timbuktu •

KEL ATARAM
    KEL DENNEG
Tchin Tabaraden •
Abalak •

KEL AÏR

Aderbissinat •

CHAD

Gao •

Tuareg of GOURMA

Bamana
Mopti •

Tahoua •

Tuareg of DAMERGOU

Nguigmi •
   Lake Chad

Tillaberi •
  Filingué •

KEL GERES

Maradi •
   Zinder •

Diffa •

Dogon

OUDALEN

Niamey •

Niger

Sokoto •

Hausa

Kano •

• N'djamena

Bamako •

BURKINA FASO

Ouagadougou •

River

Kaduna •

Bobo-Dioulasso •

BENIN

NIGERIA

Gaoua •

Korhogo •

Tamale •

Togo

CÔTE D'IVOIRE

Bouaké •

GHANA

KEL AÏR	Tuareg ethnic group	Songhai and Djerma people
Hausa	Non-Tuareg ethnic group	Hausa people
- - - -	Boundary between agriculturalists and pastoralists	Kanuri people
	Limit of Tuareg expansion	"Arab" and Toubou people
······	Northern limit of Fulbe expansion	- - - Trade routes

0   250 miles

Gulf of Guinea

1.9
Map of the Tuareg region.

1.10
Tuareg men fencing.
Photograph by Chasseloup-Laubat, Tamanrasset, Algeria, 1935. Musée du Quai Branly, Photothèque, c.64.12653.70.

The Tuareg practice both matrilineal and patrilineal forms of inheritance and succession, which is somewhat unusual in an African context. Most authorities argue that the earlier Tuareg were matrilineal and that with the introduction of Islam by Arabs from North Africa, some patrilineal features were adopted. It is clear, however, that women enjoy a high status among the Tuareg, and several origin stories feature a powerful woman leader known as Tin Hinan. Matrilineage also determines membership in each drum group.

Men sing and recite poetry to declare their love for a woman. They typically seek a mate with fair skin, a symmetrical face, dark eyes, shiny hair, and an ample body. While men tend to be lean and muscular, the ideal Tuareg noblewoman is radiant and fat, the latter trait signifying her wealth. Marriage (*ehen*) is sometimes arranged and in all cases is an economic union featuring a substantial dowry given to the bride consisting of livestock, jewelry, and in urban areas, cash. Weddings and dowries are organized and arranged by the *inadan*. The bride owns the tent (also known as *ehen*) and all other domestic items. The Tuareg have a preference for marrying cross cousins[3] as this helps maintain economic resources within the extended family. If a marriage does not work out, divorce is easily obtained and usually requires only the consent of the parents or immediate families.

The turban and veil, known as the *tagulmust*, are the most distinctive items of a Tuareg man's dress. A woman wears a head scarf known as the *erkerkey* or *adalil*, which she draws over her mouth and nose in some social circumstances. The *tagulmust* and the *erkerkey* are given at initiation and are indications of adult status. There has been much debate about the purpose of the *tagulmust*, as it is quite unique, especially in the context of Islamic cultures where women, and not men, are customarily veiled. These head and face coverings help Tuareg men maintain the required social distance from their in-laws and from strangers. It is also thought that evil spirits can enter the body through the mouth, which must therefore be covered and protected.

The cotton cloth (*aleshu*) used to form the five-meter-long *tagulmust* and the shorter women's head scarf is obtained from Hausa traders. The cotton is grown and woven in northern Nigeria where it is dyed with a deep indigo that rubs off on the wearer, coloring the skin a dark purple-blue. This distinctive indigo head covering and the similarly

1.11

Tuareg on camels.

Photograph by P. Ichac, Algeria, 1934. Musée du Quai Branly, Photothèque, c.34.1476.231.

1.12

Camel caravan en route from Tabelot to Bilma, Niger.

Photograph by Thomas K. Seligman, 2001.

dyed clothing worn on festive occasions explain the sobriquet "Blue People of the Sahara," which is often applied to the Tuareg.

Historically, the Tuareg obtained their livelihood from raising goats, camels (fig. 1.11), and, in some areas, cattle. They hunted and collected edible and medicinal plants. In the southern areas, they engaged in limited agriculture. Raiding was undertaken to obtain camels as long-distance camel caravans were essential so that the Tuareg could transport salt from the desert to exchange with southern groups for millet, cloth, and other essential food and goods. In the past, caravans of twenty thousand camels carried salt from Bilma to southern markets in Zinder or Kano. The return trip brought the above-mentioned goods to the Aïr region. After colonization by the French, a few roads were developed, and now much of the movement of goods and people is accomplished by truck. Smaller camel caravans do continue to cross the Sahara, however, especially to obtain salt from the oasis of Bilma (fig. 1.12).

The Tuareg formerly controlled many of the wells and routes through their region and "taxed" caravans or provided security so that they would not be raided. After independence, the imposition of national borders between Algeria, Niger, and Mali altered the nature of these caravan and truck routes, further compromising the traditional Tuareg caravan economy. Raiding continues to take place, but now it is more likely undertaken by "bandits" armed with automatic weapons and using 4 x 4 vehicles to rob tourists and trans-Saharan truck convoys of money and vehicles.

The introduction of a cash economy and the major cycles of drought experienced in the Sahara over the last three decades have also significantly disrupted traditional Tuareg economic practices. Many nobles have lost their herds and have been forced to work as guards for wealthy Africans and Europeans. Vassals and enslaved peoples, who were theoretically freed by the French and the governments of the independent countries, have attained some formal education and work in cities and towns or on their own farms, selling produce locally. The *ineslemen* still teach the Koran and earn their living by running Islamic schools and making protective amulets. Generally, the *inadan* have prospered, moving to cities and towns and producing jewelry and other work for Tuareg and non-Tuareg clients—who may include other Africans, government officials, aid workers, Peace Corps volunteers, exporters, and tourists.

With the significant alteration of their economic and social structure over the last fifty years, there is now considerable tension among the Tuareg themselves and between the Tuareg and their national governments. The majority populations in the countries in which the Tuareg live have marginalized them to a significant degree. They are often described as a proud and independent people, and they have repeatedly come into conflict with more populous and powerful groups such as the Algerian Arabs and the Hausa, Djerma, and Bamana of Niger and Mali. These economic stresses and sociopolitical tensions have flared into rebellions led by groups of Tuareg on several occasions, most recently during the period 1990–1997. While these uprisings have demonstrated the frustrations felt by many Tuareg, they have so far failed to produce meaningful long-term solutions and are thus likely to reoccur in the future.

The Tuareg are understandably proud of their way of life, culture, and history. They go to great lengths to demonstrate this pride to each other and to outsiders, creating what might be termed a Tuareg "mystique." Living in a difficult and hostile environment, they are especially aware of their ability to negotiate their landscape and prosper within it. While they may not be rich in the sense of having accumulated abundant material goods, they possess a spiritual, cultural, and aesthetic wealth that sustains and nurtures them. Because they were once primarily pastoral nomads, their material possessions had to be portable; nonetheless, they were always beautifully made, highly embellished, sophisticated, and elegant, embodying a rich aesthetic vocabulary and sensibility. Great care and tremendous labor was, and still is, devoted to the aesthetic dimensions of the visual, verbal, musical, and spiritual.

☑

THE SAHARA

I lead my sons away from the abodes of man,
even though there is plenty of water,
for water makes men into slaves.

FROM A TUAREG SONG

My camel is like lightning, the finest of animals
when it turns its head towards me
its hair feels soft as silk
I pity you because you suffer,
But I too have known this pain.

GARDI (1970, 34)

The Sahara was once an immense inland sea. Several millennia ago it dried up, becoming a vast and fertile plain capable of sustaining giraffes, elephants, antelope, and pastoralists with large herds of cattle. Around 2500 BCE, however, the Sahara underwent another major ecological shift, which would ultimately transform it into the world's largest desert. It is not primarily a sand desert and is characterized by numerous mountains; vast rock plains dotted with oases and dry river beds; and sand seas consisting of immense dunes.

Trade across the Sahara was made possible by the introduction of the one-humped Arabian camel (*Camelus dromedarius*) to the region around the first millennium BCE. Early traders and explorers traveling to the central Sahara encountered the Tuareg, a people who had mastered the art of living in this forbidding region. The Tuareg have always lived in the desert, and it has shaped their culture and their worldview.

Freedom for the Tuareg is mastery of the desert and reliance solely on an extended family. Whether riding a camel and using the stars and desert landforms in lieu of a road map or driving the latest 4 x 4 vehicle, guided by a global positioning system, the Tuareg experience freedom when they can go wherever they please, whenever they please, without a thought about national borders, passports, or interference from others. The Tuareg believe that the Sahara is their home.

T.K.S.

A.1 (OPPOSITE, TOP)

Marli ag Amayas changing campsite.

Photograph by Gast, Tamanrasset, Algeria, 1951-1952. Musée du Quai Branly, Photothèque, BF.64.6707.716.

A.2 (OPPOSITE, BOTTOM)

A house made in the *zereba* style.

Photograph by Thomas K. Seligman, Erefouk, Algeria, 1988.

A.3

Rock plain and sand dunes.

Photograph by Thomas K. Seligman, near In Guezzam, Algeria, 1988.

A.4

Rock formations.

Photograph by Rita Barela, Sefar, Algeria, 1984.

A.5

Sunset in Agadez. The pyramidal building silhouetted in the foreground is the main mosque.

Photograph by Thomas K. Seligman, Niger, 1980.

2

POETRY AS A REFLECTION OF TUAREG CULTURAL VALUES AND IDENTITY

Gian Carlo Castelli Gattinara

Tuareg society has not changed significantly over time, although with the arrival of the French in the nineteenth century, there were some modifications in group structure. In substance, however, the society has maintained its values, its use of time, and its philosophy of life. Today, the traditional chief (*amenokal*)[1] no longer regulates all functioning of the group because there is a prefect, a court, and a police force—people must pay taxes and respect the laws established by the state. Most individuals, however, would rather refer to the authority of the chief than that of the government (fig. 2.2). If one can no longer attack a caravan and take its cargo or forcibly acquire the necessary manpower from the southern territories for the activities of the group, the values associated with these actions and attitudes nonetheless still exist. The Tuareg have kept their heroes as points of reference, pillars upon which the younger generations can lean. These "heroes" are still those of the *rezzu* (the raid),[2] and their glorious deeds are transmitted in epic poetry (fig. 2.3).

As has been noted in the introduction to this volume, the *inadan* (smiths and artists) occupy a special position within the Tuareg social hierarchy. Specialists in woodwork, leatherwork, and metalwork, they are capable of making a camel saddle, twisting a rope, sewing and decorating leather pillows, and making and repairing traditional arms (swords, lances, daggers, knives, etc.). Furthermore, they know how to melt and mold silver to create bracelets and necklaces. Because they work with fire, bending and dominating metals with their forges, the *inadan* are held in high esteem. This ability is presumed to give them access to the underworld, the world of the spirits beyond the grave. They are feared because it is believed that if they are slighted or irritated, they can cast terrible spells or invoke the evil eye or stop the rains and cause droughts in the pastures. They live at the margins of the camps of those for whom they work and to whom they feel they belong. As the *inadan* are always aware of what is happening, whether gossip or matters of great import, the noblest chief will usually want one of their number as a secretary—in the etymological sense of the term—among his counselors. Thus, the *enad* is considered the guardian of secrets; an emissary; a man of trust; an ambassador; and a person who can arrange an appointment, transmit information, and organize feasts. Significantly, the *inadan* are also frequently "singers," the people who know and recite poems at every occasion. They are therefore keepers of tradition.

The oral poetry one hears today reflects Tuareg society very well—a society that belongs to the past as much as it does to the present. Tuareg poetry is like a mirror, a chronicle, a daily journal of prominent and everyday matters experienced by the group. The events it records are historical, geographical, political, and anthropological. Poetry also defines the beautiful and the good, as well as the despicable and the ugly, or inharmonious.

2.1

Taitok *inadan* women playing a drum (*tende*).

Photograph by Gian Carlo Castelli Gattinara, Azawak, Niger 1965.

2.2

Mohamed, leader of the Tuareg group known as Kel Nan, and his nephew, Ghumar, who holds a portable radio.

Photograph by Gian Carlo Castelli Gattinara, Azawak, Niger, 1965.

2.3

Camel riders at dawn.

Photograph by Gian Carlo Castelli Gattinara, Aïr, Niger, 1966.

Tuareg oral poetry opens a door on the past and the inner workings of this society. It explains values and customs, ideals and sentiments, religious and moral sense, relationships between the sexes, and the awareness of the social and environmental realities faced by a group of shepherds and caravan guides who happily inhabit one of the most arid and difficult regions on earth.

The Tuareg do not write their poems. This is not because they lack a written language,[3] but because they do not want to relegate the most important matters of group life to a material as transitory and as perishable as paper. Tradition (facts, events, and models that become the norm) is entrusted to the noblest attributes of mankind—the mind and memory—and is transmitted thus from one singer to another over the centuries. As generations change and memories grow dim, however, much is lost, and today we are incapable of collecting and transcribing poems more than 150 years old. Poems composed and recited before the nineteenth century have been lost, dispersed like a trace on the sand that is cancelled by the wind (fig. 2.4).

CASTELLI GATTINARA

2.4
Dassine oult Ihemma (left), a
female poet of the Tuareg group
known as Kel Rela from Algeria,
with Khemiche oult Ibrahim, a
woman from Adrar des Ifoghas,
Mali, at an oasis.

*Photograph by P. Ichac, near Tamanrasset,
Algeria, 1930. Musée du Quai Branly, Photothèque, c.54.1417.716.*

The predominant themes of Tuareg poetry are war,[4] love, and the pastoral lifestyle.
Epic poetry is a hymn to courage and to action, to a man's worth, and it establishes the
parameters within which new generations grow and are formed, as shown in the poem
below:

I planted myself in front of enemy warriors	*əs zənga ən Gawaddaran əknegh*
I tucked up my clothing,[5] I am like a bull,	*tatəbt tazara nəqqal esheg*
dismounting from the camel I do not think	*nəgmad-du tədəgnast wər ordegh*
of anything but fighting, I will return victorious.	*a tət-d-əqqəlagh tijəwənkegh*
[Warriors] are like the rains that beat the hills	*megh tagawt təwatat s əkashwar*
the arrows are off like a storm	*imarran sawatan d əzozzar*
they will plant themselves in the chests of men	*ghattinen də meddan də gugar*
we take the sword out of the sheath	*nəlbay shin təbenen də shitar*
ready for the encounter, we refuse to escape	*nəsigarfan əgdala shiswal*
we vow to kill each other	*ege-de ənniyat n əmsəghəssar*
our bodies are a mountain.	*əmosan fədəghnan-nana adrar*
At Baniwalki we catch up with the enemy	*Baniwalkiy a ghur tan nosa*
and inflict a fatal attack	*nəg-asan tesawdat ta n Alla*
we strip Issani bare of his riches	*nətsha Issaniy əd tamghar a ila*
....	....
Because no one in our army	*id egan –nanagh a wər eha*
there is no one who has not plundered a camel.	*eshegh wər nəwegh agədəbba*

Under colonization a new enemy was added to such traditional adversaries as other Tuareg federations, the Arabs, and the Toubou.[6] This enemy was a foreign one, the French.

people are stunned	ojaban aytedam
nothing similar ever existed,	eges wala a italan
...............it is true	...............illikan
on top of you gallop	fəll-awan əsrayan
foreign soldiers	sojitan a əmosan
they have short hair,	win sattakalkalan
they do not wear the veil	əs kul wər əngedan
they wear a kepi on their heads	kəbbutan a taggan
Wakhil saw them.	Wakhil tan-inayan
Abruptly everyone stood up	igan hərəgdidan
quickly everyone dispersed.	igan fəziwikan

With the arrival of the foreigners, firearms entered the honor code of Tuareg warfare, replacing swords and spears. Fighting styles changed. One no longer confronted the enemy with sharp swords in hand, but shot at him instead, while hidden behind a bush:

We point steaming guns at them	təzzar narway-asan busatta yəha agad
the bullet crackles, it gets tangled in the acacia	ibidagdag aldom ighyay fəl təbəssagh
the powder smells like incense.	əlbəhru yətaggu teghney tan əsəffegh

The feeling of impotence occasioned by the scarcity of suitable weapons manifested itself as anger toward those who unfairly held the advantage:

If I had men	ənnar nəla meddan
well equipped	əs kul-dagh əttafan
with firearms and courage	temsey wər-əggifan
I would salute the captain	əssələmagh kabtan
with a whistling shot	s-əgerəs izyakan
that would smash his temples	wa irazzan anaran
that would crush his cranium	addagdag ilkasan
with another shot I'd ask him	əssəstənaq-q s-əyyan
puncturing his chest	irdaghan idmaran
cracking his shoulders	iffizfaz izeran
what harm did the men do	d-awa ghshadan meddan
to be slaughtered, enchained	win igzam əkradan
what harm did the necks	d-awa ghshadan rawan
of the women with swaying their hips do,	ən dad təhilaggan
that he cut off, adorned	win ifras ədlagan
and beautified with gold?	s-urəgh tan-idraghan

In 1960 France conceded independence to various Sahelian "regions" that had been part of her colonial empire. The Tuareg from Niger placed their hopes in the constitution of a Tuareg state, which was to have united the groups actually included in the new states of Mali, Niger, Algeria, and Libya. This state was never established. The Tuareg took exception to the fact that they were now under the jurisdiction of individuals they considered to be their "ex-slaves," that is, Africans from the Hausa and Djerma groups, or of their traditional enemy, the Arabs. The new governments deprived the Tuareg

2.5
Tuareg camp with leather tents.
Photograph by Gian Carlo Castelli Gattinara, Azawak, Niger, 1965.

nobles of their authority, and the Tuareg found unbearable the limitations placed on the absolute freedom they had always known (fig. 2.5). Borders, customs, and passports were shackles, and this is once again reflected in poetry:

we are in a nation that harms us
where the police and customs were created
and they will not allow a goat to leave
we are banned, now there are identity papers
we will never see the country of Touat [Algeria] again.[7]

Resistance against these new governments was organized several times. It proved, however, too weak and divided to constitute a valid opposition to the established authority. It was, nonetheless, sufficient to engender dreams of greater autonomy. Spontaneous oral poetry immediately gave voice to this desire. The poet, now a partisan, thus speaks of hiding in the mountain, as shown in the two poems below:

he with the strong braids[8] will not be captured,	*awa–dagh ekankan igdalan atərməs*
he moves toward the mountains…	*adghagh n əkizamzam mər ijwar iwan dəs*
He who wants a battle should follow him…	*er irhan akənnas allaflafet-əd dəs*

Oh people of useless gossip	*kəl-tənnawən annat tsiwdam*
I am sent to prison for you who are resting.	*hawan nəggəz səllul sunfam*
Modibo Keita, who told you	*Modibbo-Kaitt ma hak-innan*
that I called you ugly face?	*əs hak-gannegh iket n udəm*
Tell the slave[9] to forget arrogance,	*annat y akli d-ayy arufən*
a slave only thinks of the herd	*agna n akliy ad iha əsgən*
and about squeezing the belly of the ox	*dad izimmu tarfa n azgar*
the Ifoghas[10] do not want him for a chief.	*wədden ad-t-gan Fughas y amghar*

In epic poetry, in addition to the assertions made about valor and courage, there is always a reference to the feminine presence (fig. 2.6). At the beginning of poetic works on war, one often turns to women, to loved ones, as in the four examples that follow:

O Mariata who was created by the Lord
a perfect work of art, he did not betray himself
a mare with well-drawn eyebrows
with black eyelashes wetted with light...
I too am valiant
and strong, and abstain from escaping...

kuk Marəyyata s iga əmakhlakh
amaknaw dagh igzal wər ighder
tahorbeyt dagh izzillat anar
s-əshwan laggan ilhay-tət ənnur
nak deghen nəmoos agawaddar
shargagga əs wər imməkkan azzal

Daughters of our tents, daughters of Musa,
think of the evening of our departure,
the saddles of the women are ready on the
    camels, lined up
and among them is beautiful Manta
as fresh as a young plant...
The power of the Damergu has been crushed
We stole it, we shattered it...

asshet nan-nana shin dəd Musa
tishenan n əjil-di du-nedwa

əganət təkhiwa admar ogda
təh-enat təməjgolt ən Manta
tətagg aməzəzray ən tanna
tamghar tan Damargu təmmətsha
təffika nəg-et shifənzuza

Manta and Halban of the long braids
and Mariata, beloved by the young
is frugal with herself, with that which pleases,
with her forms hidden under her garments,
with her voluptuous breasts and hips
this year we made a raid of hand-picked warriors.

Manta Halban ən ləggənatan
əd Marəyyata a-ran baradan
wər tənəzzal ih-et awa-ran
isan a təghabbar s aylalan
əd win daw aghil əd səgəttan
tene-wa nəga egan zəddigan

Innocent daughters of our tents
who ride majestic camels
take the Kel Aghlal in your arms...

asshet nan-nanagh shin təmənhag
s-ak-əyyat təwan anamaggag
taggimat Kəl Aghlal dagh ləngag

It is during the most difficult times of battle that one thinks of these "innocent daughters of our tents." The poet often begins with declarations of pride and defines himself as "a tempest of wind crashing over the mountains." Nonetheless, he does not lose his humanity, and during times of weakness, nostalgia emerges. This weakness, in addition to courage, can be considered a model for young people. Love should never prevail over honor, over the protection of the camp and of freedom, over one's own independence (fig. 2.7).

I was ready to follow
the mass of faraway clouds [to escape]
when I thought of the tent
of Nofa, beloved by the men
she who has long hair
and small gaps between her teeth[11]
and well separated breasts
...I get up...

sammadrana ad nəftan
ignawan iggugan
nəkta-duw as ehan
wan Nofa aran meddan
təha təla izaggan
s əmmizayan shenan
əftaghan idmaran
təngay tadist daw-san
nənkar

CASTELLI GATTINARA

In another poem the poet confesses to shaking at the sight of the enemy:

Fear brings an ugly thought	*tos-i-du tasa d ark əmedran*
I thought: if I had never been born...	*har səmmadrana iba n təhut-in*
I remember the tent filled with people	*əkte-d ehan idnayen orshan*
the murmuring of the old women,	*d anagamnagem ən tamgharen*
the flirtatious staring of the women...	*d anazagnazeg wan tədoden*

But this is only a moment's hesitation:

Then I take up the faithful shield	*iddi-za obazagh-d ən tiremen*
I shake it, the buckles tremble	*nənnəgnag-tuw asəggagan dan*
I hit it with my foot	*nəwat s eləgh-in ghur tilazzen*
and I make a pledge that will be eternal	*nəga Alwashiy iksan dagh aman*
I attack the enemy like a demon	*nərrəmbak-kan əstannagh aljayn*
I turn them into a tangled mess of dogs	*nəga dər-san aməqqəs ən dan*
who find a leftover carcass...	*əgrawnen tamakhsayt wər ətshen*

2.8
Chemo Saidi.
Photograph by Thomas K. Seligman, Agadez, Niger, 1980.

2.9 (OPPOSITE)
Camels and goats at a well.
Photograph by Gian Carlo Castelli Gattinara, Niger or Mali, 1967.

In love poems the praise given to the beloved throws light on the concept of beauty (fig. 2.8), especially when it is compared to the unsuitable or decidedly ugly:

I know how Fatima looks among the young women:
she is like a she-camel with black stripes on her nose and her flanks
among old goats who are burned by the wind,
like a docile she-camel rich with milk from the steep hump
among ten gaunt goats hit by smallpox,
like a limpid moon with resplendent light,
in the circle of pale stars,
like an arrogant noble with ample riches
among the blacks who wear only rags,
like young grass washed by the stream
beside a dry bush thirsty for clouds,
like a date palm, splendid and blue
among small trees that the wind has turned to rock,
like a tunic made of a hundred deniers and heavy with indigo
among old shreds of horrid rags,
like a soft cloth with red designs
among old washed-out carpets stained with time,
like a necklace that has the sound of precious gold
in a heap of old steel coins,
you know how different these things are
and thus Fatima is different among the other women...

ənken təga Fatəma dagh taraghen əlmadaq-q
shilan təsakayt təgat tadgak təga tetawaq
tige də rədghan n-əhud s akk-iyan ibibbagat
tamnəst təgat tadafort tonaan təmoos telabat
ma-yofan ənten maraw boghaman iha ərkəshək
tellit təmilawlawat wər nəmmələd təssəkhat
tige də təkwənkuwet n-etran n-ehad temarawt
eləlliy əmməjgalan ket-net təsinafflayəq-q
ma-yofan əd tefənan win wər nələssh esuwət
əmshekən immar eshel aynayan ijijjarat-t
ma-yofan əd ghərfəza win wər niney tegarak
telazdaq ən-Albaday təkhalladat zawzawat
ta ənnəgbalan fantakan tərattak ak assaghat
tige də bəssagh yəgar jibrir igen tazalaq
Kura n-temeday n-sələy təshwat də baba tələk
tige də tərkijəghil ən-kaywaten wassharat
tabroq təgat təzaghant təmməjgalat kurəsat
ma-yofan əd təkrəren shin təsmaghat tabbakat
tədnit tesiraghraghat n-urəgh raghat təzgarat
tige də tərshinshənit ən-səndəran wassharat
ənkən igan mudaran wini d wini əlmədat
ənka a-təga Fatəma də shin nənay zəgzənat

The source of comparison is always drawn from the immediate surroundings of the Tuareg, the only world they know. It is a reality made of sand, dunes, steppes, tender grass during the rains, gazelles, ostriches, desert wolves, the products of the earth cultivated in the oases, herds of cattle, flocks of goats, and, most of all, the camel, an animal that is cared for and idealized for its extraordinary qualities (fig. 2.9). This may be seen in the following excerpts from a single poem:

As beautiful as two mares, she appears to my desire	*idwan-i-tət agna s-əsnatat təwaggen*
Her skin resembles palm trees, the tender grass, a garden of wheat, a flowering acacia…,	*elam tizdayen alwat ashaghor* *lambu n alkama torfen ən Tədaz*
Her braids are similar to the wings of a bird to ostriches with fine necks…	*təsaltaf-tan ofan ifrutan n-tiwəghsen* *arrawan ən-tənibzag shin rawan sədodnen*

It is again apparent in the fragments from the two poems below:

The skilled angel God entrusted her to has fallen in love with her, he has shaped her on the model of a gazelle with the golden skin of melons that is washed by the rains on the dunes of Tedbeken.	*tash ifad Yalla angalos goni də-wa yimməzen* *ig-əs-də kira ən tenert elam dada ən tilkəden* *tinad təshishum tagawt fəl gefan ən Tədbəken*
The hair covers the head like ostrich feathers, and falls on the shoulders, confused with the amulets, If you look at her hips, you are seized with madness, her hips enclose a healthy belly her thighs are those of a well-nourished filly.	*s-afalla n-eghaf tinnyal a dəs-d-iknan ejiwəl* *ad tilalnat izeran də shira iknaan əmjəljəl* *as təzgazda tisəgwen a kay immər dəs əmkəlkəl* *əd ləttadan ogganen wan ghəbberan ədbənbər* *taghmiwan wələt Bagzan tosaat ənta təbbilal*

The male poet does not hesitate to confess his weakness in front of a woman as in the following verses from two separate poems:

At this point I am a prisoner
taken, lost, trapped in the soft flesh
of her hips, rippling with pleats
on top of where the fat[12] is abundant.

nak əgmeda nəshghal
əmishaməsha ərbegh iwwaghana afəlfəl
insaan fəl əghəbber iwaar-t iyan əkfəl
ənibaabən əkkoz dagh iqqirəs aggəl

————————

————————

Thinking of her my heart turns into grass on fire.

itat-d-əktəta at-təqqəl tibərmen əha emammal

The Tuareg sense of humor is also apparent in love poems. It shines through in moments of amorous frustration or in situations that border on the ridiculous:

I come near you, my veil brushes against
your cheeks, and decided, I turn to you
with gentleness and murmur words of love,
you say to me: you are old, go away...

nərrənbak-kət as ogda əmawal
əd maddan nəga-əs adaghanghar
n-əsəttəktək iwaran idrar
tənn-i he-kay id kayyuw amghar

On another occasion, the poet is even less fortunate:

I walk in the night, wander, I get lost
when I find myself near the tents, no one is wakeful...
she is dressed in indigo; you could call her a young plant,
she sleeps and does not hear, her sleep is deep
I take the hand she uses as a pillow from under her head
she moves her arm away, uttering cruel words
she feels my body on the mats; I come near to her
the bed creaks, a piece of wood breaks, falls...

s-əsirarama ehad nətaadaz nəraddal
ad id idharan nan wər okey əmudar
əd baba təmos d-əs tənna ankom n-ənəzər
takhlad wər təla iggi dagh edəs tənakhar
nərkəb daw eghaf-net tawshet das-tədəfar
təghtəs-in dagh-i əfus tiga awal n-əmasshar
tofray-id də tisgar nak da a tət-nədahar
əghwisan fasasan wa yərzan inaaddar

A disdainful and almost cynical attitude is also common toward religion, in particular those aspects of it pertaining to relationships with the opposite sex, as in the verses from the two poems below:

The day I die my friends,
the beloved garments of Kannow will be my shroud
cover me tightly in this one
so I may feel the perfume of sin.
Hell may do what it will.

imidawanin mər katayyegh
tifət afər ən Kənnow a əregh
taknim-i dagh-əs degh ədəbbugh
ad-əggatagh adu n abakkad
tagu temsəy a wa əs təsarag

————————

————————

What more can Paradise give you?
These words are from Efellan
who neither observes or knows prayers,
he only respects young girls.
When united, they spend the day in the tent
I join them and take the place
of he who is traveling and sleeps far away.

wər ira dagh aljannat a əggen
shifir za a di itagg Efellan
wər nəssəfrar amud wər t-issen
wər issəfrar ar tibaraden
da-d tiddawnat əklanat inan
sinufagh-tanat taggagh aman
i wa isshokalan dagh-san ins-in

2.10
Woman and child from the Tuareg
drum group known as Kel Fadey.
*Photograph by Gian Carlo Castelli Gattinara,
Aïr, Niger, 1965.*

Tuareg poetry, as previously noted, does not only concern itself with love and war.
It also chronicles and is an expression of daily life—composed of extraordinary and common events and of the continuity between them. It is made of reflections and of rules
that must be respected to insure the proper management and harmony of the group and
the family (fig. 2.10). Objects that form part of daily life also represent it. Poetry thus
becomes the reflection of an unwritten moral code to which one can always refer using
the formula "as the poet says."

She who wishes to marry	*azalaf iri izallafan*
wants to be given	*ira i-dəs isimatagan*
cows and suckling calves	*shitan ərwasən barkawan*
and young gurgling camels.	*iwaran əghinannasan*
When she wants some garments	*as tənna təra a təlsa*
she will have clothes of indigo,	*anzin win Bagay tals-en*
when she will ask to drink	*as tənna təra a təshwa*
the she-camels will be milked	*əzzəgnat təməkkula*
when she wants to eat	*as tənna tera a tətsha*
the throats of the rams will be slit.	*əgzəmnat təməggəgra*
And to you who gave yourself for nothing	*ta təsməlkawat bannan*
God will send suffering	*ikf-im əməli timmam*
atrocious suffering...	*timmam shin tənəzzəmmar*
I swear I will not give myself without a dowry	*wəll səmməlkəwaq-q bannan*
without the testimony	*sadəgh d i tigəyyawen*
of the saintly marabouts.[15]	*n əlfəqqitan əghdalnen*

2.11

Oubala Ouha in a garden.

Photograph by Thomas K. Seligman, Aouderas, Niger, 1980.

The Tuareg realize that times are changing. They know they can no longer make raids, that group unity has weakened, that young people tend to leave the group and move to the city, and that their traditional way of life is degenerating. In the same way that the elderly bemoan their youth—generalizing their loss to encompass the decline of society and the environment—poetry reveals a certain nostalgia for the past and speculation about periodic natural disasters, which are linked to the deterioration of traditions:

...How many changes	...awa n-tighərwen
did the generous Lord want	ig-enat-d əmakhlakh ilallan
in the daily destiny of human beings.	y-əddənet fəl a tət-gətəqqen
When the groups were not destroyed	anin as wər əkhreban ghərfan
and life was not led in the city	wər təqqel taməddurt ighərman
....	....
the wind blew, carrying the clouds,	igar-d aduw ibat tignawen
all of a sudden you could see the lightning	walayhogan as oggan esman
the swamp filled with big trees	əsshin as balazzen fəl ghərman
and entire hills of rain flowed,	tətkar Tinwalamban tan eshkan
the frogs let out their cries	aman əqqalan tikashwaren
to thank the generous Creator	əndawan garan tigharaten
fresh grass sprouted on the dunes	agoda y-əmakhlakh ilallan
fattening the heifers,	yel add-igmadan fəl təgefen
the goats, and the she-camels with milk.	a tu-tazzagan win təbəgwan
	əd win wəlliy əd win tiliten
....	....
This is the way we live and the years go by	nəha ten-da har əglan elan
until disgraces befall us	təzzar osanat-du teqqaghen
the grasshoppers cover the grass and the plants	osa-ddu sharo wan yel d-eshkan
all of the areas we live in empty themselves	ikallan-nana kul əffofen
and the livestock is lost.	nəghassar-tan itiba ihərwan

In spite of this apocalyptic portrait, the situation today is not dire. The percentage of young people who leave the camps to move to the cities is nonetheless significant. An important chief has replaced the camel of which he was once so proud with an expensive

Toyota four-wheel drive. Another has left the large skin tent, once a reference point for the entire group, to move into a walled house, which is warm and not very comfortable. It, nonetheless, represents the "modern," according to Western tenets, a step in the direction of progress.

The Tuareg are an optimistic people, a happy people, they are facetious and they are always ready to see the glass as is half-full as opposed to half-empty. They are happy with what they have, aware of the free life they have been offered, of the gifts received from the Lord:

Thank the Lord for what he has given you and take care of it:	*a kay ifa əmeli n-tarna shelshe təghrəda igodan*
he has given to his servants everything I nominate,	*ənta a itaaffan eklan-net fəl-a dak-nəmel shadan*
some have camels that are meant to be ridden,	*wəyyad əgrəwan imnas wər əmkhatəran s-aggan*
others have cows and goatskin bags with butter and cheese,	*wəyyad əgrəwan shitan təsagne a ədnəyan d-əzman*
yet others have goats and flocks that give meat,	*wəyyad əgrəwan wəlli d-ayfəd gazzəman kəl san*
others taste the sweetness of fruit on the palm trees,	*wəyyad onofan tagayt timsəlmadən əd kokan*
others who are merchants in the markets are always working,	*wəyyad məra jolatan d-əssuk fawda iga ənəkhdam*
others have faith in God and turn to the sacred books,	*wəyyad əngəran Yalla d-əlkəttabən inəghtam*
others are artisans, a group that works at the forge,	*zannet tan nadan tawshet tay təngharbash əd lokan*
others tie, braid, and twist ropes	*wəyyad əkkan izərwan a tan-tassəsan s-ellam*
to capture animals, others hunt them with the dogs	*fawda əbbazan iwəghsan sambagan wəyyad əs dan*
others make salt loaves from sand and water	*wəyyad amadal d-aman a dagh kannan idaqqan*
flavorful bricks that are sold to the caravan guides.	*ən-bəlghan təha tənbay zanzin-tan də kəl salan*

All the economic aspects of Tuareg life emerge in the poem above. Agriculture is not mentioned, however, because it is regarded as a demeaning activity:

The government, I have learned has risen and has decided	*əslegh əlkhəkumat tənkar tənna tanat*
that we are to go to the fields, we are to change lifestyles	*ad-nəmbəg də fərgan nəsmətti taməghsurt*
that the dust we shall raise will be with the spade and the hoe	*nəssənkar təboqqa tan felu d-təgomayt*
that we shall grow melons, plant onions	*nəkrəz ak malotan nəmbəl təzməzəllit*
and potatoes and we will abandon transhumance	*nəkrəz konbateran namazzay d-tanəkkert*
take this decision for yourselves, for you it is better than nothing	*tanat-tay-za agat-tat tof-awan təbannint*
because you only live, but not to be happy…	*fəl-as təddəram ghas wərge fəl tənaflit*

Despite the stance of the poem above, which is more a criticism directed at the government than a reality, the Tuareg of the oases are farmers and are proud of what they produce and of the security derived from irrigated land, as opposed to a random rainy season (figs. 2.11, 2.12):

My garden this year is the most beautiful of all gardens,	*tene-ta afarag-in ənta ofan də-fərgan*
I made an enclosure with the branches of the trees,	*agegh-as afarra dagh ədwalan ishkan*
I have finished the work and have chosen	*əssəmda shəritan nəfran-du də-zəgran*
two big oxen from the herd, raised by Khataman	*əsshin kəmhəriran yəsshonan Khataman*
I attach the well rope to one of them	*as du-nobaz əyyan nosaq-qu dəghunan*
the pulley creaks, my soul is happy	*har təzyək takarkart ad-ak-əgrəzan man*
misery will cease, and hunger will desist from the tents	*təsawəqqəs əsshil əd laz igməd inan*
now my garden gives me serenity	*əjil-wa afarag-in issins-ana əmedran*
the wheat is high; there are tomatoes in abundance	*ibdad alkama-net tarawnat timutan*
I spend the day there while the water runs	*ənta dagh nəkallu faw əngayan aman*
far away are the worry and anxiety	*wər t-illa asshawasha wela iba n-ənəgri*
of the shepherd during the dry season	*win-itagg əmawal tamert tan əzərgu*
when the pool is dried up and the pastures are lacking…	*dad-iqqur əgəlman əsawagh d-aba-tu*

2.12
Well and garden.
Photograph by Thomas K. Seligman, Tewart, Air, Niger, 2001.

In the poem below, allusions to female beauty are not made with reference to animals from the steppes, such as gazelles and ostriches, but to the yield of the garden:

Alghamia and Thali are more beautiful than a field of millet,	*Alghamiya əd-Tahəli shin offanen karkara*
their skin is like palms, like an expanse of wheat…	*elam da tilazdaghen məda afarag n-alkama*
Young mint plants, untouched by the wind	*anaghnagh infag s-əket wər tu tedes genəwa*
peppers and cucumbers, which form a mixture,	*ifalfalan telagast win da əs iga ganbaza*
gourds all intertwined, gleaming like green glass	*izna(gh) əmisalsanen insa d-asan soniya*
potatoes and spices nestled among high tomatoes	*dəkudəku d-aghəjiy ighta d-asan natəma*
corn born among the sweet potatoes	*ənten abora n-Masar inninfag əd dankala*
spots of melons with entangled leaves	*imammanan d-aggotnen əshigdan aghraw d-ala*
aromatic plants from Teguidda n Tagayt	*səlmitan ən-nekaran winad n Təgədda n Kaba*
Bindweed from Tabzagort moist with water	*əmshekən ən Tabzagort ijijarat hadara*
grass from the pastures on which the rain flows,	*misilmisil telabot win fəl iga jankama*
coming down from noisy clouds washed by the earth	*n-agnaw əhinagnagan iga amadal luləma*
....	....
Alghamia, you resemble all of this.	*ishim əffilazlazan a-dər sawa Alghamiya cc*
I will give you up to no one, even if it is an armed man.	*wər za-kəm-ayya i-barar wala ad-ila babəsa*

2.13

Salt caravan preparing to depart from an oasis at Bilma, Niger. Note the conical salt castings in the foreground.

Photograph by Gian Carlo Castelli Gattinara, 1989.

In addition to breeding camels, cows, and goats, some Tuareg groups are also caravan guides. Twice a year, in November and in February, the men leave their camps. After rounding up and equipping a large number of camels, they leave Agadez and cross the Tenere[14] for the oases of Fachi and Bilma in Niger (fig. 2.13). Others leave from Timbuktu in Mali for Taudenni or from Iferouane in Niger for In Salah in Algeria. These itineraries range from one thousand to two thousand kilometers round trip. The Tuareg accomplish the trips in thirty to sixty days, walking eighteen to twenty hours at a time. They often walk at night and are guided, as they say themselves, by the Ashet Ehad, the daughters of the night (the Pleiades).

The preparation for a salt caravan is extensive. Men have to choose camels, buy goods to exchange for the salt, stock many bales of hay to feed the camels during the desert crossing (camels can do without water for a month, but they must eat every day). They must also divide the loads, prepare the ropes, and secure the goods. For the Tuareg, a salt caravan (*azalay*) is an important commercial venture. It is also a good opportunity to make money for small-scale camel breeders. Those who are able join the caravan with two to ten camels and make a nice profit. Many families who have camels (preferably male and in good health) often lend them to caravan guides and will earn 50 percent of the profit on the product being transported. Thus long lines of camels, ranging from two hundred to a thousand loaded animals, proceed patiently, slowly, surely, and silently across the sand (fig. 2.14).

The road toward the salt oases is not an easy one, even for those who have crossed it ten times. Every year there are uncertainties. Every year some camels are lost or die of fatigue, lack of food, and infections from wounds caused by poorly arranged loads or bites inflicted by other camels. Worry is the constant companion of the caravan guide:

In the *azalay* departing today,
those who live softly cannot participate
only a strong person can participate
a person who can endure the heat and weariness.
Last year I went there without knowing
without knowing, I was the salt seeker.
We arrived at a solitary well
called Tafagak and filled the goatskin bags
in the Tenere we immersed ourselves, and in the mirages,
we arrived in a poor desert village
we load [salt and dates] and we gather together
we pack, we tie, the camels kneel down and we stay
on the sixth day some were discouraged
on the tenth day problems arose
the camels are tired and the charges are abandoned
we are burnt, starving, thirsty
while crossing [the desert] mercy be upon us

taghlamt ezal-ada ad təsagmad
wər tat-s-iggəz iddar də-təlmad
wər tat-z-iggəz ar alawantag
ikbalan təfuk ad tələyyagh
naydan əggazaq-qat dagh ədrug
wər əssenagh a ymos ənafrad
har nosa anuw issufan iggug
igan Tafagak nədnay ibyagh
nuda dagh tanere d-təjujab
as nosa aghram irhanan indagh
nərzak-du nəmos azarereg
nəkarraf nətaqqan nəsagan nəsabdad
əjil wan sədis əzran wəyyad
mashan wan maraw ad iga əghshud
eddaz ən mənas d-abadagdeg
nətaqqad nətullaz nətufad
as nəghras yəha ser-na amarked

In the months that precede the arrival of an *azalay*, the inhabitants of the small oases who await the caravans either accumulate a large number of salt bars, dug up in open-air mines, or patiently decant salt water found close to the surface and prepare salt loaves (figs. 2.13, 2.15). These they will sell or exchange for subsistence and comfort goods brought by the caravans (wheat, textiles, tomatoes, dried meat, sugar, coffee, tobacco, tools, radios, lamps, gas, flashlights, etc.). For those dwelling in the oases, the *azalay* represents contact with the outside world, the possibility of touching manufactured or imported goods. It is an opportunity to hear new stories and to break the monotony of

daily existence. The arrival of a caravan is an occasion for a big feast, which will be discussed for weeks to come. The young girls, who surely notice the most handsome young men among the camel breeders, will fantasize about the world outside their remote oasis.

The Tuareg buy salt at a predetermined rate and sell it for twenty times that in the southern markets. Transportation is almost free considering that the men and camels would have been eating anyway had they remained in their camps. Work, understood as time in this society, does not have a price. Today, trucks would seem to offer serious competition, but they are costly and camels are not; so camels are usually chosen (fig. 2.16). Trucks and camels loaded with their products (salt and dates) can arrive in the markets of the Sahel on the same day. The caravan however, would have left the oasis a month or two earlier. The products carried by caravan can be used or given to resellers at a lower price than those transported by truck, and the Tuareg note this in their poetry:

Merchants and truck drivers
have goods that are too expensive for us
a glass of tea costs a thousand.[15]

If it is true that a culture approaches crisis when men lose the taste for conversation—when speech is no longer a creative act—then the Tuareg are far from this state. Conversation is central to Tuareg society and may be considered an art in its own right. After the cattle return, after the she-camels, the cows, and the goats have been milked, when the sun sets, the air becomes cooler and the glare of daylight fades, the Tuareg sit in small groups and talk. They talk in low voices of the happenings of the day, while stirring the embers under an enamel teapot. The strong tea that they brew will be poured into small glasses and handed to all those present. They tell stories of the past as if faraway events had happened yesterday. Time, among these nomadic people, does not

2.14 (OPPOSITE)
Caravan en route to Bilma, Niger.
Photograph by Gian Carlo Castelli Gattinara, 1967.

2.15
Salt ponds.
Photograph by Gian Carlo Castelli Gattinara, Fachi, Niger, 1967.

2.16
Tire tracks and tracks from a camel caravan intermix in the sand.
Photograph by Gian Carlo Castelli Gattinara, Tenere, Niger, 1967.

2.17

Tuareg chief.

*Photograph by Gian Carlo Castelli Gattinara,
In Gall, Niger, 1965.*

progress in linear fashion as it does in the West. It is a cosmic time, not a historical one. Here, the past, the present, and the future exist serenely together. This concept of time prevents these breeders and caravan guides from thinking ahead to a possible drought or an epidemic.

Sitting in a circle in the evening, the Tuareg will speak late into the night (fig. 2.17). There are many things to consider: the government's policies toward them, the new rules dictated by the regional administration, and the efficiency of the new advisory center opened in the town. They discuss a passing guest, the wounded cow, the fight between two camels caused by a she-camel in heat, and a Buzu (servant)[16] bitten by a scorpion while she was digging to plant a tent post. Also discussed are the levels of the water in the wells, the presence of mouflons on nearby rocks, a caravan of Toyotas with foreign tourists on the road to Agadez,[17] and then the news of the world transmitted in Tamasheq[18] on the local radio station and picked up by the transistor radio that everyone owns now. They also talk about the excessive heat and the cold, the coming of the rains,[19] or their lateness, the drought, the eventual cattle plague. Sometimes some Fulbe[20] arrive unexpectedly in their territories. They are usually followed by large herds of black-mantled oxen with big lyre-shaped horns. The questions are inevitable: Will they move on? Will they stop? How long will they use our pastures? Then discussion turns to new areas with abundant pastures. These are the facts of Tuareg existence.

A more organized "conversation" with an audience is called a *tende*. It is often accompanied by the rhythm of drums (fig. 2.18). The stories and poems recited during these meetings are not monologues but dialogues with the audience. The audience relives, contests, comments, and contributes. Sometimes those in the audience modify a verse to make it clearer or to illustrate an event in a more felicitous manner. The participation and joy in listening reside principally in the content of the story, the exploits described with which one can identify. The *tende* is a spontaneous event. It may occur during a wedding or at a child's christening or when a person returns after a long absence or when

CASTELLI GATTINARA

2.18

Tende with camel riders.

Photograph by Gast, Tamesna region, Niger, circa 1955. Musée du Quai Branly, Photothèque, BF.64.6788.716.

there is a visitor. Usually a middle-aged or elderly woman starts a *tende*. She is assisted by other women and brings the wooden mortar used to pound millet for the meal out of her tent. She carries it into an open and comfortable space, fills it with water, and covers it with a skin, which she stretches taut with two sticks. This is the drum. Softly, one begins to hear a melodic lullaby in the air. Sometimes the song is accompanied by the sound of the *imzad* (*anzad*), or one-stringed violin (fig. 2.19),[21] and by the duller sound of a small, whole gourd that is shaped like a flask. This is also filled with water and is rhythmically pounded by a woman with the palm of her hand or with the flexible sole of a sandal. The women rhythmically drum the most famous melodies and sing while the men listen, speak, and recite poems by famous singers or improvise new compositions that are often polemical or ironic, commenting in verse on news events.

The children and young people are the first to come running at the sound of the *imzad*. Then the men arrive, then the young women come, followed by some elderly men. Everyone takes a seat on the sand. They create a vast circle around the group of women who sing and play the instruments. Other women come out of their tents and join the small group. They clap their hands and mark the rhythm of the syllables *ten-de*, stopping for a moment on the letter *n* and dragging the final *e*. They alternate the song with cries of "yi-yis" hurled into space. Sometimes young men take the initiative during the *tende* and show off with their camels. They make them twirl with a dancer's grace, or they arrive at a gallop right up to the drum. They do this in jest to scare the musicians. They also make their camels bow in front of their favorite maiden, to pay homage to her and prove their agility. The *tende* can last for hours, late into the night, until the women who started it decide it is time for sleep. Then, in the same quiet manner in which they arrived, the attendees disperse and a lukewarm silence returns only to be interrupted by the bleating of a camel or the continuous sniffling of the goats.

The *tende* is always in the thoughts of the Tuareg when they are far away from the camps, on a trip, or during a battle:

2.19
Young Tuareg girl playing an *imzad*
or *anzad*.
Photograph by Gian Carlo Castelli Gattinara,
Aïr, Niger, 1967.

I remember the day of the encounters...
and the *tende* playing incessantly it is never enough
and the race course where we compete and follow each other
playing difficult games where you need experience.
....
I remember the encounters of days gone by
and the poetic competitions with pretty girls.

With the sound of the violin in their hearts, the men advance
    on their hands and knees...

....wər din-z -attawa anəbdad
tende fawda təggatat təglam-du təla n-aggad
nəgraw etaghas n-əbdan nəgharrad d-əs anmiwad
khay iket za tibeten san ewadnat emjərrab
....
əkte-d anəghima ən azəl nad
d-awshənnan əgegh əd təmənhag

as d-emmoradan gharran anzad

This is also apparent in the following poem:

The [courageous man] will delight in conversation, he will
    play with the braids
of the young women gathered around the violin.

And I think of the young women with nostalgia
those one plays with during the time of the transhumance,
those one need not speak to during encounters...

ad ammandəy awal d əzəlli n-tijəkkad
ən-təlmam əzəl-nad as ikrabbat anzad

nak əndanna d elwa d əsuf ən təməjgal
shinad dər nətaddal tamert tan tanəkkert
sas nəffur sər-əsnat way tasansagh awal

When these meetings are larger and more formal, they are called the *ahal*, or the love courts. *Ahal*s are actually literary and musical encounters that take on amorous undertones only later at night. They usually end when young couples disappear into the darkness. Famous poets and personalities participate in these encounters, as do young men and women and married men far from their wives. The *ahal* are organized a couple of days ahead of time and are announced: one knows that on such and such a day there will be an *ahal* in such and such a camp. An experienced woman is the president. She organizes the songs, the music, and the reciting of ancient poems or of improvised compositions, which may celebrate a current event or simply praise a beloved young woman.

During the *ahal* other groups are teased with allusions to embarrassing incidents in the past. Some individuals are ridiculed through exaggeration as well. Riddles are also recited, such as: "What can put a hole in the sand without having arms or hands? Urine"; or "What can't be hidden between two camels? An elephant"; or "What is the small sapling you can lean on and be sustained? A young Tuareg." If it occurs that two love rivals are present during an *ahal*, the improvised, oral poetry takes on a challenging tone:

He who wants neither wounds	*ey wər nəra ad ubas*
nor insults nor slander against his father	*attarbad asl i-ti-s*
he should let Elweter sleep.	*ayy əlwətər təttas*

The rival responds immediately:

Bodal, the wounds	*Budal kay-ak abus*
you mention, what do you think they are?	*wa təttafagh ma ymos*
A man, even if he is wounded	*aləs ghala itubas*
and insulted and his father is slandered,	*attarbad asl i-ti-s*
will not give up caressing	*aglu degh ira edes*
the breast of a woman, and her womb.	*ən-gər nəfaf d-ilghas*

The next response:

I, what I can tell you	*nak za a dagh-ak-əssana*
is that if you come to me armed	*as ku sər-i-d təkhsala*
and our weapons are equal	*togda təzoli-nnana*
and we each have a shield	*nəla ighəran ket-nana*
I do not promise you	*wər ak-za-zəzzigəza*
that you will be able to open your mouth to scream	*ad taragh imi thala*
or to cry.	*wela ad təzərrurəwa*

The response is ready:

Perhaps the man who says he is stronger than I am	*awak aləs a ygannan orn-i*
thinks he is a prophet	*awak ənnəbi megh əghali*
or has the strength of a stallion	*megh əqqurəd a yga ən əmali*
or that of a lion near a well	*megh inn-eləgh iwaran anu*
enraged because of the heat and hunger?	*igraw-t ezəz ih-ay barori*

The language used in Tuareg poetry isn't a written language, and while I transcribed and translated these poems, I had the impression that in a certain sense I had altered the true meaning of the message. To speak means more than to translate. Precisely, it is something untranslatable. This is why, when I heard these poems being recited for the first time, I immediately wanted to meet the author, and then the singers, and the group who shared both form and content. This is why I stayed in Tuareg country for five years with my wife, my daughter, and my dog, until I was no longer considered or felt like a stranger.

The spoken language, unlike the written one, cannot be reproduced. It is addressed to listeners who are present, it responds to their anticipation, it reacts to their "vibrations." To allow an oral communication to be published is almost a form of betrayal. The alternative, however, was to lose these poems and with them the true understanding of a people. This knowledge comes from the inside, through the words of the players. It stands apart from the usual descriptions of groups written by anthropologists, who are by all means observers and are thus inevitably on the outside of the group. The "news" related here is situated in this perspective. Through their meanings, words hide, let us glimpse, conceal, and unveil variable situations. Once they are printed they remain there, fixed, motionless, arid, and are exposed to any misinterpretation without the possibility of an answer. The spoken language is an expression of identity. The people who used those words did not do so solely for the sake of conveying news. They wished to express something, which is difficult to understand for those who do not belong to the culture and who do not speak the language. Tamasheq is considered a minority language because it is only spoken by the Tuareg. What matters is not how many people speak and understand a language but what it expresses. This is where its energy comes from. Otherwise, monolingualism (which the world is headed toward anyway) would be optimum. If everyone spoke English, for example, they would have the impression that they understood one another, but we know understanding goes beyond words. In this sense an exhibition of silent objects is a more efficient form of communication than reading a book or listening to a speech. In addition, to even out cultural differences (like language) to a unique standard would make things simpler in a practical sense while destroying mankind. What to think if all of humanity dressed in the same fashion, in sweatpants manufactured in a large factory, or if everyone ate hamburgers and salad?

In the past years the Tuareg have in fact modified certain habits and certain equipment, but this only concerns groups who have been affected by the road across the Sahara uniting the Mediterranean and the Gulf of Guinea. For the others, and they represent the majority, life continues to follow the pastures and the seasons. Their revenue is based on livestock breeding, caravan marketing, and, for some groups, small-scale farming of fruit and vegetables sold at Sahelian markets. Livestock still conditions Tuareg lifestyles and continues to represent much more than a meager income. Besides furnishing meat and milk, livestock symbolizes prestige; it is smells, sounds, dust, and fuel. It is the raw material for the making of bags, satchels, cushions, and tents. All of these things, are essential elements entering into the identity of a Tuareg during the first days of life and continuing, along with the climate and the environment, to forge character and determine culture. The few Tuareg who have become tour guides or Toyota drivers or who have studied and found jobs in cities often return to their camps and organize a *tende* on their days off.

Transistor radios and battery-run televisions now expose the Tuareg to a bombardment of news and images that were heretofore foreign to them. The young are intelligent, curious, courageous, and resourceful, it will be difficult for them not to accept the challenge of competing, of experimenting with the new, certain that they will remain themselves even if they enter the field and face these temptations. They do not realize the immense power wielded by Western culture and its economy. The basis of the lack of understanding between the two cultures, that of the West and that of the Tuareg, does not lie in the different aspects available to each, but rather in the meaning of existence.

This explains the dislocation and confusion that some Tuareg experience upon entering Western society. It seems that to be modern, developed, progress-oriented today, you must be Westernized. I have faith, however, that the Tuareg will find their own definition of development and modernity without refusing their past.

TIFINAR

The Tuareg speak a language known as Tamasheq. Regional variations of Tamasheq occur, and it is not uncommon for members of various social strata within a single Tuareg group to pronounce words differently. Furthermore, some *inadan* (artists or smiths) speak a language of their own among themselves, which is called Tenet (see chapter 4 of this volume). Tamasheq has an alphabet called Tifinar, which is known in most Tuareg groups. Tifinar is related to ancient Libyan scripts dating to 150 BCE and shares letters with the Phoenician alphabet and with cuneiform characters as well. Some of the rock paintings at Tassili-n-Ajjer display ancient Tifinar motifs.

The Tifinar script is composed of lines, circles, and dots; its style is angular, linear, or oval. It can be written horizontally, vertically, from right to left, and from left to

B.1

Tifinar alphabet. From Francis James Rennell Rodd. *People of the Veil.* London: Macmillan, 1926, p. 267, pl. 33.

Published with permission of Macmillan Publishers Ltd.

B.2

Petroglyph with Tifinar.

Photograph by Thomas K. Seligman, near Sefar, Algeria, 1984.

B.3

Detail of a Tifinar inscription on the back of a veil weight (see fig. 7.13).

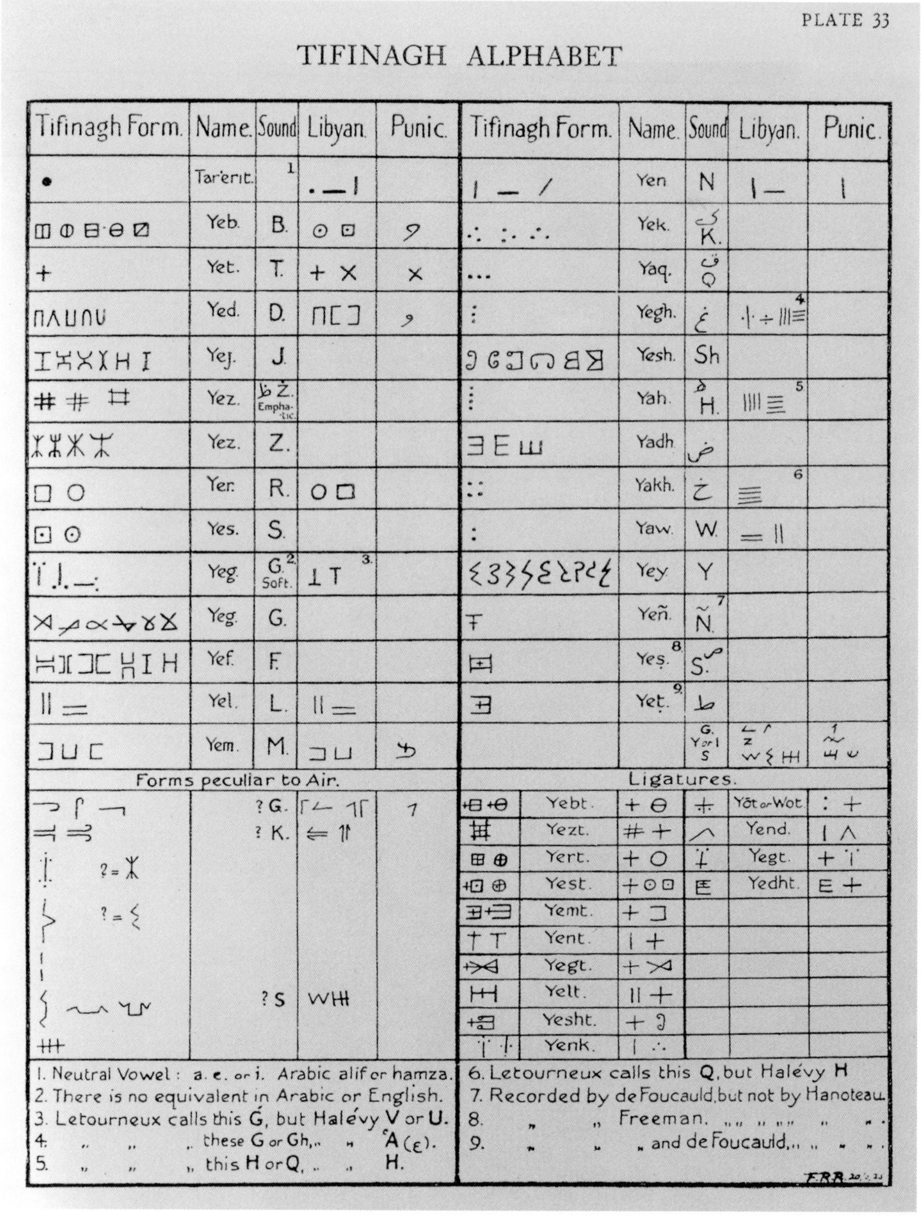

PLATE 33

TIFINAGH ALPHABET

Tifinagh Form.	Name.	Sound	Libyan.	Punic.	Tifinagh Form.	Name.	Sound	Libyan.	Punic.
•	Tarerit.	[1]	. — I		I — /	Yen.	N	I —	I
▢ⵁⵂⵀ▨	Yeb.	B.	⊙ ⊡		∴ ∵ ∴	Yek.	Ḵ.		
+	Yet.	T.	+ ×	×	...	Yaq.	Q.		
ⵏⵍⵓⵏⵓ	Yed.	D.	ⵏⵍⵄ		:	Yegh.	ġ	·I·÷·III [4]	
I⵿ⵝ⵿HI	Yej.	J.			ⵛⵛⵍⵍⵎⵣⵧ	Yesh.	Sh		
# # ⵄ	Yez.	ḍ Ẓ Emphatic			:	Yah.	Ḥ.	IIII [5]	
ⵝⵝⵝ	Yez.	Z.			�ⵎⵜ⵿E ш	Yadh.	ḍ		
▢ ⵔ	Yer.	R.	ⵔ ▢		:.	Yakh.	ẖ	= [6]	
ⵔ ⵔ	Yes.	S.			:	Yaw.	W.	= II	
ⵜ ⵍ .⵰	Yeg.	G[2] Soft.	ⵜ T [3]		ⵥ⵰ⵥⵥⵣⵥ	Yey.	Y		
ⵥⵍⵄⵗⵗⵝ	Yeg.	G.			ⵟ	Yeñ.	Ñ. [7]		
ⵎⵍⵍⵀⵄH	Yef.	F.			ⵗ	Yes.	Ṣ. [8]		
II =	Yel.	L.	II =		ⵢ	Yet.	ẓ [9]		
ⵎⵓⵄ	Yem.	M.	ⵎⵓ	ⵄ			G. Y or S / Z / S	ⵍ / ⵣ / ш ⵗ HH	~ / ⵄ ш
Forms peculiar to Air.					**Ligatures.**				
ⵄ ⵔ ⵄ		? G.	ⵔⵄ ⵄⵄ		·▢ ·ⵁ	Yebt.	+ ⵁ	ⵜ	Yôt or Wot.	: +
ⵄ ⵄ		? K.	ⵄ ⵄ		ⵃ	Yezt.	# +	ⵄ	Yend.	I ⵄ
.I.	? = ⵜ				ⵃ ⵃ	Yert.	+ ⵔ	ⵢ	Yegt.	+ ⵢ
ⵗ	? = ⵗ				·▢ ⵁ	Yest.	+⵰⵰	ⵍ	Yedht.	E +
I					ⵜⵗ	Yemt.	+ ⵎ			
ⵗ ⵄⵄ ⵄⵄ		? S	Wⵃⵃ		ⵜ T	Yent.	I +			
ⵃⵃ					ⵄ	Yegt.	+ ⵄ			
					ⵃ	Yelt.	II +			
					·ⵗ	Yesht.	+ ⵗ			
					ⵜ .I.	Yenk.	I .⵰			

1. Neutral Vowel : a, e, or i. Arabic alif or hamza.
2. There is no equivalent in Arabic or English.
3. Letourneux calls this Ǵ, but Halévy V or U.
4. „ „ these G or Gh, „ ᶜA(ε).
5. „ „ „ this H or Q, „ H.
6. Letourneux calls this Q, but Halévy H
7. Recorded by de Foucauld, but not by Hanoteau.
8. „ „ „ Freeman. „ „ „ „ „
9. „ „ „ „ and de Foucauld,„ „ „ „ „

F.R.R. 20/3/24

54

right. The presence of the script often enhances geometric patterns, which are found in most Tuareg art forms. The writing of Tifinar is transmitted by mothers to their children, who learn by tracing its lines and circles in the sand. In Tuareg culture and tradition, the important matters touching the group, such as history, politics, genealogy, and culture, have always been committed to memory and form part of the oral tradition. Tifinar is used to make notes and to write letters and messages to friends and loved ones. *Inadan* also sometimes sign their jewelry in Tifinar. Under French colonial rule, the Tuareg resisted attempts to regularize and standardize their written language. Since the 1970s, however, there have been concerted efforts to add vowels to the existing Tifinar letters and to establish a standardized cursive writing style.

Some Tuareg authors write and publish their works in foreign languages. Ibrahim Al Koni (who comes from the Ajjer region) writes in Arabic, and his works are translated into other languages. Alhassane ag Baille (who comes from the Adhag region) wrote and was published in French. Tifinar has been taken up as a language of publication as well, as the poet Hawad (who comes from the Aïr region) writes in Tamasheq transcribed in a cursive Tifinar style, with French translations. He also illustrates his poems with designs he calls *furigraphies*, which are intended to reach out beyond the enclosed space created by words.

K.L.

3

THE *INADAN*, MAKERS OF AMAZIGH IDENTITY
The Case of the Aïr Region

Mohamed ag Ewangaye

Specialist journals and scholarly studies devoted to the Tuareg, or Amazigh,[1] often contain rather hasty assertions and conclusions about certain aspects of our lives as individuals and our existence as a group.[2] Owing to the inaccessibility of our lands, we remained cut off from the Western and Arab world until a few Arab travelers, led by curiosity and a desire for adventure, managed to reach us some centuries ago (fig. 3.2). That marked the beginning of a descriptive chronicle, which, though not negative in its entirety, often betrayed an underlying ignorance. Without stopping to observe in depth or bothering to acquire the instruments and tools needed to decipher the Tuareg, a people fiercely bound to their age-old culture, these often-frightened observers laid the foundations of a literature that completely misses the point. Their writings have served as the basis of studies by contemporary researchers who thus continue to relay erroneous theses that need to be reoriented. This is a colossal endeavor that we must all undertake, inasmuch as certain simple ideas will persist for a long time to come, if they continue to be so often repeated by those who lack the knowledge to transcend them. The ongoing mission of specialists is to reestablish objective truths in order to restore to humanity its treasures in their proper contexts and with the least possible distortion. Humanity needs this to discern its future, so that all people will live in peace.

The purpose of this essay lies within this goal of reorientation, specifically in a domain vital to the objective study of Tuareg culture, namely its arts and artisanship. I will not attempt an exhaustive study of Tuareg art objects, instead looking closely at the contexts in which these works are realized in order to understand their content. Ultimately, the essay will focus on the people behind this ancient craft, a pedestal of one of the oldest civilizations in the world. Here the artisans, or *inadan*, as they are called in our language, Tamasheq, will begin to speak by themselves and for themselves (fig. 3.3). A certain narrative has heretofore usurped their true identity, but today they reclaim it, at the risk of overturning many received ideas that have been promoted and spread by some who claim to know them.

History and Evolution of the Conceptual Content of Tuareg Art Objects: Influences, Interpretations, and Authenticity

A look back in history allows us to dismiss certain fantastic notions put forth in the guise of explanations for the conceptual content of the objects produced by Tuareg artisans. This examination sheds light on certain shadowy areas and dispels all doubt so that we may finally return to the simple definition of our artisanal production—for it is surely more simple than it appears to the novice. And the simplest things are often the most exciting to discover.

3.1
Saidi Oumba in his workshop with French clients.
Photograph by Thomas K. Seligman, Niamey, Niger, 1997.

3.2

Aerial view of Agadez.

Photograph by the Armée de l'air, 1948. Musée du Quai Branly, Photothèque, c.48.2487.561.

3.3

Mohamed ag Ewangaye is a member of an *inadan* family.

Photograph by Thomas K. Seligman, Niamey, Niger, 2004.

3.4

Andi Ouhoulou working leather.

Photograph by Thomas K. Seligman, Agadez, Niger, 1988.

Since I am part of this milieu, my personal research has allowed me to understand that the Tuareg adoption of Islam nearly a millennium and a half ago has had a definite influence on the conceptual content of Tuareg art objects. Islam is largely unencumbered by spirit worship and related rites. Thus, for almost fifteen hundred years, all of our artisanal production has been stripped of aspects relating to rituals of this type. Our objects function as commodities of daily life. Tuareg artisans are guided purely by the desire for aesthetic beauty, utility, and functionality. This process induces a dialectic between the artisan and the work, and in the end the *enad* delivers it with a part of himself or herself. Thus the object reflects the personality of the one who has realized it; the artisan has a presence (fig 3.4). It is this presence that observers sense as a kind of magic, which ultimately becomes a myth. This touch crystallizes even further when the object is manipulated by its eventual owner. It thereby reflects two imprints: that of the one who crafted it and that of the one who uses it. For this reason it is alive and communicative. But the message it conveys is that of the beauty of art, not that of a mystical ritual or a representation or image that stands for faith. Even if, in the process of creating, the artisan uses chemical or physical procedures that could be likened to ritual manipulations, this action is inscribed in a purely material framework. In fact the action of fire, for example, in the melting of metals is an operation that partakes of science alone (notably physics and chemistry) and not of magic, occultism, or a traditional alchemy.

Without dwelling on the influence of Islam on Amazigh culture, it appears, generally speaking, that our present-day artisanal production is more devoted to aesthetics and functionality. It is important to emphasize this because in neighboring sub-Saharan Africa, artisans are very often the producers of physical representations of local beliefs. Given that some Western researchers tend to view all of Africa from one rather general perspective, often owing to partial research and study, it seems useful to affirm the specificity of Tuareg artisans within the global theory that concerns African art. Africa is a vast continent that encompasses civilizations that merit deeper, more discerning study. It is distressing to see the oversimplification on the part of Western researchers with regard to that diversity. In fact, from north to south and from east to west, as well as in Central Africa, of course, the sociocultural realities reflected in art and by the artisan differ. Up to now, a good deal of the research conducted by the West has concerned sub-Saharan art, although it represents only a portion of the artistic production of this great continent, about which much remains to be written.

To understand Tuareg artisanship well and Tuareg society in general, it is more profitable to orient research toward origins lying beyond Africa. Before they settled in Africa, many of our ancestors were established in the Arabian Peninsula. This little-known part of our history accounts for the Semitic and Middle Eastern influences on our art. Later came Egyptian influences, which were joined by Amazigh, Andalusian, Indo-European, and finally sub-Saharan influences. The difficulty in reconstructing this complex journey, comprised of incessant comings and goings on different routes (via the north and the east), often confines us to the simplest course, that of considering the most recent piece of the Tuareg odyssey.

In terms of the presence of Islam in Tuareg society, as it pertains to art and artisanship, we have found no representation that serves religious belief among the Tuareg. Geometric, cosmogonic, and astral representations may be discerned in the decoration of our art objects, but these stem from an approach more scientific and aesthetic than ritualistic or religious (fig. 3.5). We have an intimate relationship with the cosmos and with movement that is manifested in our art. This aspect was not crushed by Islam, for in no way does it contradict or compete with the principles of the oneness of God that underlie the religion. More profane aspects, however, may have succumbed with the arrival of Islam. Many facets of our culture did survive the conversion. This is the case with the preparation of plant-based medicines and many other traditional practices. In general our culture is compatible with Islam, given that as the Tuareg people slowly formed into a group, few were inclined to spirit worship and associated rites. Thus it is

3.5

Bracelet (samboro)

El Hadj Tchabé Ouhoulou
Tuareg, Kel Ewey
Niger
Silver
W: 2.5 cm; Diam: 6.4 cm
Cantor Arts Center
1997.58

easy to be Muslim and Tuareg without having to abandon one's identity. In the Tuareg experience, Islam is more than a set of rites or a religion reduced to its strictest sense, as perceived by the West and the East. Rather, it is a total vision that encompasses man in his physical, sociological, political, economic, cosmogonic, and spiritual definition. We believe that this is the very meaning of the Divine Word contained in the Koran. That may not always be evident in our marabouts' dogmatic reading of the Koran, which results in a highly controversial image of the beautiful original Islam that Our Almighty Lord teaches us. The Tuareg achieves a more natural spiritual relationship with the cosmos than most of these so-called marabouts.

The *Inadan* within the Social Context

Within the strata of Tuareg society (see chapter 1 of this volume), the *inadan* are the men of earthly knowledge, of history and technology. They make all the goods necessary to daily life. They also hold the power of social censure regarding the conduct expected of each individual and clan. They are the judges of social acts in relation to Tuareg social ethics. Their judgment is feared by all; for these reasons, the powerful, the *imajeren*, or nobles, cannot do without them. The *inadan* perform all duties that the *imajeren* give them.

The place of the *inadan* in Tuareg civilization and social structure is the cornerstone of Amazigh identity. The artisan realizes the physical and visual attributes of the Tuareg. He is the ferment of the living society, the link between the different elements. The artisan is also present in the exercise of power. He can be the political, military, and administrative strategist; he is also the spy or the policeman who keeps the aristocracy informed about the daily life of the community in its internal and external relations. These different roles have earned the *enad* (singular form of *inadan*) an immunity, which is recognized by all Tuareg. In fact *enad* may be translated as "immunity," the safe-conduct and tactical freedom enjoyed by the artisan. Etymologically this term embraces all the aspects of the various roles the artisan must play among the Tuareg.

The *Inadan* within the Cultural Context

Our culture is the totality of our daily acts and deeds fixed by time in our habits and customs. The material expression of these acts, deeds, and practices constitutes and defines our artisanship. Each object originates from an idea or a need, and, in turn, from the satisfaction of our daily requirements, art and artisanship are born. The fact of having repeated it every day through millennia has made it our culture. The external world designates and distinguishes us by these objects, which characterize and identify us. The artisan thus forges a part of our identity with his hands (fig. 3.6).

Those who defend and preserve culture are logically the same artisans who fashion and model it as they please. As noted above, they are called *inadan* because of the immunity and freedom that their role confers on them. In wars and internal conflicts they are spared. Thus, the matrix upon which Amazigh society is constructed or reconstructed remains safe. The respect for this immunity is often confused with fear, but the *inadan* are neither feared nor rejected, but respected. The Tuareg who forgets this is fallen; attacking the *inadan* amounts to destroying and repudiating oneself. *Inadan* symbolize the collective patrimony that all Tuareg must defend. This code of behavior at its extreme can lead the Tuareg to flee the *enad* so as to avoid even the temptation to vex the artisan.

To play the many roles of the *enad* well, the artisan needs—in addition to the necessary material and technical tools—the capacity to manipulate speech. That is why one finds many poets among artisans. This power is used to safeguard the patrimony by calling offenders to order. For the sake of pedagogy the *enad* can assume the guise of a buffoon or a clown to soften the impact of criticism or censure. It takes a good dose of humility and intelligence to walk such a tightrope, one upon which someone else might easily falter.

The French term *forgeron* (blacksmith) does not encompass the whole definition of the *enad* that we have just reviewed. It translates only the technical aspect, which we find in the generic term *ammijil* in Tamasheq, the nominative form of which is *enammajal*: he who creates and fabricates. Among the Tuareg *ounnoudou* (the fact of being *enad*) and *ammijil* are often found together in the same person. The first relates to the social function that we have discussed above, and the second covers the technical aspects of creation and fabrication. Sometimes, however, an artisan privileges one aspect over another or clings to one alone. That depends on the configuration of the microcosm of Tuareg society in which he lives. In any case, he always adapts to the needs of that microcosm by necessary constraint or by a tactical choice for survival.

Through his function as *enad*, the artisan reveals the degree of nobility possessed by fellow Tuareg. Those who respect *inadan* or preserve their good name fulfill the duty of safeguarding the collective identity and thus merit their stature: they are *imajeren* and may govern society. Those who frustrate the *enad* deviate from the norm: they are not upright and virtuous; they are *imrad* (the opposite of *akhad*, which means "rectitude") and therefore cannot lead but are relegated to other duties. The process of acquiring nobility is not complete until the individual is capable of controlling himself and his animal instincts: saving the widow, the orphan, and the weak. It is thus in the interest of every Tuareg to cherish the *inadan* and show them consideration, even to fear them.

In carrying out this role, the *enad* often makes many enemies among the other elements of Tuareg society. That is why the artisan is the object of contradictory sentiments on their part. If you question people about the *inadan*, they will rarely have anything good to say. The roles the *inadan* play as censors, clowns, and spies, among others, pit them against the regulated sections of the social corpus, who perceive them as brakes on limitless freedom. That is why for them the *inadan* are the dregs of society, although, objectively, no Tuareg can do without their services. Ultimately, these controversies are the expression of a people who have always had eventful lives and whose civilization is enriched each day by such jousts. It is a fitting form of dialogue for a rich, diverse, and solid culture.

In order to understand these culturally specific concepts, one must have access to the secrets that only the artisans and thinkers possess. Without this, every researcher misses the truth and gets lost in interpretations that sometimes egregiously misrepresent the sacred foundations of Tuareg culture. Settling for populist and popular conceptions does no honor to knowledge and research. It is further regrettable to see that the dubious sources are often provided by the Tuareg themselves, who deliberately offer a tendentious view that disorients researchers. One must not be taken in by the "exotic" character that the Tuareg assume to deceive the visitor. The Tuareg do not open up easily. A covert aspect always remains that will not be divulged. The knowledge that defines a culture

3.6

Blacksmith working metal.

Photograph by P. Ichac, date unknown, Tamanrasset, Algeria. Musée du Quai Branly, Photothèque, D.34.1506.231.

or a civilization is not the province of all the members of that group. There is always an intellectual elite that by virtue of its thought or its actions fashions social life. The researcher must remain objective, preserve a healthy skepticism, and show discernment. Fortunately, certain fallacious assertions do not stand up to time or to objective inquiry.

If we consider Tuareg culture without the *inadan*, we immediately sense a certain void. Why then should we accept assertions that characterize them as the basest element of Tuareg society? That suggests instead an egocentric process on the part of other Tuareg, whereby each person attributes the noblest role to him or herself. It is the sum of all roles, however, that makes our social framework and our culture strong. The nuances and sophistication of the Tuareg sociocultural architecture call for deeper research from a purely anthropological perspective into the whole ensemble of elements that gave birth to this civilization over time and space.

The Economic Context of Artistic Production:
Marketing in the Past and in the Present
In the beginning, all the objects produced by our artists were traded, not sold. Their value was gauged by their nature and the status of the one who had ordered them. This principle endured even after the exchange became monetary. It has only recently fallen from use. We can trace its disappearance to the crumbling of the Amazigh social system, which started in the last decade of the nineteenth century. When the Tuareg were no longer able to offer the artisan what he needed in exchange for his skill, he began to look outside his community to the exterior (*oussouf*) for his means of survival. Naturally, he turned to our closest neighbors in the Aïr and its southern and western extension. Thus the nomadic Fulbe, who traveled in the same areas as the Tuareg, were the first to benefit from our artisanship with access to such objects as camel and horse saddles, tools, and later arms and material for assembling shelters and furniture. In this case, objects were plainly sold as merchandise, even if this was initially accomplished in the form of exchange. The artisan had entered into a purely commercial logic.

Toward the end of the first half of the twentieth century, since the *inadan* no longer received any meaningful economic support from Tuareg society, the artisan began to withdraw to the urban agglomerations of the Aïr and the surrounding area. This trend was accompanied by a necessary conversion of the *enad*'s art that was dependent upon the artisan's adaptability. The potential of the *enad*, previously held back by ethnic borders, developed at a phenomenal rate. From this time on the artisan needed to satisfy a different clientele, one composed of city dwellers and foreign travelers (see fig. 3.1). His traditional clients had to follow him to the city.

Thus the production of jewelry, for example, came to be intended more for tourists and the Western market that colonization had opened; yet while the range of work broadened, the Amazigh touch remained. Artisans still draw on their rich cultural heritage and creativity, which have now found another domain for their expression. Those who buy the *enad*'s works perceive in them ancient Tuareg myth. They are right: it is there. Artisans always perpetuate their Amazigh identity. Only the form has evolved; the content remains the same. To achieve this new form of exchange at a very appreciable level of economic and commercial competitiveness, the Tuareg in general, and the *inadan* in particular, have undergone a long process of conversion.

Evolution of the Political Context and
Socioeconomic Relations in the Tuareg Area (Tamazgha)
The phenomenon of withdrawal that led the artisan to the city or into contact with other groups is a strong sign of the disintegration of Tuareg social structures, a disintegration born of French colonial policies. In the face of fierce resistance, the French studied every possible way to subjugate the Tuareg so they would no longer pose a threat to colonial interests in the new zone of influence. Thus, under the pacification that lasted from 1918 up until the independence of Niger and Mali, all the pockets of resistance were reduced,

and all the potentially rebellious chieftains were replaced. Tuareg society was carved and reshaped along the lines of French interests. Its traditional workings were deeply affected over the whole Tamazgha area (Algeria, Libya, Mali, Niger, and Burkina Faso).

Within this new context, the society no longer worked as it did before; the *inadan* found themselves, like others, disoriented. They lost part of their social power, although in theory they retained it without knowing over whom they could exercise it. They thus clung even more to the technical aspect of their identity. They began to sell their skill. It was the ultimate attempt at survival, for it was painful for the *inadan* to sell the identifying attributes of their civilization. Our neighbors and the city dwellers were the first beneficiaries of this "brain drain."

In the cities, the Tuareg still try to re-create the ancient workings of society, but it is a waste of effort; many of the parameters have changed. Social and economic relationships are no longer the same. The Tuareg nostalgically live through the end of one era and set foot in another with great apprehension. Their fate, over the course of a century, has been characterized by upheavals. They try to guide what awaits them by mastering the new strictures in order to lessen the impact. In this evolution, all elements of society watch as their roles are transformed. But into what? It is still too soon to say. History has not yet had the last word. From these conditions the revolutionary movements of past decades were born in Mali and Niger, where the identifying matrix of the Tuareg is still alive.

The armed uprisings of Tuareg in Mali and Niger during the last decade of the twentieth century were merely an extension of those that had taken place in the central Sahara over approximately two decades during the time of colonial penetration. Seventy years of pacification did not suffice to annihilate the innate freedom of the Kel Tamasheq. Beginning in the early sixties the Kel Adrar of Mali rang the death knell for this supposed "fait accompli." They established the basis for what would become the revolution of the nineties. Since that date, a process of critical interrogation has been underway in the heart of Tuareg society. The Tuareg seek the political means for a renaissance within the new African order, the most visible aspect of which is balkanization. In Niger as in Mali, the watchword is "resist" (*shimmir* or *zimmir*).

The objective of the new revolutionary dynamic is to push the Kel Tamasheq to draw on their resources in order to find the strength they will need to adapt to the challenge that awaits them: surviving while preserving their cultural matrix. In this process, the *ishumar*, or resistance fighters (the word comes from *shimmir*) undertook the mission of clearing the way to attain this objective. The Teshumra (as the political movement of the *ishumar* is known) called into question those factors that prevent us from evolving and entering into a modern dynamic without trampling on our identity, or what is left of it. The *ishumar* use every means of sensitization and propaganda at their disposal. From musical poetry to mingling with the masses, the message conveyed is that of resisting and adapting our modes of life to present realities. Internally, a new mode of operation must be found to make what remains of our social structure viable again. Externally, we must defend ourselves from the steamroller of our enemies, their systems of state control.

As we can see, the *ishumar* in some ways took the place that the *inadan* once occupied in the social body. They became the new censors, the new spokespersons, and the new guides. They indicated the social conduct that was called for at the moment. In their wake, many prohibitions exploded. The unbridled society threw itself into the race for modernity, but a modernity that would not crush the foundations of our civilization. In their propaganda, the *ishumar* do not present the same discourse at all times and in all places. The precursors of the movement came from among the fighters who had survived the insurrection of Adrar des Ifoghas in 1963. Their first place of exile was in the Algerian south, where the new Arabist authorities did not look favorably upon them. To distract attention and win confidence, they purposely concealed the political nature of the Teshumra by suggesting a French derivation with less-problematic connotations,

3.7

Mano Dayak and armed rebels.
Mano Dayak was one of the principal leaders of the armed Tuareg
rebellion, which took place in Niger
in the 1990s. He died in 1995 in
a plane crash en route to a peace
conference with representatives of
the Niger military.

Photograph by Jean Picard, Aïr, Niger, 1995.

chômeur (unemployed person) for *ishumar*. In fact *ashamur* (the singular of *ishumar*)
rhymes well with *chômeur*. The French term also suggests the destitution characteristic
of the *ishumar*. By this means the *ishumar*, now *chômeurs*, won the confidence of the
Algerian public authorities, making them believe that they were merely unemployed
men in search of jobs. The precariousness of their political and economic situation in
fact attracted international sympathy. Several years would pass before Algeria realized
that the Teshumra was a political movement that was slowly gaining ground. At the
same time the Algerian revolutionary socialist Houari Boumédienne was coming to
power with his pan-African vision of revolution. His regime was the first to offer the
ishumar the possibility of bringing their movement out into the open. They thus received
their first military and revolutionary instruction in Algeria before responding, several
years later, to the call of the fiery colonel Muammar el-Qaddafi. The international press
and specialist journals, however, had by this time conveyed the derivative definition of
the movement that linked it to unemployment and poverty. It was thus considered a
humanitarian act to create a media uproar over these emblematic Tuareg reduced to
wandering and begging on their lands, which were now divided up among several countries. Everyone had forgotten that the term *ishumar* came from the root *shimmir*, which
was itself a neologism at the time, having rarely been used before and, in any case, not
in a political context. Its true meaning was understood only within the resistance movement (figs. 3.7–3.9). The two meanings traveled together: one used to fool those who
would nip our struggle in the bud, and the other, the real one, used only among ourselves. In their warrior poems, the first fighters of the Adrar, such as Alladi, frequently
used the term *shimmir* and its derivatives to galvanize the people and incite them to
revolt. Today, we accept the two meanings explained above.

3.8

Cross of Mano Dayak

Mohammed Attako
Tuareg, Kel Aïr
Agadez, Niger
Silver, beads
Pendant: 9 x 5.8 cm;
   L (of necklace): 30 cm
Private Collection

The cross of Mano Dayak was
created in 1996, supposedly by
Mohammed Attako, to commemorate the first anniversary of the
revolutionary leader's death. A
few *inadan* made this cross type to
sell to tourists, but it never gained
much following among the Tuareg
themselves and has not yet been
added to the twenty-one crosses they
recognize for their various regions.

3.9

An armed Tuareg resistance fighter
stands in front of a door painted
with a map of Mali, a Tuareg man,
and an automatic weapon. Below
the map are inscriptions in Arabic
and Tifinar.

*Photograph by Pierre Boilley, Adagh,
Mali, 1994.*

3.10

Tuareg selling camel rides to Europeans involved in the Dakar-Agadez rally.

Photograph by Thomas K. Seligman, Agadez, Niger, 1997.

Tuareg Civilization:
Conquering the West and the African Subregion through Artisanship

Relations with the West will continue to change. Thanks to their legendary open-mindedness, the Tuareg have been able to convert conflict into active friendship. The Europeans, the conquerors of yesterday who once crushed us, have become the allies of today. From confrontation, mutual respect was born. They admire our culture, our lifestyle, our art of living, and our environment. On the basis of these friendships, the thinking about exploitation of our economic potential has changed as well. One of the most important of our assets is doubtless the desert, and especially the Tenere. Thanks to increasingly positive relationships with the West, the Paris–Dakar rally was born, and along with it, tourism developed (fig. 3.10).

These contacts, as noted above, have had a great influence on our artisanship, one of the pillars of our economy. The production of our artisans has been modified in both quantity and quality to conform to this new order. It has become an industry that has brought revenue to many people, even beyond the Tuareg community. In Agadez, Kidal, Tamanrasset, Djanet, and Ghât, a large part of the local population profits from it. In these cities, frequented by Western tourists, a veritable chain of commerce in artisanal goods has been created. The Western clientele has been won over and continues to grow. The *inadan* have traveled all over Africa, to the cities and capitals of North Africa, West Africa, and Central Africa. All the commercial events that are held in Africa, the fairs, shows, and exhibitions, include the *inadan*. Their works are often awarded prizes by organizations such as UNESCO.

The armed struggle of the nineties against the governments of Mali and Niger was accompanied by a far-reaching diplomacy directed at the West. Western governments and institutions had to be convinced that their intervention in these theaters of war could influence the politics of Niger and Mali and prevent genocide. With the new information technologies, this intense diplomatic activity widened the Tuareg sphere of activity. New relations have been formed, and the *inadan* take advantage of them by investing in European markets. These overtures toward Europe and the United States have a friendly character in addition to the economic benefits that they confer. The American market, however, given the distance and the complexity of access, has yet to

3.11
Sale of Tuareg jewelry made by the Koumama family and sponsored by Ann Elston at Fort Mason in San Francisco.
Photograph by Thomas K. Seligman, 2004.

be conquered. Although we do not share a part of our history with America, as we do with Europeans, our hope is that the beauty of our artisanship and the sophistication of our culture will win their hearts as well (fig. 3.11).

New development projects accompany the dynamic of peace, which was finally accepted as a result of the diplomatic campaigns led by the Tuareg. In Niger as in Mali, there has been a slight boost in the economy. Of course, one of the economic bases that deserves to be developed is artisanship, which attracts many local and foreign investors. The thrust of these projects is to structure this sector by organizing production around reliable economic entities, modernizing it, and introducing new techniques that do not alter the essence of the art—making it competitive in an efficient commercial dynamic. Today, thanks to aid from Luxembourg through DANI (Development of Artisanship in Niger), a program that has supported the sector for ten years, considerable progress has been made toward the realization of these goals. The battle currently underway is undertaken by a well-considered commercial process resting on sustainable grounds. In this struggle, all the actors have been mobilized: the artisans, the economic experts, and the supporting partners. New forms of marketing are being developed that rely on new information technologies, in particular the Internet.

Since the Tuareg *enad* has been present in the market, he has become an economic operative who generates wealth. In the region of Agadez, the artisan contributes greatly to the gross domestic product. Assuming there are fifteen thousand artisans in Agadez and its immediate surroundings, as has been stated by the experts who practice in the community, we can see the impact of artisanal production on the regional economy. In one year, the market value of this production can amount to billions of CFAF (African Financial Community francs).[3]

In the artisanal village of Agadez, a center of organized production, at the end of 2001, the turnover reported by the member cooperatives came to 461 million CFAF. If we consider that this number includes only a third of the cooperatives represented in the village and that those cooperatives include only a tenth of the community's artisans, we see that it is a mere fraction of the actual figure. At the national level, experts estimate the revenue generated by artisans at about 30 percent of the gross domestic product.

3.12
Tuareg selling soapstone carvings
to tourists.

*Photograph by Charles Frankel, Azel Ecole,
Niger, 2001.*

Some Characteristics of Production

The production of our artisans in Agadez is mainly artistic rather than utilitarian. Traditional utilitarian artisanship is being supplanted by modern industry, which supplies many of the tools and domestic implements required. Modern utilitarian artisanship has just made its appearance in the economic sphere, thanks mostly to the professional training program financed by the European Union and implemented by NIGETECH, as well as to other development programs that have a technical training component.

Artistic production is divided among the following trades: leatherwork, shoemaking, jewelry making, basketry, sculpting in wood and talc, sword making, cutlery, saddlery, metalworking, embroidery, tinplate making, sewing, dyeing, and knitting. Leatherwork, which is executed by women in addition to their domestic activities, has a local market. The exports are mostly jewelry in solid silver and in nickel. Initially the Agadez artisans would wait for foreigners to arrive during the tourist season. Given the recent disruptions in tourism, however, the artisans have taken the initiative by physically besieging the Western market and other markets in neighboring subregions. In the conquest of these markets, our jewelers have displayed their true genius. Today the support programs for this sector need only follow the path forged by the artisans themselves. Jewelry, given the market value of these works and their aesthetic quality, draws the most attention and constitutes an overwhelming portion of the exports for this sector. All these objects that travel far and wide captivating the viewer are the work of our valiant jewelers, who at present are the ambassadors of Amazigh culture to the world.

The materials used in making these Tuareg products are leather, wood, precious metals such as silver and gold, heavy metals such as steel and iron, and light metals such as copper, brass, and aluminum. Silver is favored by the Tuareg for whom it symbolizes purity, nobility, humility, beauty, and all the virtues that ennoble man and bring him into harmony with himself, with his environment, and with others. Gold, however, is thought to stimulate greed, self-aggrandizement, an excessive love of life and power, domination of others, and their envy in turn. The dialectical approach of the Amazigh brings him closer to the values embodied in silver. The Amazigh artisan simply bows to this necessity. To best express his creativity, he uses this metal above all, which is why the majority of pieces are worked in solid silver. In Agadez we estimate that at least two tons of this metal are worked each year.

Conclusion

As we have seen, the role of the *inadan* is in the process of evolving within the framework of the global transformation that has been observed in Tuareg social organization for a century now. In rural areas, where the traditional form of managing society essentially survives, the role of *inadan* has remained more or less unchanged. In the cities, however, the *inadan* have become independent, freeing themselves from traditional social ties that are difficult to reconcile with the new economic stakes of commercial competition that urbanization and the monetization of exchange require (fig. 3.12). Thanks to the creative genius of the *inadan*, their client base reaches far beyond the Tuareg community. Today it encompasses the world market. Tuareg artisans are central to an economic dynamic in which they play a crucial role as producers of their traditional art in a renewed form. The *enad* is irreplaceable in that role. The battle that remains for artisans to win is that of mastering the global channels of commerce while retaining the cement of their identity. The other Tuareg constituents are also concerned in this struggle to adapt to the modern world. This effort must eventually succeed and converge with the effort to recompose Tuareg civilization and give it a new face. There is growing hope that we shall achieve a modernity based on the roots of Amazigh identity. Our cultural potential is a sizable advantage in this battle, and those who bear the regenerative seed are the *inadan*. A new society is slowly being born, and the *inadan* are part of it, equipped with a new social power that will enable their success in their new circumstances.

⊟

INDIGENOUS BELIEFS AND ISLAM

Beginning in the seventh century, merchant-traders, who also served as clerics, carried the precepts of Islam with them south into and across the Sahara. In the process of its dispersion, Islam came into contact with a multitude of indigenous religious beliefs and practices. The Tuareg, who were well established and were essential middlemen in trans-Saharan trading caravans, were among those who encountered and engaged with Islamic beliefs and cultural ideas. These new beliefs were interwoven and blended with the existing Tuareg worldview. Islamic clerics (marabouts), known in Tamasheq as *ineslemen*, developed and became highly influential in some Tuareg groups and remained marginal in others.

While there are those who generalize and label the Tuareg as Islamic, this departs from my own observations.

The Tuareg believe in a powerful spirit world, where the Kel Esuf ("people" of the void) flourish after dark, and men and women must wear protective amulets to guard against them. Jinns (spirits) are thought to live in mountains and in abandoned areas. Tuareg beliefs in the evil eye and mouth, or *tehot*, resemble those found in much of the Mediterranean world. They therefore tend to be secretive and reserved about personal matters in order to avoid jealousy and bad luck. Tuareg men wear the *tagulmust*, or face-veil, over their noses and mouths to guard against penetration by evil spirits. People also rely on divination as a means of protecting themselves. This is practiced using mirrors, by interpreting animal entrails, and through tracing specific lines in the sand.

C.1

Koran board (*asselum*)

Tuareg, Kel es Suq
Gao, Mali
Wood, pigment, leather
59 x 24.2 x 3 cm
Musée du Quai Branly
71.1941.19.1010

C.2

Koran Case (*ettabu*)

Tuareg, Kel Aghlal
Abalak, Niger
Leather
12 x 10 cm
Musée d'ethnographie, Neuchâtel
00.19.2

Cases such as this one are made to hold the Koran. The delicately incised motifs signal the importance of the holy book that is contained within the case. The inscription in Tifinar says that the case was made in 1945.

C.3

The main mosque in Agadez is built of mud bricks and wood supports and surfaced in layers of mud.

Photograph by Thomas K. Selgman, Agadez, Niger, 1980.

The Tuareg have nonetheless combined their indigenous beliefs with some Islamic practices, especially those they regard as potentially efficacious in securing protection from evil and obtaining good fortune. Praising Allah to obtain benefit is not seen as harmful even to the nonbeliever. Thus, Allah is invoked to help by using Arabic expressions such as: "Praise be to God," "In the name of God the merciful," "Blessing is to the Prophet," "I depend upon God," or "It is God's will." At the same time, however, precautions are taken to protect against the world of malevolent spirits. The Tuareg believe that to be successful and free in the difficult environment of the Sahara, it is prudent to use all resources: physical, cultural, and spiritual. One can invoke power from several religious traditions without being a true believer or a cynic.

T.K.S.

C.4 (OPPOSITE, LEFT)

Koran case (*ettabu*)

Tuareg, Iwellemmeden
Gao, Mali
Leather, pigment, glue, copper
61.5 x 7.5 x 2.3 cm
Musée du Quai Branly
71.1941.19.602

C.5 (OPPOSITE, RIGHT)
Marabout El Hadj Ilias washes the writing from a Koranic board. The ink combined with water will be drunk for protection, a practice widely observed throughout West Africa.

Photograph by Thomas K. Seligman, Niamey, Niger, 1997.

C.6
Mosques, located along caravan routes, provide a place for travelers to pray.

Photograph by Thomas K. Seligman, Tassili-n-Ajjer, Algeria, 1984.

C.7
Bodies are buried in Islamic tombs, such as these, with the head facing east toward Mecca. The individual graves are marked with an unadorned stone.

Photograph by Thomas K. Seligman, Tassili-n-Ajjer, Algeria, 1984.

4

THE TUAREG ARTISAN
From Technician to Mediator

Edmond Bernus

Amma, among these people, joins to each his counterpart:
Male with female artisans;
Male with female plebeians;
The Imenan must stay with their own,
The Iforas must do the same;
One must boil wild roots in water alone
And put no butter in food that is bad,
Nor mix flour of wheat with that of the date palm.

AAKENNA AGG ILBÂK (QUOTED IN FOUCAULD 1930, 354)

4.1

Tuareg man wearing a white *tagulmust* (turban and veil) and holding a sheathed sword.

Photograph by Thomas K. Seligman, Agadez, Niger, 1991.

Tuareg artisans form endogamous groups within their society. These groups are referred to simply as *inadan* (sing., *enad*), followed by the name of the larger group to which they belong, for example, *inadan wan*-Kel Nan or Kel Fadey. The role the *inadan* play in Tuareg culture is far more important than their technical skill alone would imply. In studying these artisans, we may discern different types. The list I give below resembles that of Candelario Saenz (1980), as we both did fieldwork with the artisans of the Aïr and Azawagh regions in Niger.

- *Inadan wan-tizol* (artisans of metal) make weapons and jewelry employing the lost-wax technique and relying on basically the same implements used throughout the Tuareg region.
- *Inadan wan-talak* work in wood. Their name derives from their homeland, the Talak plain, west of the Aïr.
- *Inadan wan-tamenannad* also work in wood and are reputed to make the best camel saddles (fig. 4.2). According to Benhazera (1908), a woman named Tamanenet was the ancestor of these artisans.
- *Ikanawan* (sing., *ekanao*) are potters associated with the southern Tuareg, Tellemidez and Ayt Awari.
- *Inesfadan* (sing., *anesfada*) are the stewards or even the messengers of the chieftains.

Recent surveys have shown the number of artisans to be relatively stable within each political unit. Among the Kel Geres in southern Niger, they represent 3 to 4 percent of the population (Bonte 1976, 144); among the Iwellemmeden Kel Denneg, they make up 3.9 percent; and among the Tingeregedech of Bankilaré (Téra region), they make

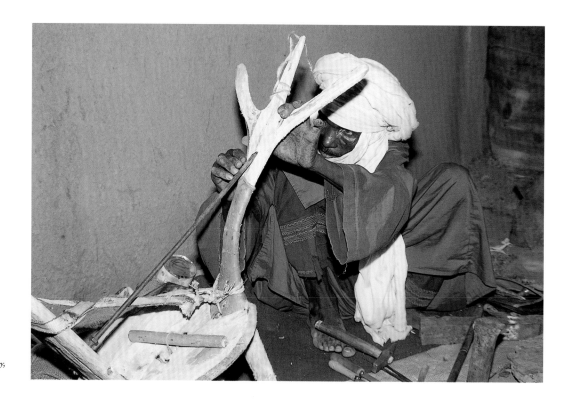

4.2

Kaggo Oumba making a camel saddle.

Photograph by Thomas K. Seligman, Niamey, Niger, 2004.

4.3

Andi Ouhoulou working leather.

Photograph by Thomas K. Seligman, Agadez, Niger, 2004.

4.4

Issighid making silver belt buckles for A l'Atelier.

Photograph by Thomas K. Seligman, Agadez, Niger, 2001.

up 3.8 percent (Bernus 1993, 358, 394). These few statistics reflect specific situations among the southern Tuareg.

Transformers of Matter

There are numerous traditions relating to the origin of Tuareg artisans, who are often referred to in the literature as "blacksmiths," although, as made clear above, they also work in wood, leather, and, in a few regions, clay. These traditions justify or explain the originality of this group, which remains apart from others in Tuareg society.

In the Ader near Tahoua, in the region of In Gall, Niger, most traditions trace the beginnings of the *inadan* to two prophets in Islamic tradition, David and Noah (Echard 1992,12–13). The blacksmith Mogha of the Kel Fadey explains that "The origin of artisans [*inadan*] is found in the prophet David. It was he who began the working of iron, which he found among the stones." For woodworking, Noah is the source. Once he regained terra firma after having built the ark, he advised others to cut trees in order to make and sell axe handles.

According to traditions cited by Father Charles de Foucauld in his dictionary, "some of [the *inadan*] were of Israeli origin, having come from Morocco in a distant age, from the ocean shores, after the Berber tribes that conquered Adghagh" (1951–1952, 3: 1300.) The hypothesis of a Jewish origin was taken up again by Henri Lhote who suggested that many of the artisans are descendants of the Jews of Tamentit, expelled from Touat in 1495, who intermixed with black slaves. "They must be the ones who gave birth to all the artisans we find today among the Sudanese tribes. In the Aïr there was a different stock, of Tripolitan origin" (1955, 323.)

Generally the tools of artisans are light and portable. Blacksmiths typically use a hammer and sledge, shears, file, burin, punch, scraper, and crucible. These are carried in a leather tool bag. In addition, however, they require two heavier and less-manageable pieces of equipment. These are the anvil, which is made of cast iron, often set in a block of wood, and bellows (*anahod*), a leather pouch with wooden handles that forces air into a piece of hardwood fitted with a metal pipe ending in a clay nozzle. A guessing game shows that the latter is thought of as alive, breathing like any living being:

> Riddle me, riddle me:
> My goat's chest is the *adaras* tree [*Commiphora africana*];
> Its neck is iron;
> Its head is clay;
> Its breath is fire;
> Its hooves are the *aboragh* tree [*Balanites aegyptiaca*].
> What can it be? The bellows.

The riddle is a complete catalog of the materials used in this essential component of the metalworker's art. With his bellows, the blacksmith is master of the elements, and of fire in particular. Woodworking requires fewer tools: an axe, adze, and iron awl for pyrography. The wives of these artisans working in metal and wood are specialists in leather (fig. 4.3). Working at a small table, the women cut the leather using a very wide, flat knife and scissors. They use metal cans to hold the glue that they apply with brushes.

Until relatively recently, the iron (*tama*) produced south of the Sahara came from the blast furnaces of rural people who were experts at smelting ore from iron-rich mineral deposits. Today, however, iron is primarily salvaged from automobile carcasses. Copper ore has been found at Apelike in Niger, and copper was produced in the very distant past with production resuming in about 1300 CE. This production stopped at the end of the fifteenth century. Today, copper is salvaged from various sources, and public faucets are especially vulnerable. Silver, the metal most often used in jewelry making, was sold at the market in the form of coins. The best known and most common of these was the Maria Theresa thaler, which apparently continued to be sold until quite recently (fig. 4.4).

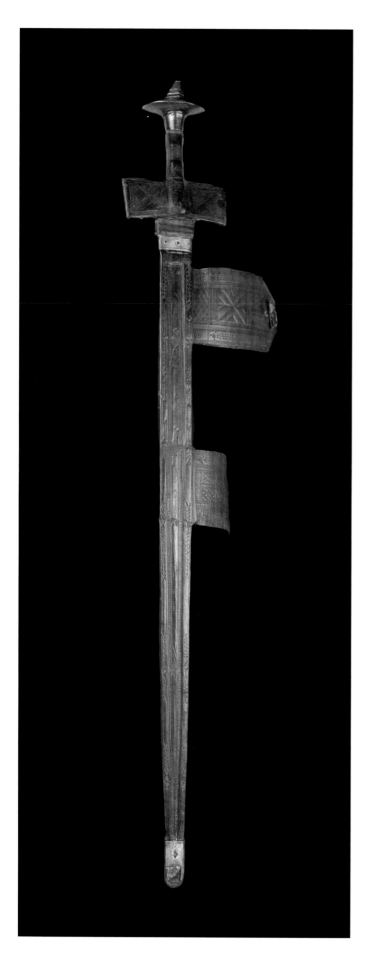

Iron was used to make weapons (swords, spears, and knives) and decorated implements (padlocks); copper and silver, and more rarely gold, were used to cast or fashion jewelry and to decorate the chiseled plates that adorned talisman cases, weapons, and padlocks. Wood was made into furniture (tent pegs and beds), as well as domestic items (cups, milking bowls, ladles, spoons) and pastoral implements (pulleys, saddles, packsaddles).

The most elaborate objects make use of multiple materials. The sword (*takuba*), for instance, requires working iron or steel for the blade, as well as copper and brass for the hilt and leather for the scabbard (fig. 4.5). The camel saddle with a cross-shaped pommel (*terik* or *tamzak*) calls for very precise woodworking of the twin pieces that fit together and are joined by leather; the cantle, at the rider's back, is decorated with colored leather embellished with brass nails and metal or copper plates (fig. 4.6). Leather is also used to make tent canopies, various sorts of sacks, water bags, buckets, and the cords that raise water from deep wells.

Guardians of the Patrimony

Throughout the Tuareg region, from Ghât to Madawa, from Tamanrasset to Agadez, there is a striking consistency among the objects made by artisans. Some of these so strongly evoke Tuareg society that they have become symbolic of it: for instance, the camel saddle with a cross-shaped pommel, the sword, and, in terms of jewelry, the cross of Agadez.

4.5

Sword and sheath (*takuba*)

Tuareg
Timbuktu, Mali
Steel, leather, bronze, pigment
88 x 18.5 x 5.8 cm
Musée du Quai Branly
74.1962.0.1317.1-2

4.6

Camel saddle (*tamzak*)

Kaggo Oumba
Tuareg, Kel Ewey
Niamey, Niger
Wood, leather, metal
80.8 x 73.3 x 36.3 cm
Cantor Arts Center
2005.102

Camel saddles require care and skill in their manufacture. The *tamzak*, the prestigious version of the simpler *terik* saddle, has a circular seat, which rests over an inverted V-shaped frame. The front of the seat has a cross-shaped pommel and the backrest is an arched cantle. The saddle is made of different pieces of wood, which are ingeniously fastened together by sewing with wet rawhide (see fig. 4.2). It is then covered with red and black colored leather. The cantle and the pommel are decorated with strips of pale green leather and red fabric, which are further embellished with strips of brass, silver, or white metal displaying geometric patterns and capped with brass or copper.

4.7

Camel bridle (*akeskabbu*)

Tuareg
Agadez, Niger
Leather, metal, pigment
22 x 18 cm
Musée d'ethnographie, Neuchâtel
48.4.94.a-b

4.8

**Woman's saddle
(*akhawi* or *ekhawi*)**

Tuareg
Boukhamia, Adrar des Ifoghas, Mali
Wood, metal, leather
120 x 96 x 75 cm
Musée d'ethnographie, Neuchâtel
49.2.35

4.9
Noblewomen riding in palanquins
mounted on camels and donkeys.
*Photograph by Gian Carlo Castelli Gattinara,
Niger.*

Miniature versions of the saddle are often seen on desks at travel agencies and airline companies. For Westerners, the camel saddle suggests the nomad crossing the desert and represents freedom in relation to time and space (fig. 4.6). The Tuareg saddle belongs to a precise cultural area. In the west, among the Moors, the comparable saddle is known as the *rahla;* in the east, among the Toubou, the *terké.* Most camel saddles east of the Tuareg region from the Toubou lands to Arabia rest on both the withers and back of the camel, spanning its hump without touching it. The Tuareg saddle, however, is placed in front of the hump, on the withers, like saddles from the Western Sahara. The rider mounts a withers saddle barefoot. Before setting out on his journey, he attaches his sandals to the hobble rope that he will use at the next stop. His feet rest on the curve of the camel's neck, giving him tactile contact with his mount and allowing him to guide it as much by his feet as by the reins (fig. 4.7).

The Tuareg have several kinds of camel saddles. One, with a paddle-shaped pommel (*tahyast*) is found principally in the western part of the Tuareg region and made mainly in Adrar des Ifoghas. The saddle with a cross-shaped pommel mentioned above (the *tamzak* being the most ornate, celebrated, and sought-after type) has its specialist artisans in the Aïr and Azawagh regions. At the markets of In Gall and Agadez both kinds of saddles are sold.

There is also a saddle or palanquin for women (*akhawi* or *ekhawi*), which is less common and mostly used by noblewomen among the northern Tuareg and the Iwellemmeden in Niger. It is rarely for sale at the market (figs. 4.8, 4.9). These saddles resemble the packsaddle (*aruku*) used for merchandise or the Arab *bassour* in that they rest on either side of the hump; however, they are far more ornate and elaborate. They have two lateral arches; each fitted with three flat pieces of wood, about sixteen inches long and four inches wide, which are sometimes decorated with brass appliqué and copper nails.

As noted above, the *tamzak,* with its cross-shaped pommel, is a complex work—one might even call it a chef d'oeuvre, in the sense of those crafted by the artisans of old in France—and it combines wood, leather, and metal.

The complexity of shapes, faithfully reproduced from one object to another, requires precise assembly of the cut pieces: the cross, the seat, the cantle are each made of two symmetrical pieces that are joined and then held together by soft white skin from a cow's belly, which connects the vertical stem of the cross to the seat back, encircling it halfway up. In general, the seat is made of the softwood of the *adaras* tree (*Commiphora africana*), while the pommel and the seat back are carved from the hardwood of the *afagag* (*Acacia tortilis* spp. *raddiana*) or *aboragh* (*Balanites aegyptiaca*) tree. Each part of the saddle bears a name that often evokes a certain anthropomorphism: the capped metallic point beneath the pommel is called "the lower beard," in relation to "the upper beard," which is represented by a leather strip that juts out below the cross. The two lateral branches of the cross are called "ears," and the upright part, from bottom to top, "throat" and "neck." The dark leather that covers the three branches is called the "veiled," in reference to the veil that men wear on their heads. On the other hand, the vertical extension of the cross and the fingerlike protrusion that tops the cantle are both named for the *Gazella dama—ener* in Tuareg—with the first called the "front gazelle" and the second the "back gazelle." [Bernus 1993, 220]

Although there is little variation in the shape of the *tamzak*, the pieces that make it up can vary in size—the seat can be wider, the "neck" longer. Sometimes the *tamzak* is covered in a white tissue to protect it, like fine furniture under a slipcover. When not in use, the saddle is placed in the fork of a tree, so as to avoid contact with the ground and the risk of termite attack.

Placed between man and camel, this saddle serves as a bond between two bodies. A riddle attests to this role: "Riddle me, riddle me: On top a living thing, on the bottom a living thing, in the middle a dead piece of wood. What is it? A camel saddle." Although the camel saddle is considered an inert object, it is nonetheless linked to the world of the living through the anatomical terms—alluding to man and to the gazelle—that are used to describe its components. Jeannine Drouin shows that this metaphorical vocabulary is above all anthropomorphic and notes that even the name of the decorated saddle, *tamzak* (lit., the deaf woman), refers to humans and to the "ears" of the cross (1982, 94-95). The elaborateness of the camel saddle demonstrates the care taken by the Tuareg, despite the precarious and unstable conditions in which they exist, to preserve the high aesthetic standards of objects that have been made for centuries.

From Swords to Jewelry

Among the weapons of the Tuareg warrior, only the sword is still carried by men. The shield has disappeared, and the spear has become extremely rare, as has the arm dagger. In his mid-twentieth-century dictionary, Foucauld opined that in Ahaggar all the blades were old and had been made elsewhere: "Almost all are of European origin, as their trademarks indicate: most come from Germany, Italy, Spain, or France; some that have Christian marks are said to have been brought from Egypt; many are from the sixteenth century.... The Kel Ahaggar classify sword blades in various types, according to their quality and the color of their steel, the thickness of the blade, the number of grooves, etc." (1951-1952, 2: 726-28).

Foucauld classified blades into ten categories, ranging from best to worst. These values are not absolute, however, as certain swords of an inferior type could on occasion be as good as those of higher categories. At the top of this hierarchy is the *tazgheyt*, "one from the Izghan tribe"; at the bottom is the *tama*, fashioned by blacksmiths of the Sudan, whereas all the other sword blades come from the north. The *tama* has the same shape as the other blades, but the Kel Ahaggar consider it worthless and unusable, as they do the *aberou* blade, thought to be "of no worth whatsoever, completely bad."

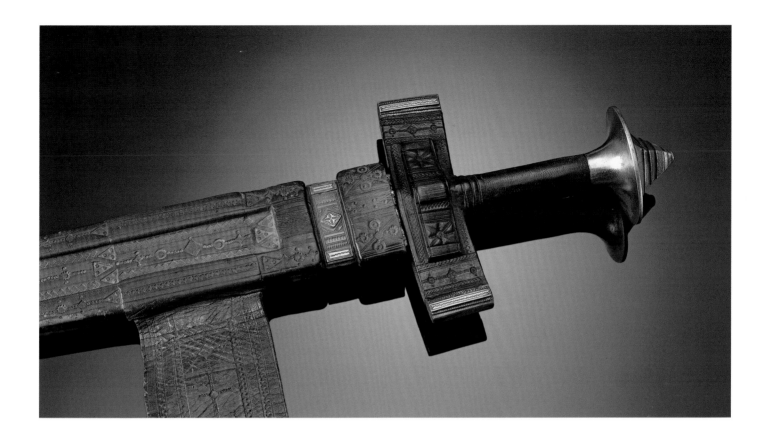

4.10

Sword and Sheath (detail)
(*tazgheyt* or *takuba*)

Tuareg
Agadez, Niger
Steel, fabric, pigment
101.6 x 12.7 cm
Cantor Arts Center
2001.190.a-b

A man receives his *takuba* upon reaching puberty and before donning the veil. It is a flat double-edged cutting sword with a cross hilt. The guard is square, and the pommel is ornamented. The *takuba* is a prestigious item and is still worn today for special occasions. Smiths sometimes impress motifs on the blades in order to indicate provenance and quality. The most prized blades in the past were those from Toledo in Spain and from Solingen in Germany. Toledo steel usually bears the mark "Carlos V," whereas the Solingen blades bear the "Wolf of Passau" mark, which the Tuareg refer to as "the Lion."

Families pass the swords down from one generation to the next. The hilts of the swords are usually metal and display geometric motifs, whereas the guards are lavishly decorated with impressed designs, and the ends are covered with metalwork that is carefully engraved. The sword is said to represent nobility and courage, and to possess supernatural powers.

4.11

Cross of Agadez
(*zakkat* or *tenaghalt*)

Tuareg, Kel es Suq
Asongo, Mali
Brass
5.5 x 3.6 x 0.6 cm
Musée du Quai Branly
71.1941.19.1286

The marks and inscriptions on the blades have made it possible to determine their origin in some cases (Briggs 1965; Gabus 1958). From the end of the fifteenth through the seventeenth century, blades made in Solingen, Vienna, Padua, and Toledo crossed the Sahara. The most remarkable of them, those belonging to the greatest chieftains, bore a name that was inventoried in the dictionary of proper names compiled by Foucauld (1940), much like Durandal, the sword of Roland. As there were not sufficient European blades to make swords for every Tuareg male, however, blades of poor quality were made south of the Sahara and given a scabbard, pommel, and hilt to resemble the high-quality blades. The *takuba* is a weapon and a symbol that is part of the Tuareg patrimony. According to M. H. Morel, the different parts of the sword (fig. 4.10), like the components of the camel saddle, have names referring to the human body: the pommel is "she of the white head"; the grip, "bone marrow"; the guard, "the shoulder"; the blunt edge, "the back"; the sharp edge, "the mouth" or "that which eats"; the point, "the tongue" (1943).

In the realm of jewelry, the cross of Agadez has likewise come to be widely considered emblematic of the Tuareg, and today it is sold around the world (see chapter 9 of this volume). This piece takes various forms and is worn by women of all social ranks. In the west of Niger, Bella women, who belong to formerly enslaved groups, all wear silver, or rarely copper, jewelry of many different styles in the form of long necklaces or hair ornaments. An article by Germaine Dieterlen and Ziedonis Ligers includes numerous photographs of women wearing jewelry in this manner, accompanied by photographs and drawings of the ornaments. In these photographs, the cross of Agadez and other pendants are worn hanging from a cord that passes through a hole or through a ring (fig. 4.11); thus, when the piece is hung, the ring or aperture is at the top and the cross or crescent is at the bottom. According to the authors, the pendant is therefore worn upside down. The top, the cross or crescent, always connotes the sky, and the bottom, with its open-worked circle, the earth. Based upon their forms, their marks, and the way they are worn, Dieterlen and Ligers argue that "On certain pieces of jewelry, all that is represented on the 'sky' part connotes masculinity (the grandfather, father, uncle, son, husband, or the objects pertaining to them); likewise, what appears on the 'earth' part connotes femininity (the mother, daughter, wife, etc., and the utensils pertaining to women)" (1972). Jewelry, like weaponry, introduces us to a world of symbols that have up to now been little studied and that Dieterlen is able to approach due to her knowledge of the Tuareg who have remained on the fringes of Islam (Bernus 2001, 68).

There is still a great deal of speculation concerning the origin of the cross of Agadez, as one recent study illustrates: "Even though the Tuareg blacksmiths in Niger told me that this cross was the symbol of the unity between man and woman, which would support the hypothesis of an Egyptian or Indian origin with sexual symbolism, I maintain the hypothesis that it is a Christian symbol, a representation of the Trinity" (Hureiki 2003, 462). Given that this cross is now sold worldwide, it will no doubt generate many more hypotheses as its popularity continues to spread.

The *Enad*'s Multiple Roles

Tuareg society disparages the artisan, projecting various character flaws on the *enad*. The artisan is said to be a coward, incapable of self-defense; a liar, unworthy of trust; and so filthy that it is best to keep one's distance.

> You, artisan, or rather slave who keeps camels,
> of no dazzling feats are you capable;
> it's known that at war you killed not even a fettered donkey.
> [Moussa agg Amastan, quoted in Foucauld 1925, 1: 408-9]

4.12

Inadan performing a "sword dance"
for tourists.

*Photograph by Thomas K. Seligman,
Timbuktu, Mali, 2001.*

4.13

Camel riders parading in front of
women at a *tende*.

*Photograph by Gast, Tamesna region, Niger,
1954–1955. Musée du Quai Branly, Photothèque, BF.64.6799.716.*

The *enad*'s reputation as a liar before God and man is revealed in the proverb: "Men of words say, 'I'd as soon expect wool on a donkey's back as truth from an artisan.'"

The description of the artisan by Francis Nicolas is more subtle but equally spiteful:

> He is not bound to his work; he need only belong to "the caste" in order to be wholly supported by the master, for whom he occasionally serves as interpreter and clown, intermediary and spy.... The blacksmith always knows how to make himself indispensable, even though he is always a born traitor; he's fit to do anything, and he's often useless; he has no needs or ambitions, and doesn't know how to save or to take charge of a herd.... The master or the foreigner must always be ready to defer to his demands, and his mendicancy is proverbial; more-over, it would be dangerous to offend him, for he is skillful at satire and if need be will spout couplets of his own devising about anyone who brushes him off; thus, no one wishes to risk his taunts. In return for this, no one is as ill esteemed as the blacksmith. [Nicolas 1950, 191]

Nicolas emphasizes the supposedly ambiguous character of the artisan: indispensable yet useless, the *enad* is capable of becoming an interpreter, an intermediary, a spy—and this implies a nobler, quasi-official, role, which could, should an *amenokal* (supreme chief) wish it, be transformed into that of an emissary or even an ambassador. The artisan takes advantage of this disgraceful reputation by behaving in a manner unconstrained by the rules of propriety that everyone else must follow. The *enad* thus enjoys a freedom of speech that allows him self-expression without the reserve that is the hallmark of good manners among the Tuareg.

The artisans' social status becomes clear when an animal is sacrificed by them at the camp for religious festivals (such as Eid al-Kabir or Eid al-Fitr, the end of Ramadan) or social celebrations (weddings, the visit of a distinguished guest; figs. 4.12, 4.13). Usually a sheep or a goat is slaughtered, although very rarely a steer may be sacrificed for a big wedding, or among the northern Tuareg only (Ahaggar and Tassili-n-Ajjer), a camel. After the animal's throat is slit, its carcass is jointed and hung from a branch to be carved. The distribution of the different parts of the animal varies depending on the occasion; certain people at a religious festival, a visit, or a wedding will be given the best pieces, which everyone recognizes as such.

One piece, however, is always reserved for the *inadan*: namely, the part of the back known as *tanazermeyt*. The animal's back is in fact divided into three parts: *tanazermeyt*, from the neck to the lowest rib; *isegbas* (pl., no sing. form), the lumbar area from the last rib to the coccyx; and *asellankam*, between the loins and the base of the tail. Among the southern Tuareg (Iwellemmeden Kel Ataram and Kel Denneg, Kel Fadey, Kel Geres), the *tanazermeyt*, is often called *seknes inadan*, which means "make the artisans argue," for it can provoke quarrels if several are present and all want this same piece.

Tenet: Secret Language or Slang?
The general mistrust of artisans and the fear that they arouse are heightened by their use of their own language, Tenet, which is reputed to allow them to communicate among themselves without being understood by others.[1] Until recently, authors would write about Tenet without knowing the language. In his dictionary, Foucauld gives the first account:

> A dialect of artisans of the Tuareg region (a special Berber dialect characteristic of Tuareg artisans) // These *inadan* of the Ahaggar have a special dialect that they speak among themselves; it is a Berber dialect that only they know. Most of the *inadan* from the Adrar, the Aïr, and the Iwellemmeden speak it as well. [Foucault 1951-1952, 3: 1301]

4.14

**Drum (*ettebel*)
and beaters (*itekar*)**

Tuareg
Agadez, Niger
Wood, leather
H: 22 cm; Diam: 52 cm
Musée d'ethnographie, Neuchâtel
48.4.108 a-c

The Tuareg are grouped into several
federations, or large political units,
such as the Kel Ewey. A federation
is made up of one or several drum
groups often named after the most
important noble group. The *ettebel*
shown here is a large kettledrum,
but the word *ettebel* also denotes
the drum chief and symbolizes his
political power. An *ettebel* carries
the notion of belonging, of being
the member of a descent group.
Various taboos relating to the drum
dictate that it must never come into
contact with water or soil.

Lhote essentially repeats this information, with only one difference: he says that
Tenet is unknown in the Ahaggar, which seems rather unlikely (1984, 57).

Not until Johannes Nicolaisen's study do we get a very short vocabulary list—seven
words—from the Tuareg in the Aïr who were in contact with *inadan*. On the basis of
this limited sample, the linguist Karl Prasse opines that the language is "a kind of slang"
derived from local Tuareg words (Nicolaisen 1963, 19-20; Prasse 2003, 2: 589). But what
is slang? It is an oral collection of nontechnical words that a certain social group likes
to use, as with Parisian slang, military slang, or schoolchildren's slang. In this case,
members of the artisan community can sometimes speak in the presence of foreigners
or other Tuareg and transmit messages that are comprehensible only to themselves.

I was able to investigate this question in In Gall among the Kel Fadey artisans and
to compile a somewhat more ample vocabulary consisting of seventy-seven words and a
few short phrases (Bernus 1983, 245-49). It appears that the syntax, conjugations, and
feminine and plural forms of Tenet are the same as in Tamasheq. And although some
words clearly derive from Tuareg terms, many others do not. According to Casajus the
presence of the same affixes could imply derivation from Tuareg words that have disappeared (1989, 125).

Courtier and Emissary to the Chieftain

Made of a very large receptacle carved from the hardwood *ahtes* (*Faidherbia albida*)
or *tuwila* (*Sclerocarya birrea*), the drum known as *ettebel* was traditionally covered with
white cowhide (fig. 4.14). The inner surface bore inscriptions taken from the suras of the
Koran. Inside the *ettebel* were placed amulets—leather envelopes holding Koranic verses
on paper—and small, round gold nuggets that would make a sound whenever the drum
was moved or beaten. In the tent, the *ettebel* was hung from two posts and was brought
out when it was to be used. Two *inadan*, one holding it in his right hand the other in
his left, would hit it with two soft beaters called *itekar* (sing., *atakor*) made of braided
leather stuffed with rags at the tip. During travel one of the artisans would carry the
ettebel on his camel. The vellum of a tent, folded up in place of the saddle, would hold
and support the *ettebel*, which was solidly secured; the *enad* would sit behind it, beating
it at regularly spaced intervals to signal his position. At stopping points the drum would

be brought down and placed on a wooden plate, thereby avoiding any direct contact with the ground. When beaten at a faster rhythm, the drum would be used to rally warriors.

Thus, the *inadan* would beat the war drum at the behest of the *amenokal*, as was recounted for the year 1867 when the Kel Denneg set out on a raiding expedition in the Aïr, under the command of Moussa ag Bodal:

> That year we carried out a true *razzia*
> worthy of the ones the prophets had led;
> for Moussa had summoned Badidan and his companions
> and told them, "Take the war drum,
> beat the call to the youth!"
> [Efellan, quoted in Ghubayd agg-Alawjeli 1975, 82]

In his dictionary, Foucauld distinguishes within each region among artisans who work in wood, those who work in metal, and a third category of artisans who are versed in neither skill but "serve as personal valets to the wealthy." Artisans of this last group are said to be especially numerous among the Iwellemmeden. The term "valet" resonates with the derogatory traits applied to all the *inadan*. I encountered artisans of this type on a visit to the Kel Nan chieftain in Niger. Upon our arrival an *enad* who fulfilled this role was instantly sent to prepare tea for us and arrange a site for our tent; he was, in a way, the majordomo of a very important chieftain, accustomed to entertaining numerous foreign guests.

Formerly this type of artisan, called *anesfada* (pl., *inesfadan*), not only looked after day-to-day affairs but could also stand in for the chieftain, serving as his ambassador before other chieftains or foreign authorities, such as the French military officers who sought to subjugate the Tuareg. At the end of the nineteenth century, two famous warriors—El Kabus of the Kel Fadey and Aghali of the Kel Nan—wounded Moussa agg Amastan, the future *amenokal*, and killed his young brother, Bello, as the two returned from a *razzia*, or raid, launched by the Kel Ahaggar. Moussa made it back to the Ahaggar and recovered from his injuries. Several years later, he led a large troop back to Izerwan to avenge his brother's death. When they had arrived in proximity of the enemy, he sent Abbas, his *anesfada*, to ask Mohammed El Kumati, the Kel Denneg *amenokal*, to hand over El Kabus, who had killed his brother. In response, Mohammed sent his *anesfada*, Badidan, with the following message: "Go tell Moussa that tomorrow morning the battle will take place: for as long as the Iwellemmeden shall live, you will not see El Kabus; and even if the Iwellemmeden are down to their last man, you will not see El Kabus." The role of the *anesfada* was to avoid a direct, and thus offensive, oral refusal. The battle took place, and the Kel Ahaggar killed numerous adversaries thanks to their superior rifles.

In December 1901 this same Mohammed—who normally traveled to the Tchin Tabaraden region during the dry season but that year had remained south, near In Gall, to avoid encountering the French army—once again sent Badidan, his most trusted *anesfada*, to Tamaské to sign the requisite submission to the French. This signature by proxy was far less binding and allowed him to avoid presenting himself as defeated. In both cases, the third-party diplomacy of the artisan enabled the *amenokal* to save face. Regarding the signing at Tamaské, Ghubayd agg-Alawjeli relates the following in his history of the Kel Denneg:

> The Kel Denneg, who up to that time had had no contact with the French, kept out of the cities and settled in the Azawar.... Only on 31 December 1901 did Makhammad [Mohammed] send the [*enad*] Badidan in his place, and the latter signed in his hand the letter of allegiance that said roughly this:

> I, Henri Gouraud, representing the French president, have accepted
> the allegiance of the Iwellemmeden tribes who recognize the authority
> of Makhammad, on the following conditions:
> The Iwellemmeden will not incite battles with anyone without
> permission of the captain who is in Tahoua; nor will they provoke fights
> with anyone without permission of the captain who is in Tahoua; they
> will neither kill nor raid the Hausa or the other Tuareg. [Ghubayd
> agg-Alawjeli 1975, 142]

It was a major treaty committing the Tuareg to dependence vis-à-vis the French army and putting an end to their freedom of action, as well as to any possibility of launching attacks to seize the property and harvests of others, as they were wont to do. The *enad* Badidan was the mere representative of the *amenokal*, not an *amajegh*, a leader of the great noble tribes.

The artisan can also be a poet: this was true of Badidan, who recounted several great battles. In 1850 he took part in a *razzia* together with Menaka and composed a poem about it (quoted in Ghubayd agg-Alawjeli 1975, 76). In 1896, at the famous battle of Izerwan, where the Kel Ahaggar came to attack the Kel Denneg north of Tahoua, several poets recounted tales of the combat: "There was a third poet, named Badidan, who was Makhmmad's blacksmith; he did not take part in the battle but composed the following poem about it" (Ghubayd agg-Alawjeli 1975, 130). This example clearly shows that the Tuareg do not have griots who belong to a caste dedicated to producing histories to glorify their leaders. Here anyone with sufficient talent—a nobleman or an artisan, a freedman or a Koranic scholar (*ineslemen*)—becomes the narrator of a collective adventure.

Conclusion

Artisans occupy an important place in Tuareg society. It quickly becomes clear that they cannot be confined to the role that they ascribe to themselves (fig. 4.15). They play on a number of registers, which frees them from purely manual activity and gives them a more ambiguous character. In their service of important figures, their freedom of speech occasionally allows them the chance to play an active role in history.

Today, however, they have slipped past the control of their traditional chieftains, realizing that their products have a market beyond Tuareg society. They travel abroad; they open boutiques at the medina of Tunis and doubtless many other cities. They still produce the jewelry one expects of them, but they use different metals and create new objects in stone for the tourist trade. They thus preserve their patrimony while enriching it with new creations.

Ⓓ

4.15

Tende players at a wedding.

Photograph by Thomas K. Seligman, Talak, Niger, 2001.

THE STUFF OF LIFE
Tent, Food, Weapons

D.1

Tuareg tents are made by sewing together either fiber mats or goatskins. Some tents are fairly large, whereas others are only big enough to contain a bed. Women stretch the tent covering over wooden arches—often using a central support beam—and they secure it to the ground with small pickets.

Photograph by William F. Wheeler Jr., Niger, 1970s.

D.2
Model tent—miniature (*ehen*)

Tuareg
Region south of Niger River, Mali
Leather, fiber, wood, pigment, clay,
cotton, sand
34 x 67 x 48 cm
Musée d'ethnographie, Neuchâtel
85.20.1

Offering containment and protection from the elements, the tent—symbolic of marriage, family, and the womb—was at one time central to the lives of most Tuareg. In fact, the Tamasheq word *ehen* denotes both the tent and marriage. Although tents are still in use, over the last thirty years many Tuareg have become sedentary and now live in adobe or cement-block houses in towns and cities. The ritual role of the tent is re-created to some extent in urban situations, but women no longer have the same property rights they once did, as it is often the men who now own the dwelling place.

The Tuareg tent belongs to the wife, and among the Kel Ferwan, the tent and its furniture are given to her by her family on the occasion of her marriage. Different groups organize their tents in different ways, but the inner space is usually delimited by a windscreen woven of reed and leather; the bed; entrances; and the hearth. Beds are often placed in the center of the tent where people gather, sit, and drink tea. The bed belongs to a married couple, whereas other members of the family often sleep on mats on the ground. Generally, a man keeps weapons, tools, saddles, and clothing on his side of the tent. A woman keeps her clothes, leather bags, saddle, cooking implements, and other belongings on her side.

With the exception of the elaborately carved tent poles, beds, stands, and wooden implements such as bowls and spoons, women make all of the tent furnishings. As is the case with many nomadic peoples, the objects used in daily life are beautifully embellished with colorful geometric designs. Women weave the supple mats (*esaber*) with finely twisted *afezu* reeds and decorate them with geometric motifs created using leather strands or colored wool. Mats are moved around the tent during the day and become: windscreens; interior panels to create privacy and reconstruct spatial areas; and covers for bed frames. Smaller examples are used to cover food. Women smiths (*tinadan*) make elaborately decorated bags, cushions, and saddle blankets. They cut hides with small knives; assemble different pieces; and make fringes, tassels, and decorative designs such as triangles and circles. They also embroider designs with leather strands and incise motifs with knives and metal stamps.

Wooden implements are made by the *inadan*, who carve pieces from a single block then decorate them with geometric designs using hot iron pokers. The *inadan* also make knives, daggers, spears, and shields. Knives hold an important place in Tuareg marriage rituals and in other beliefs. Some believe, for example, that a blade becomes soft if a woman touches it. The sword (*takuba*) is possibly the most prestigious of Tuareg weapons. The handle, blade, and sheath of the *takuba* are manufactured with great care and beautifully decorated with excised and engraved motifs. The blades of these swords, which in many cases came from Europe and the Middle East, are prized for their strong and flexible steel. They are often fitted with a new handle and sheath when these become worn.

K.L.

D.3

Windscreen (*esaber*)

Tuareg
Mali
Leather, reeds
97 x 685 cm
Cantor Arts Center
1996.288.a

D.4

Windscreen (*esaber*)

Tuareg
Niger/Mali
Fiber, leather, pigments
90 x 599 cm
Cantor Arts Center
2001.109

D.5

Tent Poles (*ehel*)

Tuareg
Mali
Wood

a. 137.5 x 17.2 x 2.5 cm;
b. 142.2 x 17.75 x 3 cm
Cantor Arts Center
2003.25.a-b

a. 140 x 18.5 x 3 cm;
b. 141 x 18.5 x 3.5 cm
Cantor Arts Center
2003.26.a-b

Tent poles are used to build the
tent, to hold up the tent wall mats,
and to hang leather bags and clothing. This particular kind of tent pole
is used to secure a wall mat that is
placed around the bed. The intricate
carved designs indicate that these
are prestige pieces intended to
embellish the tent.

D.6

Tent Poles (*ehel*)

Tuareg
Mali
Wood
120 x 19.5 x 3.5 cm
Cantor Arts Center
1996.288 b-c

D.7

**Bowl (*tazawat*), stand (*taseskat*),
and cover (*teseit*)**

Tuareg
Gao, Mali
Bowl and stand: wood;
Cover: leather, fiber
Bowl: 17 x 24.8 cm;
Stand: 118 x 31.8 cm;
Cover: 42.5 x 37.5 cm
Private Collection

D.8
Basket (*aghouzou* or *tafakemt*)

Amina Alga
Tuareg
Timia, Niger
Straw
H: 7.6 cm; Diam: 19 cm
Cantor Arts Center
2001.199

D.9
Bowl (*tazawat*)

Tuareg
Agadez, Niger
Wood, metal
H: 16.5 cm; Diam: 36.2 cm
Cantor Arts Center
2001.171

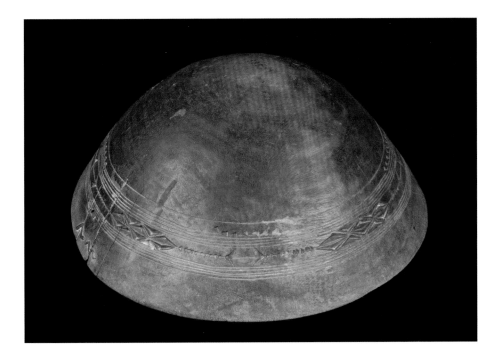

D.10
Child's Bowl
(*takerouas* or *akerawas*)

Tuareg, Kel Tacriza
Aderbissinat, Niger
Wood, metal
H: 8.5 cm; Diam: 20 cm
Musée du Quai Branly
71.1941.19.335

D.11

Bowl cover (*teseit*)

Tuareg, Kel Antassar
Goundam, Mali
Leather, *afezu* grass
H: 14.5 cm; Diam: 32.5 cm
Musée du Quai Branly
71.1941.19.722

D.12

Bowl (*tazawat*)

Tuareg, Iwellemmeden
Tchin Tabaraden, Niger
Wood, metal
H: 19 cm; Diam: 40.5 cm
Musée d'ethnographie, Neuchâtel
71.6.60

The Tuareg cook their food in
earthenware pots or in imported
enamelware. Bowls used for eating
are usually made of wood by the
inadan. When such objects break,
they are repaired with strips of
brass or copper, which are then
engraved, illustrating the Tuareg
concern with the aesthetics of even
the most utilitarian of objects.

D.13

Plate (*takerouas*)

Tuareg, Kel Antassar
Goundam, Mali
Wood, copper
H: 16 cm; Diam: 57 cm
Musée du Quai Branly
71.1941.19.855

96

D.14

Bowl cover (*teseit*)

Tuareg
Agadez, Niger
Leather, metal
H: 12 cm; Diam: 31 cm
Musée d'ethnographie, Neuchâtel
48.4.42

D.15

**Bowl (*tanast*)
and hanger (*timatrak*)**

Tuareg
Tiffert, Algeria
Copper, brass, leather
H (bowl): 7 cm; Diam (bowl): 26 cm
Musée d'ethnographie, Neuchâtel
48.2.75-77

Drinking bowls like this one are attached to camel saddles. This bowl is an import and is fastened to a long leather cord created for ornamental display. The cord or hanger is made of three tubular cords attached to one another and embellished with strands of braided leather.

D.16

Ladle (*tamulat*)

Tuareg, Iwellemmeden de l'Est
Tchin Tabaraden, Niger
Wood
L: 20.5 cm; Diam: 10 cm
Musée d'ethnographie, Neuchâtel
71.6.87

D.17
Spoon (*tesukalt*)

Tuareg
Niamey, Niger
Aluminum
22.9 x 5.7 cm
Cantor Arts Center
2001.197

D.18 (OPPOSITE)
Ladle (*tamulat*)

Tuareg
Niger
Aluminum, leather
L: 25 cm; Diam: 12.5 cm
Cantor Arts Center
2002.51

This ladle is made of scrap aluminum and decorated with copper and brass overlays, which are engraved with delicate motifs. The Tuareg usually eat twice a day and have a small early morning snack. The men usually eat together, and the women and children eat separately. Their diet is largely based on milk and its derivatives, such as buttermilk, cheese, and butter; dried fruit, such as dates; and bread, millet porridge, and gruel. Goat and cow meat is not eaten on a daily basis; rather, it is reserved for festive occasions and roasted either under the hot ashes of the fire or on a spit, or sometimes boiled.

D.19

Spoon (*tesukalt*)

Tuareg, Kel Icheriffen
Gao, Mali
Wood
24.2 x 4.4 x 7 cm
Musée du Quai Branly
71.1941.19.1287 bis

D.20

Cup (*akus*)

Tuareg
Algeria
Wood, leather
H: 21 cm; Diam: 15 cm
Musée du Quai Branly
71.1941.19.1960 bis

D.23

Cushion (*adafor*)

Tuareg
Abalassa, Algeria
Leather, pigment
86 x 29 cm
Musée d'ethnographie, Neuchâtel
48.2.56

D.21

Milking bowl (*akus*)

Tuareg, Kel Rela
Tazerouck, Algeria
Wood, leather
H: 13.5 cm; Diam: 15.5 cm
Musée du Quai Branly
71.1941.19.18

D.24

Cushion (*adafor*) (OPPOSITE, LEFT)

Tuareg
Mauritania
Leather, pigment
Diam: 56 cm
Musée du Quai Branly
74.1962.0.1255

D.25

Cushion (*adafor*) (OPPOSITE, RIGHT)

Andi Ouhoulou and Abou Efat
Tuareg, Kel Ewey
Agadez, Niger
Leather, pigment
H: 19.1 cm; Diam: 52.1 cm
Cantor Arts Center
2001.204

This beautifully made cushion is
decorated with cut and sewn designs
and impressed squares. Its round
shape and height recall North African and Arabic examples. Round
cushions have more stuffing and
padding and are usually used for
seating. This cushion was one of
two made by Andi Ouhoulou and
her daughter Abou Efat for Abou's
wedding in Agadez.

D.22

Salt block (*fosi*)

Tuareg
Bilma, Niger
Salt
H: 7 cm; Diam: 21 cm
UCLA Fowler Museum
x88.1471

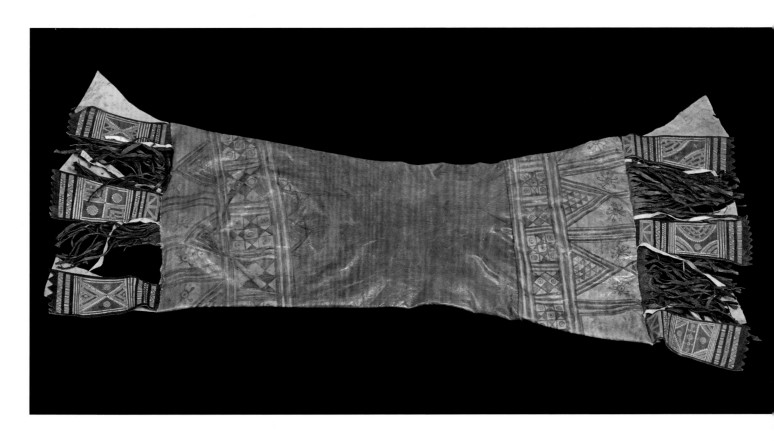

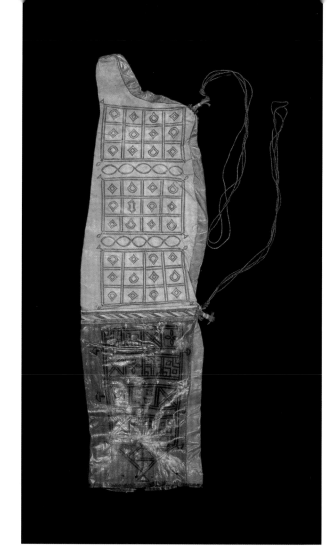

D.26

Cushion (*adafor*)

Tuareg
Agadez, Niger
Leather, pigment
123 x 44 cm
Musée d'ethnographie, Neuchâtel
48.4.78

D.27 (ABOVE, RIGHT)

Bag (*abaun*)

Tuareg, Oudalen
Boularat, Mali
Leather, pigment
111 x 33 cm
Musée du Quai Branly
71.1941.19.605

D.28 (RIGHT)

Bag with tassels (*ettabuk*)

Tuareg
Niger/Algeria
Leather, pigment
73 x 30 x 3 cm
Musée du Quai Branly
74.1962.0.1158

D.29 (OPPOSITE)

Bag (*eljebira*)

Tuareg, Kel Ahaggar
Ahaggar, Algeria
Leather, pigment, silk
78 x 69 x 6.8 cm
Musée du Quai Branly
74.1962.0.1463

D.30

Bag (*shekw* or *abalbed*)

Tuareg, Kel Assakan
Bourem, Mali
Leather, pigment
70 x 40 cm
Musée d'ethnographie, Neuchâtel
48.3.16

Movement is an essential aspect
of Tuareg aesthetics. The Tuareg
are constantly rearranging their
garments and head veils or wraps.
When men walk, their clothing
moves or billows in the wind. The
same is true of women's jewelry,
especially hair pendants, which sway
with movements of the head. This
aesthetic of movement applies to
leather bags as well, and they are
richly decorated with fringes and
tassels that shake as the camel or
donkey carrying them walks along.

D.31

Bag (*taseihat*)

Tuareg, Iwellemmeden
Tchin Tabaraden, Niger
Leather, pigment
70 x 77 cm
Musée d'ethnographie, Neuchâtel
71.6.28

D.32

Bag (*ettabuk*)

Tuareg
Mauritania
Leather
63 x 23.5 x 5.8 cm
Musée du Quai Branly
74.1962.0.1165

D.33 (BELOW)

Bag (*taseihat*)

Tuareg, Kel Icheriffen
Gao, Mali
Leather, pigment
50 x 135 cm
Musée d'ethnographie, Neuchâtel
48.18.3

D.34 (OPPOSITE, TOP)

Bag (*taseihat*)

Tuareg, Iwellemmeden
Tchin Tabaraden, Niger
Leather, pigment
49 x 140 cm
Musée d'ethnographie, Neuchâtel
71.6.23

D.35 (OPPOSITE, BOTTOM)

Bag (*taseihat*)

Tuareg
Niger
Leather, pigment
48 x 129 cm
Musée d'ethnographie, Neuchâtel
66.1.13

This leather travel bag comes from the Musée d'ethnographie in Neuchâtel, Switzerland, an institution with a lengthy history of collecting Tuareg art. The museum's Saharan collection missions began in the late 1940s under the direction of Jean Gabus and other colleagues working in Algeria and Niger. The museum's Tuareg collection includes objects in wood and leather, basket-work, metalwork, and jewelry. Along with the former Musée de l'homme in Paris (now part of the Musée du Quai Branly) and the National Museum in Copenhagen, the collection of the Musée d'ethnographie houses many of the earliest and finest pieces of Tuareg art.

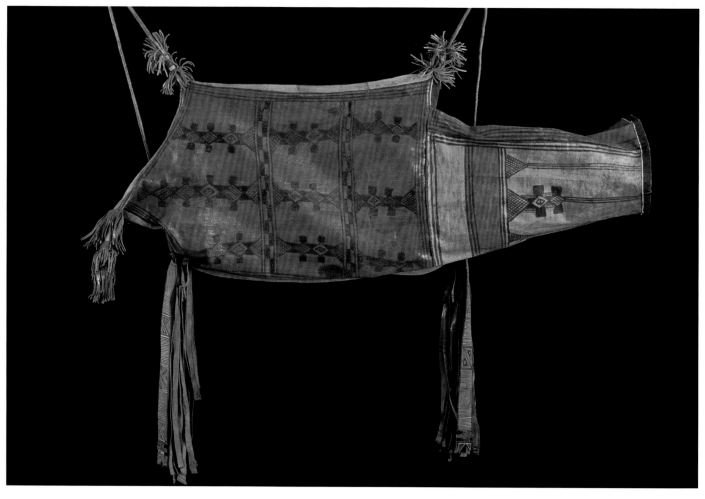

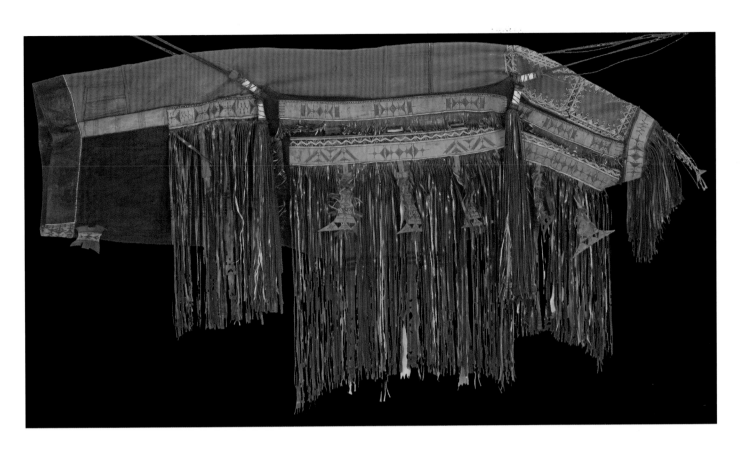

D.36

Bag (*eljebira*)

Tuareg, Kel Aïr
Agadez, Niger
Leather, pigment, silk
80 x 82 cm
Musée d'ethnographie, Neuchâtel
48.4.90

D.37

Woman's saddle blanket (*asetfer*)

Tuareg, Kel Icheriffen
Gao, Mali
Leather, pigment
58 x 48 cm
Musée d'ethnographie, Neuchâtel
48.3.4

D.38

Bag for teapot (*tekabawt*)

Tuareg, Iwellemmeden
Tahoua, Niger
Leather, pigment
H: 85 cm; Diam: 21 cm
Musée d'ethnographie, Neuchâtel
48.7.32

D.39

Bag (*alegutgut*)

Tuareg, Kel Aïr
Niger
Leather, fiber, pigment
38.1 x 15.2 cm
Cantor Arts Center
2001.170

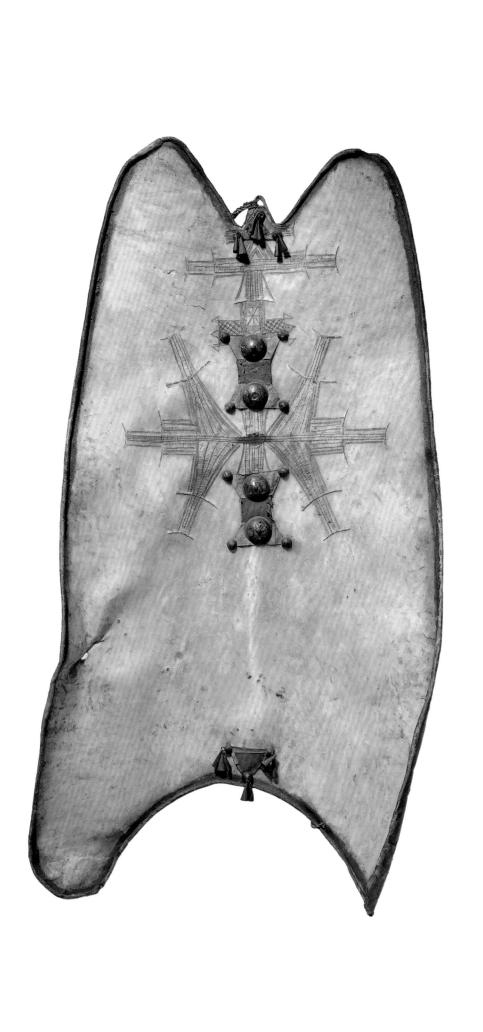

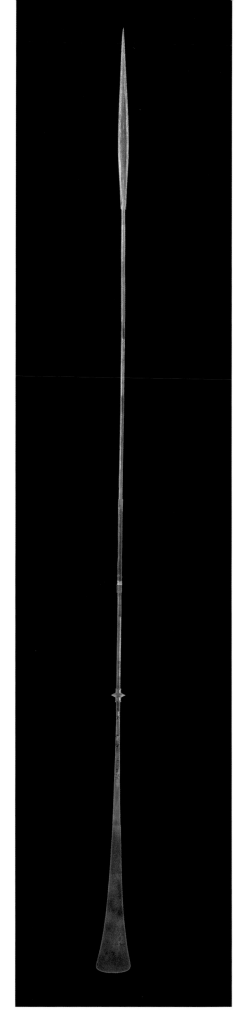

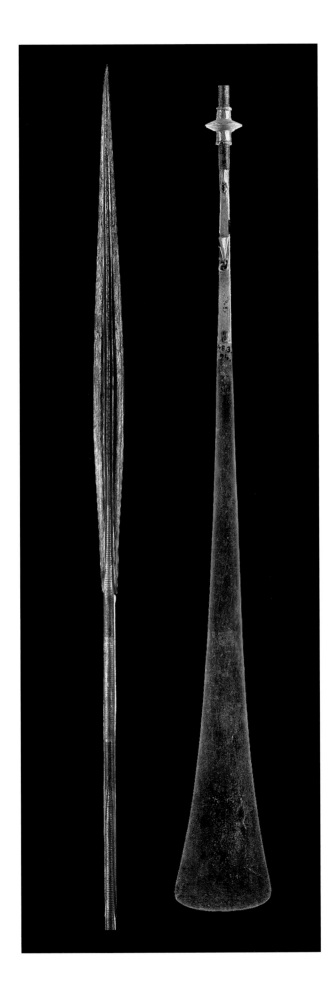

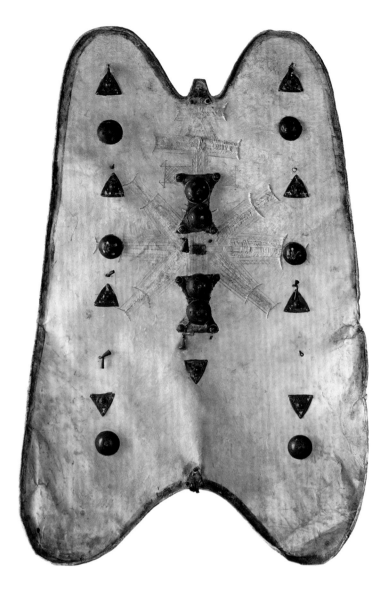

D.40 (OPPOSITE)

Shield (*agher*)

Tuareg
Leather, metal, cloth, pigment
130.8 x 66 cm
Cantor Arts Center
2002.21

The Tuareg shield is usually grasped
by its handle using the left hand. Its
size is such that it offers protection
for the whole body. This shield is
embellished with leather and cloth
decorations, metal studs, and pyrography. The most coveted Tuareg
shields were made of oryx hide,
which is supposedly tough enough
to withstand sword cuts.

D.41a,b (OPPOSITE AND LEFT)

Spear (*allagh*) (and details)

Tuareg, Kel Assakan
Gao, Mali
Leather, iron
L: 200 cm
Musée d'ethnographie, Neuchâtel
48.3.94

D.42 (ABOVE)

Shield (*agher*)

Tuareg
Timbuktu, Mali
Leather, metal, cloth, pigment
121 x 74 cm
Musée d'ethnographie, Neuchâtel
60.7.317

D.43

Sword (*takuba*) and sheath

Yahaya Hamouda
Tuareg, Kel Aïr
Niger
Steel, brass, copper, leather,
cloth, pigment
Sword: 96.8 x 12.4 x 5 cm;
Sheath: 83.8 x 78.7 x 1.27 cm
Private Collection

D.44

Knife (*elmoshi*) and sheath

Tuareg, Kel Aïr
Niger
Wood, metal, leather, cloth
35.6 x 5 x 1.4 cm
Private Collection

D.45 (OPPOSITE, LEFT)

Dagger (*telek* or *gozma*) and sheath

Tuareg
Timbuktu, Mali
Steel, leather, copper, bronze, cloth
L: 65 cm
Musée d'ethnographie, Neuchâtel
60.7.339.a-b

This type of dagger is worn on the
forearm, concealed under the man's
gown.

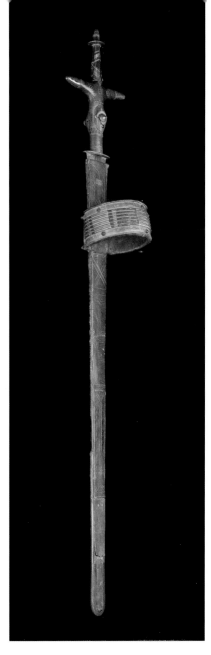

D.46 (LEFT)

Dagger (*telek*) and sheath

Tuareg
Niger/Algeria
Steel, bronze, leather, wood
78 x 11.2 x 9.5 cm
Musée du Quai Branly
74.1962.0.1322.1-2

D.47 (BELOW)

Leather-working knife (*tezigiz* or *telmusit*)

Tuareg
Agadez, Niger
Steel, brass, copper, wood
24.8 x 4.5 cm
Cantor Arts Center
2001.174

When women artists (*tinadan*) work leather, they use sewing awls, a small wooden cutting board, a wooden implement for smoothing, a heavy stone, and a knife. In earlier times many of the dyes used by leatherworkers came from plants such as indigo, pomegranates, sorghum, and minerals, which yield black, green, yellow, reddish brown, and white. Many dyes today are synthetic. Leatherwork knives are small and used to cut pieces before assembly, as well as to incise and excise detailed decorative designs. The wooden end is used for impressing or scoring the leather. Designs refer to the natural and animal world and are similar to those used in metalwork. This particular knife has been decorated with a copper base in keeping with the belief that women should not touch iron and that copper neutralizes it.

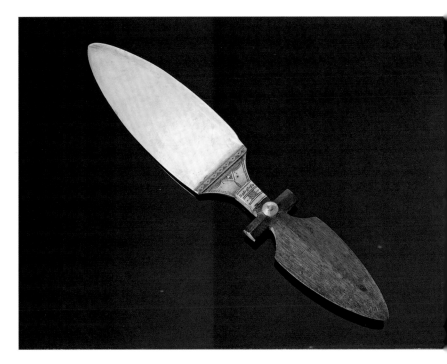

5

TUAREG MUSIC
From Acoustic to Electric

François Borel

Over the past three decades, the Tuareg have undergone a number of sociocultural transformations as a result of droughts, famines, and the crises to which these have given rise. Furthermore, the governments of the states of Niger and Mali compelled the Tuareg—often brutally—to settle or to go into exile. This in turn provoked the creation of clandestine armed-resistance movements whose existence (officially recognized in the mid-1990s) and actions eventually led to peace accords that have been more or less respected. This dramatic course of events has markedly influenced Tuareg musical life, and today so-called traditional music is disappearing. It is instructive, however, to examine the precise causes and nature of this disappearance, which is customarily explained by the vague term "musical acculturation."

Tuareg music is exemplary in many respects. First of all, this population, spread over a vast area that spans five nations, is in continual contact with other musical cultures—borrowing from and influencing them in a perpetual exchange. Urban settings encourage this sort of musical fusion, but even among the most remote rural groups—those that up until recently were purely nomadic and considered the guardians of the traditional music repertory—changes are taking place. The most interesting example is the adoption of a musical genre very different from "traditional" Tuareg music for largely political and ideological reasons, which will be discussed below. To set the stage for this discussion, however, I will initially present a regional panorama of traditional Tuareg music, focusing primarily on Niger, the country with the largest Tuareg population.

Tuareg Traditional Music in Niger

Among the Tuareg groups in Niger that still practice seasonal nomadism, women hold the monopoly on instrumental music. Those of the highest social classes can play the *anzad* or *imzad*, a one-string fiddle, while women of the *inadan* (artisan) or formerly enslaved classes usually play only the mortar drum, or *tende*. Women solo singers are always accompanied by a responsorial chorus, whereas men sing solo a cappella or in duet, sometimes accompanied by the *anzad* (fig. 5.2). These diverse vocal and instrumental forms can be combined to create several types of music; the most common types are *anzad* songs, or *anzad* airs, and *tende* songs.

The repertory of men's songs and *anzad* songs is closely linked to the past and to the epic tradition of Tuareg groups, although there are also many songs that evoke the beloved or simply recount the poet's state of mind. In general, everyone in the group knows the composers and lyricists. It is not customary to create new songs, and interpreters must simply reproduce the repertory, sometimes introducing minor stylistic variations. On the other hand, the women's songs accompanied by the mortar drum

Anghelen playing an *anzad* (*imzad*).
Photograph by François Borel, In Gall, Niger, 1983.

5.2
Singer Mejila and *anzad* (*imzad*) player Almuntaha.
Photograph by François Borel, Kao, Niger, 1981.

5.3
Curative *tende* ritual.
Photograph by François Borel, Tiggart, Niger, 1987.

provide an opportunity for improvising poems that serve as chronicles and sometimes social satire of life in the camps.

Music is generally not sung or played unless there is a specific occasion for it. Two of the most important occasions—and those most often mentioned by the nomadic Tuareg—are gatherings for "songs for the spirits," during which the *anzad* or the *tende* is played (with or without singing) to cure a sick person (fig. 5.3)—that is, to drive the spirits from the ailing person's body—and celebrations (e.g., baptisms, weddings) at which men parade on their favorite camels in a "camel round" that circles the drummer. In the latter instance, only the drum is used, along with a female chorus. In times past, when the Tuareg still launched wars and raids against neighboring groups, caravans, and colonial troops, the *anzad* would be played to encourage and celebrate the warriors' feats of bravery. Warriors were said to "deserve the *anzad*," an expression still used today in reference to a man of valor.

These musical forms therefore reflected social differences within the group itself— the division of players and singers by sex and by their status and role in the traditional hierarchy. Schematically, the music of the Tuareg in Niger was thus made up of: (1) vocal music for men (nobles, vassals, artisans), which is called *asak* in the Azawagh region and *ezale* in the Aïr; (2) instrumental music (played on the *anzad*) for women of the noble and vassal classes; (3) vocal and instrumental music (played on the *tende*) for women of the artisan and formerly enslaved classes. This hierarchical classification is, however, subject to numerous exceptions, especially in regard to the *tende*, which many vassal women (*imrad*) also play. It is also called into question by the current crisis affecting these groups: the growing scarcity of pasturelands, transhumance routes, and herds of camels and cattle. As the nomadic Tuareg society evolves into an agro-pastoral one, the continuity of social practices that guarantee its identity is jeopardized. One of the few customs that remains structured and continues to be repeated and reproduced by its members is the practice of music. It represents a sort of refuge for Tuareg identity, regardless of the social category to which its practitioners belong. Together with the language (Tamasheq), writing system (Tifinar), and veiling of the face (*amawal*) by men, music remains one of the most powerful elements through which the Tuareg show themselves to be distinct from their neighbors.

Vocal Music

SONGS OF THE EPIC TRADITION

Epic poems (see chapter 2 of this volume) are the backbone of Tuareg oral history. Chronicles of war predominate, but they are often drowned in a sea of metaphorical digressions on the inaccessible love of a cherished woman, life in the camps, camels, or cattle. The personal creativity of the reciter or singer is only rarely demonstrated. It is nonetheless permissible for the singer to mix in other poems and to intersperse verses borrowed from other writers. The singer must, however, carefully respect the meter, rhyme, and "poetic rhythm" that confirm the noble warrior origins of the sung poem and must cite at least one verse of the original poem.

The various rhythms and melodies are the "property" of one or another faction of the Tuareg. At one time, in fact, and often even today, the texts and songs attached to a warrior's "personal" rhythms could be recited or sung only by their author or his appointed artisan (*enad*). Only the *anzad* players had the right to perform the rhythm and the melody, and only in instrumental form. Even today, when you ask these women to tell you the name of the tune they are playing, they reply with the name of the rhythm or one of its derivatives.

LOVE SONGS

All Tuareg men, regardless of their origin, are allowed to compose and sing love poems. This is a genre where men never seem to be short of inspiration. Women are often mocking, critical, and demanding, and the prospective lover must outdo himself in order to rank among the suitors of the woman he desires, hoping one day to be the chosen one, or at least one of her favorites. He thus takes great care in the composition of his poems and strives to personalize them so that he won't be accused of plagiarism. That is why the suitor, when he recites or sings a love poem, customarily cites his own name as author at the beginning or end.

His declamation takes place at night, in a small group of men, during the oratorical contests of which the Tuareg are fond. Usually the only family members who participate are "joking relations" with whom there are no ties of *takarakit* (modesty or respect): male and female cross cousins (*tabbubaza*) and relations through marriage (*tellusa*). The other women and girls who are present remain in the background; they will bring to the woman who is the object of the poet's desire the verses that are dedicated to her. It would be inconceivable to recite a love poem in the woman's presence, unless it were done in private.

LEARNING TO SING

The song repertoire is passed on through imitation of a renowned performer. Vocal practice requires the singing of known and recognized melodies. It is unthinkable to rehearse—unless one is alone in the bush—by humming melodies without lyrics, for without words they have no meaning. It is thus impossible to "sing about nothing" (*argangan wan asak*), an act considered childish and unworthy of an adult.[1] For the Tuareg, every adult must observe *asshak*, a certain reserve, a rigor in conducting oneself that could be translated as "nobility." Moreover, and especially in the presence of family members or foreigners, the Tuareg male is bound by the rules of modesty, shame, and respect, which demand that he refrain from externalizing his feelings or speaking of certain subjects, notably music. In short, a man can sing in public only in the presence of an audience belonging to his age group and to his family of "joking relations." But above all, a man cannot sing before an audience unless he has fully mastered his repertory and deems himself capable of presenting it in a way that respects the aesthetic rules of vocal technique that have been passed down from generation to generation. The learning process unfolds through imitation that takes place in the absence of the master, even if he is the singer's father. The adolescent is thus left to his own devices, with only his own judgment to go by (and sometimes today the aid of a cassette recorder) in assessing his talents.

AGENTS OF TRANSMISSION AND REPRODUCTION

The repertory of traditional songs is transmitted through *inadan* (artisans or smiths) and literate Tuareg (*ineslemen*). *Inadan* often serve a nobleman (*amajegh*), and they will collect his words and deeds. They are the first to recite his poems, a privilege that had formerly been theirs alone. The *inadan* are themselves remarkable composers of poems of praise or satire; woe to whomever treats them badly! The reputation of that person can be damaged forever. The *inadan* are the group with the greatest number of poets and singers. If the rules of conduct (*asshak, takarakit*) must be scrupulously observed by nobles and vassals, they are less rigorous, if not nonexistent, for the *inadan*, who characteristically lack reserve. Their social status enables the *inadan* to bypass many constraints. Like griots in areas of West Africa, they are thus the main transmitters of the repertory, the only difference being that they are not professionals, as their musical activity accounts for only a small part of their income.

The *ineslemen* are accustomed to transcribing Arabic texts, since they are, generally speaking, the only literate Tuareg group. Paradoxically, from among those most respectful of the Koranic proscription of profane amusements come the most reliable perpetuators of the oral tradition. One of these is Sheikh Hamed Ibrahim ag Hamed el Mumin, who maintains a rich and valuable library at Abalak. For years he has been meticulously compiling the titles of airs and rhythms in a large hardbound notebook to which he adds remarks, in Tamasheq transcribed in Arabic, on the particulars of their origin and the circumstances of their creation.

Instrumental Music

THE ONE-STRING FIDDLE

Considered the emblematic instrument of Tuareg women, the *anzad* (in the dialect of the Iwellemmeden Tuareg of the Azawagh region of Niger) or *imzad* (in the dialect of the Ahaggar Tuareg) is still played in several Tuareg communities of Niger and Mali, whereas in the Ahaggar and the Tassili, women fiddle players are becoming rare (fig. 5.4).

Nonetheless, the one-string fiddle remains, in itself and through its repertory of tunes, the symbolic medium blending notions of war, class, and femininity that the Tuareg delight in perpetuating and enriching through proverbs, orations, and poems—all the more so now that the instrument is one of the few remnants of their glorious past. Charles de Foucauld described its evocative power in his *Dictionnaire touareg-français*: "The *imzad* is the favorite musical instrument, preeminently noble and elegant; it is the one that wins all preferences, the one that people sing of in verse, that they yearn for when far from their homeland, of which it serves as a symbol and whose sweet pleasures it recalls…. It is played for guests whom one wants to honor" (1951–1952, 3: 1270).

More recently, Paulette Galand-Pernet analyzed the female image in Charles de Foucauld's *Poésies* and inventoried the elements of an aesthetic code that includes teeth and violin:

> There is, in effect, a series of terms referring to significant elements of the female aesthetic code: choice physical features, accessories that bespeak a high social rank and refined cultural tastes—these become cultural symbols…. These linguistic features are highly instructive: besides their use in reference to cultural facts, "teeth" and "violin" have poetic uses in which the usual meaning blurs, but the image of beauty and refinement remains, associated with important moments in the sentimental life of the individual and in the social life of the *ahal* [courtship gatherings]. [Galand-Pernet 1978, 32]

Today the Tuareg language retains several expressions that include the word *anzad*. As noted above, *ihor anzad* (he deserves the *anzad*) means "he is worthy of praise,"

5.5

Fiddle and bow (*imzad*)

Tuareg
Ahaggar, Algeria
Wood, leather, fiber
L: 61 cm; W: 14 cm; Diam: 29 cm
Musée d'ethnographie, Neuchâtel
97.13.1.a,b

5.6

Dassine oult Ihemma playing an *imzad*.

Photograph by P. Ichac, date unknown, Tamanrasset, Algeria. Musée du Quai Branly, Photothèque, c.34.1576.231.

implying courage and valor. Khamed Ibrahim, the head of the Kel Aghlal *ineslemen*, observes that "in the word *anzad*, we find *izod* [that which is gentle and sweet, which pleases the soul]" (personal communication, 1980).

· THE REPERTORY

Anzad players are content to perpetuate rhythms and airs based on the repertory of men's songs. The women keep the original titles and usually play them in a set order, which facilitates memorization. Among the eastern Iwellemmeden Tuareg in Niger, this body of melodies can number up to 150, some of which are simply ornamental variants of the main airs. Some are first learned by singing in solitude and are then reconstructed on the instrument, always accompanied by a soft murmuring in the throat. This technique, perceptible to listeners attuned to throat movements, is called *asak dagh iman* (singing within the soul). The occasional nighttime gatherings of young people not only provide an opportunity to get better acquainted with members of the opposite sex, they also lend themselves to curative sessions on the one-string violin, during which the ailing person is immersed in a warm atmosphere that restores his or her contact with the community.

· THE INSTRUMENT

The resonating body of the *anzad* is made up of a hemispheric receptacle (*aghezu*) of *adaras* wood (*Commiphora africana*), an imported enameled bowl (*teghert*), or half a gourd (*alkas*). Use of the wooden receptacle, common among the *anzad* players of the Iwellemmeden Kel Denneg Tuareg of Azawagh, gives the instrument an ephemeral quality, since the receptacle will be used for food again after it serves as the resonating body (fig. 5.5). That is not the case for the half gourd, which is worth far less and thus need not be reused. Use of the half gourd is common among Tuareg in the plains of the western Aïr and in the Aïr mountain range itself, as well as in the Ahaggar. The sounding board is made of the skin of a buck (*egashek*), or a goatskin (*abayogh*) that is worn out (*agadod*). Most of the time, because of the mounting holes and acoustic holes, the

5.7
Women gather to watch a men's *tende* dance at a wedding. An *aghal-abba* drum with the characteristic submerged half gourd is visible to the right of the *tende*.
Photograph by Thomas K. Seligman, Agadez, Niger, 1988.

agadod is carefully stored, rolled up with the strings and the bridge. The neck of the instrument is a branch of the *aboragh* (*Balanites aegyptiaca*), freshly cut, lightly curved, its bark peeled (wood for the neck and the bow must be acquired secretly, out of sight of the spirits known as "forest guards"). It is carved to a point at its lower end (the future "tailpiece") and furnished with a notch at the upper end (the "nut"). The string is made of a bundle of animal hair (*anzaden*; sing. *anzad*; hence the name of the instrument), about a hundred strands taken from the tail of a horse. After it has been carefully moistened with saliva so that the strands stick together, the bundle is fixed at each end to a skin strap that allows it to be attached to the top and the very bottom of the neck, passing over the resonating body. The length of the string is on average two-thirds of the total length of the instrument. The bridge is made of a crossed pair of short sticks, the upper ends of which are bound by a small strap made of leather, vegetable fiber, or a scrap of cloth (fig. 5.6).

At about age fifteen, when she is old enough to wear her first head scarf, a girl will build her own instrument from salvaged materials and cow hair, horsehair being reserved for the instruments of the adult women. Before she will play the airs (*izelan*; sing., *azel*) of the classic repertoire, she begins with a learning exercise known as *melloloki*, which allows her to practice, first of all, the movements of the bow (*esawey*): the upstroke (*huket*) and downstroke (*aseres*), and especially the light taps that mark the rhythm (*asatarekhtarekh*); next are the movements of the fingers (*azzemezeri n duduan*) and their position, their "meeting" (*ameni*). It's only after several years of rehearsal, when she considers herself ready, that a girl will dare to perform in public.

THE *TENDE* OR *TINDÉ* DRUM

· *TENDE* DRUM SONGS

Among the eastern Iwellemmeden and the Tuareg of the Aïr region, with the exception of the Kel Ewey, *tende* song (*izeliten n tende*) is an exclusively feminine domain (fig. 5.7).

5.8

Making a *tende* drum using a mortar.

Photograph by François Borel, Tarazeyna, Niger, 1978.

5.9

Lallawa playing a *tende* drum.

Photograph by François Borel, Aghaljen, Niger, 1982.

A woman beats the drum that is constructed from a mortar, and she also sings as a soloist accompanied by a female responsorial chorus.

The *tende* is played on two very different occasions: the "camel races" that take place at weddings, baptisms, official meetings, or any event that serves as a pretext for men to show themselves in their best light and the sessions of "seated" dancing (*takbest*) that effect a healing process for certain physico-psychic afflictions that are referred to as "illnesses of the spirits" by the Tuareg. These two genres can be distinguished by the rhythms that are beaten, but the distinction between their song repertoires (in terms of content and expression) is less obvious. In fact, the themes evoked—praise of or anecdotes concerning an individual—are found in both genres.

The *tende* repertory differs greatly from the male song repertories in that the soloist can create and improvise the lyrics and melody, drawing on themes of her own choosing and giving them form with no restriction besides the rhythm. She may also use texts or fragments of texts created by other singer-drummers in the region. Surely one of the best representatives of this musical category was Khadija, a former captive of the warrior group Ighalgawen Kel Fadey. She had no match in her camp or in the region of In Gall. Her talent was so widely recognized that she was often invited to perform at festivals and at the official receptions that follow the period of the Cure Salée,[2] and she composed a song for the visit of the French minister Yvon Bourges in 1971. Her songs principally evoke the people of her camp and regional history.

· THE INSTRUMENT

The *tende* is a skin drum made of a mortar used to crush millet. The mortar is covered with a goatskin attached by ropes and is fitted with two parallel pestles arranged horizontally on each side of the mortar (fig. 5.8). These serve as seats for the two accompanying singers, while also ensuring the proper tension of the skin. This kind of drum is typical of nomadic Tuareg and is not known to be used elsewhere. In all Tuareg dialects the word *tende* means "mortar" and, by extension, "mortar drum." The instrument is present throughout the Tuareg world, even though the women drummers of the Ahaggar replaced it long ago with a jerican (a metal gas can). The jerican requires no preparation or maintenance, and its timbre can be adjusted by opening the hinged lid. There are, in addition, two other configurations for the *tende*. The first does not require the use of a second rope since the pestles, or poles, are attached directly to the skin on each side of the mortar. The second merely has the skin attached to the mortar with a rope but with no pestles. Normally two women are seated on the crosspieces of the *tende* to balance it and ensure the proper tension of the skin. When there are no accompanists, two blocks of stone or sacks of sand may serve this function. And among the Kel Ewey of the Aïr Mountains, men rather than women beat the drum with leather beaters at rites of passage such as name days and weddings.

The skin is moistened before setting up the instrument to facilitate assembly. During playing, the drying skin becomes increasingly taut, making the sound sharper. It must therefore be periodically moistened to keep the drum in tune. In some groups, a moist cloth always covers the drum while it is beaten (fig. 5.9). The fastest and most frequent method of tuning the drum, however, is to beat the edges of the skin and the pestles with a stick or a small rock, sometimes even in the course of playing the instrument.

It would be quite convenient to view the use of the *tende* by women of the formerly enslaved class as a reflection of their original servile status, which is given concrete form by virtue of the fact that it is constructed from a kitchen utensil. According to the Kel Fadey Tuareg of the In Gall region, however, the *tende*, as a rhythm instrument, was formerly played only by women of the *imajeren*, or noble, class. They were in fact the only ones to play an instrument, while those enslaved could merely sing and clap the rhythm of the dance performed by the men. It seems therefore that great changes have taken place in the traditional attribution of instruments among the Kel Fadey and their neighbors, since today it is the "formerly enslaved" and "vassal" women who beat the drum, whether for camels or for spirits. Moreover, it is rare in these groups to see a noblewoman crush millet and even more rare to see one beat the mortar drum. The fact that a certain number of old songs were created by noblewomen supports the hypothesis of the noble origin of *tende* playing and the oral transmission of the repertoire of songs to the servile classes. The nobles do retain the rights to sing the songs dedicated to spirits on occasion. Furthermore, the Kel Fadey report that among them the *tende* was originally played for healing. Only later did its use in the camel round arrive from the Ahaggar.

Tende playing is learned very early and in an informal manner with the aid of drums fabricated by young girls from recycled materials (empty cans of food or powdered milk covered with a rag). Here the learning process is not kept from view, since *tende* playing is a favorite childhood amusement, enjoyed especially by the little girls of *inadan* and of the formerly enslaved group. The different rhythms (*iwetan*; sing., *ewet*; "to beat") are learned gradually through the numerous nighttime drum performances, during which a young girl can easily beat the motif on the ground or on any object at hand.

· RHYTHMS FOR CAMELS

The Tuareg apparently have no general term for the rhythm of a drum. This notion seems to be subsumed by the names of diverse rhythms. Thus, one would say, "beat the *illigwan*," for example, the *illigwan ewet* being the name of a particular rhythm. Rhythms for the camel round are the most numerous type. They function to direct, in some sense, the camels' movements through the mediation of the camel riders (although one might wonder if it isn't the camels who react from experience to the changes in rhythm). The names of these rhythms are closely linked to the camels and to the different kinds of steps that they take. Moreover, it is likely that each step has its own equivalent motif struck on the drum. Their tempo is characteristically quite lively, presenting a rather syncopated structure and establishing a compound meter.

· RHYTHMS FOR "THE SPIRITS"

As noted above, another type of *tende* rhythm is played for people afflicted by "the illness of the spirits." As one Tuareg described it,

The ailing person dances, sitting or standing. When he is sitting, he moves only his head, chest, and arms. When standing, he moves his whole body. Sometimes during the *tende* another man or woman will "fall" ill. At that point they may remain silent, prostrate, eating nothing but only drinking water. They can be healed in one day or one night, but if not, we rest and start over the next day. All nomad groups have people possessed by spirits. There are people from sedentary groups in the west who are also possessed, but they speak when they are ill. Among certain nomads, especially in the west, the spirits are called *aljeynan* or Kel Esuf. The healing music can be played on either the *tende* or the *tazawat* [see below], but among the *ineslemen*, only the *tende* is played. [Personal communication, 1978]

Regarding the Tuareg of the Ahaggar, Marceau Gast wrote: "At Idélès in May 1961, Jouma, the daughter of Khaned, fell into a trance during an evening celebration, blinded by the flash of a camera, in the middle of the group that was beating the *tende*. Her state of trance lasted about one hour, in spite of the repeated songs of exorcism sung by a group of men in the midst of whom she walked" (1962, 150ff.). For the Kel Fadey of Niger, the *tende* has more power than the *anzad* to heal the illness of the spirits, but that also depends on the personality of the one afflicted. On the other hand, playing the *tende* without singing "is not worthwhile," since one must "say proverbs so that the sick person may heal."

Most of the rhythms played during these healing rites have a rather slow tempo and a rather "obsessive" four-beat pattern. Among the Kel Fadey, the main rhythm is called *gumatan*, a term of obscure origins. Two other rhythms can alternate: *egishen*, or "the horses," the motif of which does in fact recall the gallop of a horse; and *azamayzamay*, the meaning of which is uncertain. Among the Iwellemmeden, the rhythm most often played for the spirits is *isanaghalebbuten* (a word that contains the name of the water drum *aghaleb*; see below). Its structure is complex, with the *tende* accompanied by the water drum and by hand clapping but no singing.

OTHER INSTRUMENTS

· THE *AGHALABBA* OR *ASAGHALABBO* WATER DRUM

The water drum consists of a large wooden (or enameled metal) bowl filled with water that has an inverted half gourd floating on its surface (see fig. 5.7). The diameter of the gourd is from about a half to a third that of the bowl. The gourd is struck with a stick. The amount of water in the bowl does not affect the drum's tone, but the volume of the gourd does. It is thus possible to tune the instrument by submerging the gourd at different depths, since this modifies the volume of the "cavity" formed between the interior of the gourd and the surface of the water. The bowl itself must be filled almost to the top, so that the back of the gourd emerges sufficiently to allow its percussion.

The water drum is beaten in unison with hand clapping by the female chorus. Sometimes it is difficult to discern the very low frequency of the instrument. In fact, it is often the sound of the stick striking the gourd that predominates. It may be that the low frequency of the water drum is necessary to complement the sound spectrum of the hand clapping or the *tende*. Evidently the water drum is never used alone.

Sometimes the water drum is replaced by another type of receptacle with a similar sonority. The receptacle can be a clay-neck jar, called *talikint*, whose opening is struck with a sandal or a basketry fan, producing a deep sound. Another variant is a long-neck gourd (*tazenut*) that is usually used to hold milk, and whose neck is struck with a sandal or basketry fan.

· THE *TAZAWAT* DRUM

In Tamasheq the word *tazawat* is used for a wooden receptacle similar to that containing the water for the *aghalabba*. Goatskin or cowhide is stretched over the opening of the receptacle, and the corners of the covering are knotted underneath it. The sides of the skin are held tight with circular straps made of bark fiber. Structurally, it is a skin

5.10
Women clapping and drumming.
Photograph by Thomas K. Seligman, Agadez, Niger, 1988.

5.11 (RIGHT)

Lute (*tahardant*)

Tuareg
Gao, Mali
Wood, leather, fiber
L: 68 cm
Musée d'ethnographie, Neuchâtel
48.18.42

5.12 (BELOW)

Playing the musical bow
(*fadengama*).
*Photograph by François Borel, Abalak,
Niger, 1980.*

drum of the kettledrum type with no opening at the bottom. Observed and recorded in eastern Iwellemmeden noble tribes in the region of Tchin Tabaraden, the instrument is not found among other Tuareg groups. Possibly its morphological relation with the *tobol* or *ettebel* (see below) led to its being amalgamated with the latter.

The water drum and hand clapping normally accompany the *tazawat*, but it can also be played by a drummer independently of the female solo singer and can even accompany the *anzad*. That explains, no doubt, why the drummer shows great imagination in the choice of her accompanying rhythms. In fact, almost every song has its own rhythmic motif. This diversity is probably due to the greater freedom that the drummer enjoys in choosing her motifs, unlike the *tende* player, who besides drumming must improvise her song or follow a text while also making sure that the melody is appropriate.

· THE *TOBOL* (*ETTEBEL*) DRUM

Although the *tobol* looks like the *tazawat*, it differs in the manner of playing and especially in its use. In fact, this instrument symbolizes the chiefdom's power, and in this capacity it was once used to alert and assemble nomadic groups under an *amenokal* (chief of the confederation). Francis Nicolas established a list of code beats used for this purpose (1939, 585; 1950, 192). The *tobol* is beaten alternately by two men (*inadan* or members of the formerly enslaved) using a supple leather beater (*atakor*). With their other hands they hold the instrument by its handles. Today an *amenokal* always has his *tobol* in his tent, but he uses it only to bring his chief vassals together or to give an alert, for instance, if a child is lost.

· *EQQAS* HAND CLAPPING

Hand clapping always accompanies the *tende*, the *tazawat*, or dance, and sometimes even the *anzad*. In general, one claps in unison with the water drum to a regular tempo and rhythm that serve as a sort of rhythmic "meter" (fig. 5.10). In the Ahaggar, women clap "à l'Arabe," in a syncopated fashion, forming motifs independent of the rhythm of the *tende*. This practice is not used or accepted by Tuareg in Niger, who make a point of distinguishing themselves from the Arabs.

· THE *TASENSEQ* FLUTE

Played by herdsmen throughout the Tuareg world, the flute is called *tasenseq*—a noun derived from the verb *ensegh* (to whistle)—in the Aïr region and among the Iwellemmeden of Niger. The instrument is played solo exclusively by herdsmen, whose occupation is reflected in the repertory of tunes. In fact, most of the titles evoke the life of the herd, the behavior of animals (running, galloping, and the gait of camels), and the solitude of vast spaces—a sort of musical narrative.

The *tasenseq* is a four-hole flute with a simple mouthpiece at the end that is sometimes lightly beveled but otherwise unfashioned; traditionally it is made from the bark of a *tamat* root (*Acacia seyal*), but more often today it is constructed from a section of tubing, either plastic (electrical conduit) or metal. Its length varies between forty and sixty centimeters, the bore is from two to three centimeters. It is held obliquely so as to facilitate the "capture of sound" that occurs by blowing the air stream formed by the lips against the rim at the end of the tube, which enables one to modify the timbre of the instrument at will and impart its characteristic texture, rich in rushing air.

· INSTRUMENTS AND VOCAL GAMES OF CHILDREN

From the age of five or six, Tuareg girls of all social groups try their hand at *tende* playing (learning to play the *anzad* comes later) by making a drum with recycled materials, for example a can covered with a rag. That is why, in almost all the camps, most women know how to beat the rhythms for the camel round or the seated dance, which confirms the very important place that the playing of this instrument holds in daily life. One might even say that it forms a part of women's domestic activities, much like crushing millet.

The musical bow *fadengama* is played by girls ten to fifteen years old (fig. 5.12). The instrument is set up vertically, the shaft resting on the ground, held in this position by an inverted metal bowl (*tazawat*). The string is plucked with the right hand to make two different tones, while it is strummed with the left to accompany the refrains sung by the young girls.

While the adult herdsmen play the *tasenseq* flute while tending their herds, the boys make small clarinets, or *wodili*, from stalks of millet. They carve one or two holes in the stalk and decorate the flute with multicolor fringes made of leftover strips of leather or plastic.

The girls perform a type of "mouth play" called *belluwel*, singing at a high pitch with a slight vibrato produced by one hand tapping the throat while the other hand is curved into a tube shape and placed before the mouth to amplify the sound. This practice, which imitates the playing of the small children's flute, *wodili*, is used as a lullaby for the babies that the girls take care of. The *belluwel* enables them to "cut up" the words that they sing so as to render them thus incomprehensible to noninitiates (the adults). It is also used in humming nursery rhyme tunes.

These same girls also use a rhythmic play of throat and mouth called *akhaguwwen*. To form a resonating cavity, they place their two hands, joined and held half-open, over their mouth and nose, while pressing their throat with both thumbs. In this way they produce a hoarse sound from the throat, modified by the pressure of the thumbs, and a rhythmic noise as the air is forcibly expelled through the half-closed lips. The result is a sort of motif evoking animal cries and the sound of the *wodili* flute.

· THE *TAHARDANT* LUTE OF THE RIVER TUAREG (NIGER AND MALI)

The body of the *tahardant* lute is made from a wooden log hollowed out in the shape of a boat hull or a dog bowl. The name of this part of the instrument is in fact borrowed from the latter utensil: *efaghir n tahardant*. Both the resonating body and the neck are entirely covered in skin (*egheyt*), usually cowhide, although camel skin might possibly be used as well (fig 5.11). The sounding board is pierced at its base with a sound hole (*tanabad*) that allows the three strings to be fixed to the tailpiece constituted by the lower end of the neck (*ashik n tahardant*). The three strings made of catgut or nylon are given names: *ahar* (the lion) for the longest; *tezori* (the hyena), for the second longest; and *ebag* (the jackal) for the shortest. A small bridge made of a fragment of gourd (*talkast*) raises the three strings at their base before they are fixed to the tailpiece. The strings of the *tahardant* are strummed with a pick (*eshkar*) made of goat or sheep bone, which also allows the lutenist to beat the skin of the sounding board while playing. To enrich the timbre and the vibration of the strings, the top of the neck features a "noise-maker" consisting of an iron plate furnished with small metal rings (*tifraghraghin*).

Although the instrument was probably borrowed from the Moors or other sedentary groups in the region of Timbuktu near the bend of the Niger River, the origin of its name remains disputed: for some, it is a corruption of the expression *tan hartani* ("that of the Haratines," the latter being former slaves and dependents of the Ahaggar Tuareg); for others, the word is derived from *tidinit* or *ardin*, the first the name of the lute of Moorish griots and the second the harp of Moorish women griots. The repertory of those who play the *tahardant* and sing is made up of old epic airs, played to commemorate great feats of arms, and newer songs, sung for dancing at "amusements," in honor of famous women.

Regional Influences and the Contemporary Scene

Two types of musical influences come from the areas bordering Tuareg lands. The first reflects older contributions that affect and determine regional styles, as seen, for instance, in the eastern Iwellemmeden, where women playing the *anzad* have adopted a certain bow stroke and sometimes even phrasing reminiscent of that of their sedentary neighbors, the Hausa *goge* players. In this case, the purely Tuareg components (instruments, forms, scales, and repertory) remain present, and the process can be considered a normal and inevitable evolution—one might even say an unconscious one—that every music based on oral tradition undergoes. The second type of influence results in more radical changes, for example, the adoption of the Arab *ûd* by the Tuareg of the Ahaggar or the Tassili, or the use of the Hausa *goge* by the Tuareg of Niger, borrowings that have obviously also entailed the masculine practice of these instruments.

Among the Tuareg of Mali, the situation is a bit different. Two musical practices coexist: that of so-called traditional music, which follows with few exceptions the same rules enumerated above, and that of a caste of musicians that holds a monopoly on playing the *tahardant* lute (see above), the origin of which is probably Moorish. These musicians have become instrumentalist griots (*aggutan*), and this function of professional musician exists nowhere else in the Tuareg world. These *aggutan* enjoy great freedom in improvising, adapting, and creating new songs, and their presence and playing are also greatly appreciated at festivals of traditional dance (*ewegh* or *taggagh*) or "modern" dance (*takamba*), during which women dance while seated, swinging their arms from side to side to the rhythm that the musician plays.

5.13

Takres n akal band performing at
a wedding in a dry river area in
northern Niger. Electrical power
came from a portable generator.

*Photograph by Thomas K. Seligman, Talak,
Niger, 2001.*

At the beginning of the 1970s, with the appearance of cassettes, the younger generations of rural Tuareg discovered Malian *tahardant* music with its satirical songs, which
were critical not only of the rulers but also of the traditional hierarchy. The new repertories unleashed awareness among these youths of the rigidity of their musical patrimony
and the difficulty of modernizing it, given that it was so bound up with the hierarchical
social structure. It is not surprising that these young people were on the lookout for new
references for their cultural identity, and that is what the songs of the *ishumar* offered
them.

REBELLION SONGS

The term *ishumar* (sing., *ashamur*) came to be associated with the French *chômeur* (one
who is unemployed) and designates the members of a generation of Tuareg from Niger
and Mali, generally single, who left their families and their country to flee oppression
or to seek work in Libya or Algeria (see chapter 3 of this volume). They are the product
of the crises of the past twenty years (droughts and famines) and the repression that
accompanied them. After 1989—and some attempts at repatriation and reintegration
on the part of the government of Niger—many of the *ishumar* organized in groups
espousing open rebellion and secretly took up arms, relinquishing their adherence to
one Tuareg confederation or another and demanding a single ethnic identity for all.
They thereby hoped to be freed of allegiance to their lineage within the social hierarchy,
which was a source of division and antagonism, and to promote Tuareg unification and
political unity within the states that governed them.

In the course of their wanderings and through their contacts with the outside world,
these *ishumar* progressively adopted new signs of identity—for example, the wearing of
turbans in the manner of the Polisario guerrillas of the Western Sahara (see below); the
occasional replacement of the traditional two-edged sword (*takuba*) with the Kalash-
nikov assault rifle; and, more relevant to the subject at hand, the acquisition of martial
songs. These songs were composed primarily by Tuareg exiles from Mali and constitute

a sort of sung popular press, a political news bulletin for propaganda and mobilization, disseminated largely through cassettes. These revolutionary songs evoke an array of subjects including the cultural submission imposed by traditional Tuareg society, the collaboration of certain Tuareg chiefs with the governments in place, the mismatch of young Tuareg girls with young sedentary men, the need to have a territory and a homeland, and so on. In general, these songs explicitly illustrate the upheavals that have affected Tuareg society.

THE INSTRUMENTAL REVIVAL

The model of instrumental accompaniment that inspired the emulators of this new genre was provided by, among others, the Tuareg musical groups from Niger called Takres n akal (Building of the Country; fig. 5.13) and Terbyia. The accompaniment consists of two guitars, and sometimes a third used as a percussion instrument; a solo singer; and a responsorial chorus of young girls. For Westerners hearing these groups, the ambience of an evening scout-troop gathering might be evoked. The guitar accompaniment mitigates some culture shock, lending a bit of familiarity to the scene. The instrument is used essentially to produce a few chords, three in general, interspersed with a few arpeggios inspired by the traditional lute (*tahardant*) playing to mark the succession of verses. The music is repetitive, since the key of the accompaniment and the rhythm rarely varies in the whole repertory.

Since these elements, with the exception of the language, are completely foreign to Tuareg musical culture, it is interesting to consider where and under what circumstances the rebellion songs were created. The answer can be found in the contacts established by the *ishumar* with other movements that inspired their effort to bring their armed struggle to fruition. Surely the songs of Polisario, the Western Saharan liberation movement (established by those living in the formerly Spanish Saharan territory that was claimed by Morocco), served as a model, not only in the use of the guitar but also in the rhythms, which are clearly of Spanish origin. This resemblance is particularly striking between the song *Kel akal nin* (Those of My Country) by the group Takres n akal and *Adelante ejercito popular* (Onward People's Army) sung by the Grupo nacional de cantos y danzas populares of the Polisario Front.

In spite of its uniform nature, far removed from the diversity of the traditional repertoire, this music affords several advantages for young people. First of all, given its familiarity, it is accessible to all, even to the sedentary groups. Moreover, it breaks the constraints imposed by Tuareg society and offers a sense of modernity that the young Tuareg from rural areas demand. In fact, the musicians justify their use of acoustic (and sometimes electric) guitar by citing the freedom it gives them. This instrument has no social connotation; it can be played by men—unlike the one-string fiddle—regardless of their social status and at any time, under any circumstances.

This new music, which for a long time was transmitted clandestinely and pirated on countless cassettes to promote the cause, has already been rehabilitated by the political establishment of Niger. Numerous groups have formed, some of which have toured Europe, and record producers have begun to pour money into this "market." It will probably undergo further transformations, as it develops into a familiar genre or even assimilates to the genre of popular world music. Today, after having met with real success among Tuareg youth—for whom traditional music evoked a sense of scorn mixed with repressed nostalgia, as though it had become "politically incorrect"—this new music is already beginning to tire its audience, precisely because it is progressively losing its original militant character and resembling all other popular world music. Actually the Tuareg have more and more difficulty identifying themselves with a music, which, mostly for commercial reasons, is "formatted" for the European and American audiences by "modern" Tuareg musicians (like the groups Tinariwen and Tartit) and Western producers who want to profit in the international records market by taking advantage of the current "Tuareg trend."

⬚

Selected Discography of Tuareg Music

1. TRADITIONAL TUAREG MUSIC

Tuareg Music of the Southern Sahara. Recorded by Finola & Geoffrey Holiday. 1 CD Folkways Recordings 004470, 1960

Touareg du Mali: Collection prophet vol. 12. Teharden and *mzad.* Recordings, texts, and photos by Charles Duvelle. Recorded in situ in 1961. 1 CD Philips Kora Sons 464488-2, 2000.

Hoggar: Musique des Touareg / Music of the Tuareg. Recordings by Michel Vionnet, Jean-Louis Garnier (1990), and Nadia Mécheri-Saada (1980). 1 CD Le Chant du Monde LDX 274974, 1994.

Niger: Music of the Tuaregs. Vol. 1: Azawagh; Vol. 2: In Gall. Recordings by F. Borel and E. Lichtenhahn (1971–1998). 2 CDs AIMP/VDE-GALLO CD-1105 and CD-1106, Geneva, 2002.

2. MODERN TUAREG MUSIC FROM TASSILI (ALGERIA) WITH ARAB-BERBER INFLUENCES, ACCOMPANIED BY ÛD AND GUITAR

Tis Ras. Collection Touareg, vol. 3. Song, choir, guitar, 'ûd, darbouka. 1 CD Al Sur/ Média 7 ALCD 124, 1995.

Libye: Musique du désert: Touareg de Fewet. Musiques du Monde. 1 CD Buda Records 1978312.

3. NEO-TRADITIONAL TUAREG MUSIC

Amazagh: Ensemble Tartit, Touaregs Kel Antessar. Troisième festival voix de femmes. Fonti Musicali, FDM 210, 1997.

4. TUAREG FUSION MUSIC

Assouf: Baly Othmani and Steve Shehan. Song, 'ûd, synthesizers, sampling, and various ambient sounds. 1 CD Al Sur/Média 7 ALCD 136, 1994.

Imuhar. Production and orchestration by Philippe Eidel. Sony Music, Saint George, CB 791, SAN 486711-2, 14-486711 10, 1996–1997.

TEA

E.1a,b

a. Tea glasses
Imported to Tuareg, Kel Aïr
Mauritania/Niger
Glass
Diam: 4.6 cm
UCLA Fowler Museum
x88.1404a,b

**b. Teapot (*albirade*)
and tray (*atabla*)**
Imported to Tuareg, Kel Aïr
Mauritania/Niger
Metal
Teapot: 13.8 x 17.8 cm;
Diam (of tray): 31.5 cm
UCLA Fowler Museum
x88.1403a,b

E.2

Hamidan Oumba making tea.

*Photograph by Thomas K. Seligman, Azel,
Niger, 2004.*

E.3

Sugar shears (*temoda ton essukor*)

Amrar ag Amareouat
Tuareg, Kel Rela
Algeria
Steel, copper, aluminum
30.3 x 7.6 x 2.9 cm
Musée du Quai Branly
71.1941.19.158

Whenever Tuareg visit and socialize or when they seek relaxation after traveling or working long hours, it is time for tea. Tea is served as a gesture of hospitality, and the caffeine it contains—along with the ample amounts of sugar added—help to assuage hunger. Three glasses are usually consumed in sequence, at least three times per day. The three consecutive glasses of tea are—in order—one strong, one medium, and one sweet. They are poetically conceived of as corresponding to youth, middle age, and old age. Tea is enjoyed by men and women, and even children sip it in small amounts.

Tea, tea-making equipment, and sugar have all come to the Tuareg through trade. In the past, the tea was whatever variety was available at the moment, and sugar came in large, densely cast cones that had to be broken up with hammers, pincers, and shears. To brew tea in the Tuareg manner requires fire; expert skill at mixing the right amounts of tea, water, and sugar; and proper aeration, which is achieved by accurate pouring of the tea from a considerable distance back-and-forth between the teapot and another vessel (a second teapot or large glass). For the first glass approximately four to five tablespoons of black tea are mixed with an equal amount of sugar in half a teapot of water. For the second and third glass, the same tea leaves are reused, but an additional four to five tablespoons of sugar and half a teapot of water are added. As a result, the tea becomes increasingly sweet. The decorated teapot (today from China), the elegant locally made sugar hammer and pincers, and the fellowship and conversation that attend its brewing and serving combine to make tea drinking a rich and integral part of Tuareg life.

T.K.S.

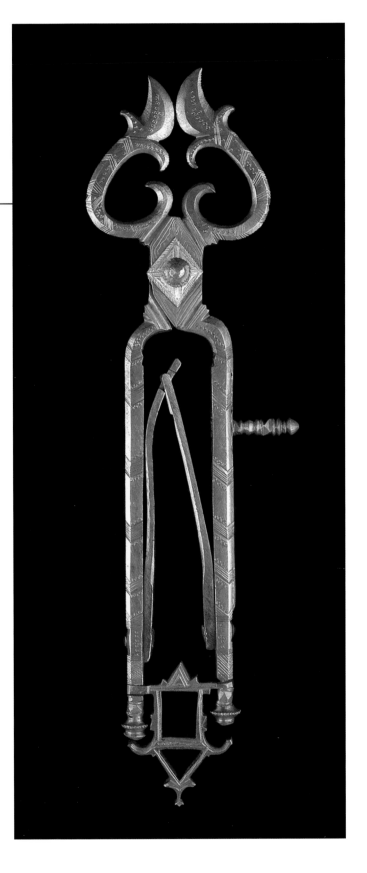

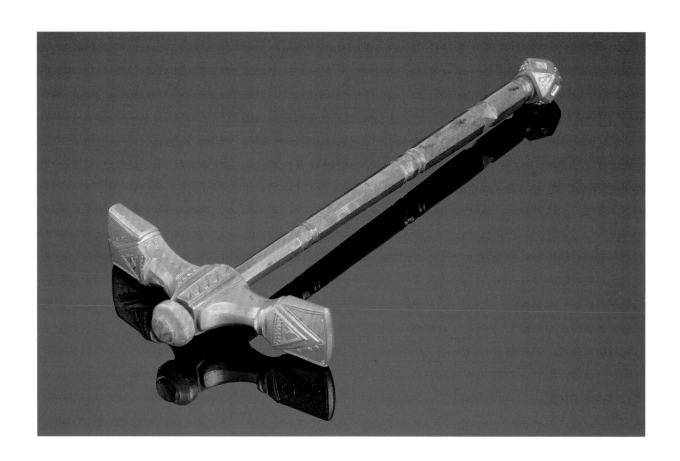

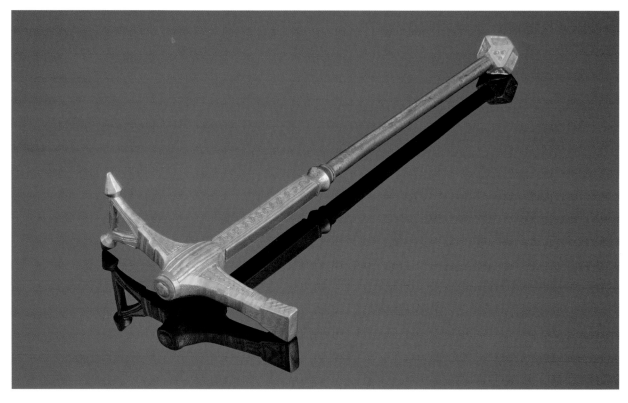

E.4

Sugar hammer (*tefedist*)

Tuareg, Iwellemmeden de l'Est
Tchin Tabaraden, Niger
Brass, copper, steel
23 x 10 cm
Musée d'ethnographie, Neuchâtel
71.6.72

E.5

Sugar hammer (*tefedist*)

Tuareg, Iwellemmeden de l'Est
Tahoua, Niger
Brass, steel
21.5 x 9 cm
Musée d'ethnographie, Neuchâtel
49.3.96

E.6

Sugar hammer (*tefedist*)

Tuareg, Kel Fadey
In Gall, Niger
Steel (Land Rover valve)
L: 13 cm
Musée d'ethnographie, Neuchâtel
83.17.16

E.7

Sugar shears (*temoda ton essukor*)

Hunna (Tuareg)
Abalassa, Algeria
Brass, steel
L: 26 cm
Musée d'ethnographie, Neuchâtel
48.2.124

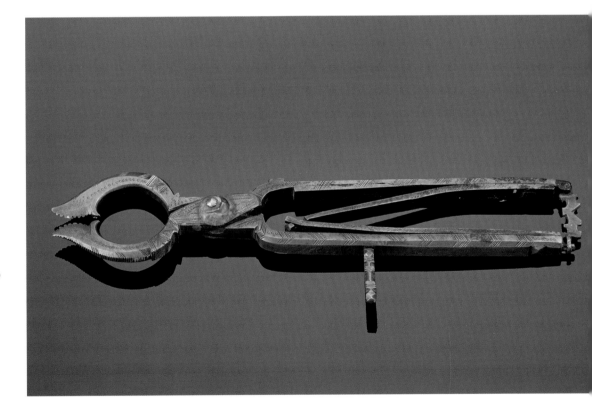

6

DRESS, IDENTITY, AND GENDER
IN TUAREG CULTURE AND SOCIETY

Susan Rasmussen

For any visitor arriving in a community, clothing and dress styles are crucial to communication and acceptance, and learning the subtle and nuanced meanings of dress as a communicative system is often more challenging than learning the local language (figs. 6.1, 6.2). In my early field research among the Tuareg people of Niger and Mali, I was often struck by the importance of dress and accessory ensembles, among both women and men.

On one occasion, when my American husband came to visit me in rural northern Niger, I led him into the compound of the mother of my field hostess, intending to introduce them. To our astonishment, upon seeing my husband, the older woman hastily raised her head scarf over her mouth and fled, laughing, into her tent. Suddenly, I realized the reason for her flight: although my husband and I were both outsiders, she nonetheless regarded me affectionately as her fictive daughter, and thus she likely viewed my husband as her fictive son-in-law. There is a strict relationship of reserve and respect between Tuareg mothers-in-law and sons-in-law that requires the son-in-law to be polite and wear his veil (*tagulmust*) high over his mouth and nose in the presence of his mother-in-law. I had forgotten to warn my husband of this, and he had entered the compound without the *tagulmust*, the turban/face-veil customarily worn by Tuareg men. Although our relationship suffered no long-term damage, my hostess's mother had fled in embarrassment.

In another Tuareg community, in rural northern Mali, I found it awkward to adjust to the regional women's dress: a long, voluminous, elegant, but (in my perception, at least) somewhat cumbersome robe, which resembles the ancient Greek toga and the Hindu sari. On my walks about the neighborhood, women often stopped me, invited me into their compounds, and gently but firmly unwrapped and rewrapped this robe, called variously a *tesoghelnet* (from the verb "to go around" or "encircle"), a *leger*, or a *burqa*. This garment has several sections to it, all named, and each needs to be draped in a specific manner in a given social context. The upper section, for example, should be draped more closely about the head when in the presence of respected chiefs, Islamic scholars, and parents-in-law. When I complimented one woman on her own dress, she thanked me, but indicated that it was hot, saying, "we wear this because it is the fashion, but it is not really that comfortable." Many women insisted that "a married women must wear this garment and also cover her head [though not her face]."

Thus clothing and dress—like language, food, and other patterns of communication—are sources of elaborate cultural symbolism. Dress fabrics and styles are not always strictly functional, or even comfortable, for members of the group. Clothing and dress are symbolic. Among the Tuareg, they have traditionally conveyed highly charged messages concerning social categories, in particular, gender, age, and class. Given its importance

6.1
Ami, granddaughter of Saidi Oumba and Andi Ouhoulou, attired in a voluminous blouse decorated in red embroidered bands with yellow accents. She also wears an indigo head wrap.
Photograph by Thomas K. Seligman, Agadez, Niger, 2004.

RASMUSSEN

6.2

Seated astride a prestigious white
camel, this Tuareg man and his
companions wear the characteristic
tagulmust made of shimmering blue
aleshu cloth.

Photograph by Thomas K. Seligman, Talak
region, Niger, 2001.

6.3

Rakia ag Boula wearing an indigo
gown and head wrap and gold
jewelry at a wedding.

Photograph by Thomas K. Seligman, Agadez,
Niger, 1988.

as an expression of an individual's social identities, relations, origins, and allegiance to
or alienation from cultural values, clothing is almost an extension of person and body.
Thus the relationship of an individual to his or her clothing is at once different from,
and more intimate than, his or her relationship to all other material objects (Kuper
1973, 366). Clothing is a form of nonverbal communication, composed of symbols developed from cultural, religious, social, artistic, economic, and other contexts (Barnes and
Eicher 1992; Goldstein-Gidoni 1999; Joseph 1986). Often, clothes communicate political
debates concerning "authenticity" and identity (Weiner and Schneider 1989; Eicher
1995; Lynch 1999; Abu-Lughod 2002).

Different types of Tuareg dress convey cultural values and social distinctions that are
undergoing change, and thus they represent not only internal cohesion but also diversity
and transformations of identity. On the one hand, there is the deliberate use of clothing
to demonstrate status and identity at different levels and at different times (Kuper 1973,
348–67). On the other, there is an unconscious assertion of meaning through personal
elaborations of dress styles (fig. 6.3). This chapter considers Tuareg dress in all these
dimensions. Distinctions between women's and men's dress styles will form a particular
emphasis of this study. Such distinctions convey traditional ideas concerning gender and
relations between the sexes, which in turn reflect long-standing local cultural values, for
example, those regarding transformations over the life cycle and interpretations of the
official religion, Islam. Dress styles also reveal social changes throughout history, such
as the quest for identity in the wake of upheavals in the precolonial stratified order and

the concomitant emergence of new classes, polities, and economies. Women and men of different social origins, ages, and regions experience tensions between tradition and change and express them in dress. These tensions arise from ambiguities in male and female roles and challenges to the old order of social relations.

Traditional Dress

Much "traditional" (i.e., long-standing, customary, and still conventional) Tuareg dress tends to persist, albeit with modifications; there is no abrupt cutoff point between old and new. Local dress has always displayed some degree of cultural unity, as well as regional, social, and individual variations. Many of these variations and changes occurred before colonization and globalization; others are more recent.

Up until about the 1950s, an older garment of leather, called a *tebetik*, which resembled a tunic with fringe decorations was worn in the Ahaggar and Aïr regions (Nicolaisen and Nicolaisen 1997, 363). Some sources report that in Ahaggar, poor persons and the formerly enslaved wore the leather tunic, and a few boys from among the "vassal" class, or *imrad*, in some groups also wore leather (Nicolaisen and Nicolaisen 1997, 361). Others report that the hide dress was held in esteem (Duveyrier 1864, 406). The meanings of leather are therefore ambiguous, or perhaps vary according to region, or have changed historically (fig. 6.4).

Since there was no local tradition of weaving cloth, all fabric was obtained through trade. The Tuareg have acquired a great variety of woven fabrics from the regions of the Sudan and southern Sahel (Burkina Faso, Mali, and Nigeria). Many of these fabrics were dyed with indigo. The dark bluish black indigo-dyed cloth called *aleshu*, which shimmers when worn, is most often seen today in rural communities (fig. 6.5). The *aleshu* was traditionally favored by nobles (and nowadays, anyone who has the means) on ceremonial occasions. Tuareg love of this pounded, dyed indigo cloth and its blue tinting of the wearer's skin caused some early explorers to call them the "Blue Men." This cloth is the product of a long tradition of commerce with Hausa, Bornu, and Egypt. The indigo-colored, iridescent *aleshu* cotton cloth, composed of many narrow woven bands sewn together, is expensive, and nowadays it is used mainly for festive events, while daily dress, including the *tagulmust*, is now usually made of European woven cottons. Many rural men and women still wear white, blue, or black gowns that are lightly embroidered. Some other cloths are made up of sewn bands, in various, usually dark, colors. Among more conservative dressers, particularly in the countryside, the traditional sobriety of nobles contrasts with the elaborate ornamental decoration, multiple accessories, and exuberant colors that traditionally signify more "popular" (i.e., non-noble) tastes.

As noted, traditional or conventional dress for many Tuareg, although changing, remains prevalent in the countryside and has not completely disappeared from the towns. For many rural men, this still consists of the long blue or white cotton gown and the *tagulmust*, a long piece of generally blue or white cloth that serves simultaneously as a veil and turban. This is wrapped around the entire head in diverse styles with apertures of various sizes left for the eyes. Many rural women still wear long clothing of a dark color and a head covering draped in a usually more relaxed manner than the man's veil. In the Aïr region of northern Niger, women wear a scarf perched on the head, a short, "bolero" type of overblouse, and a wrapper-skirt (fig. 6.6). With the exception of the smaller type of head scarf, the following garments are typical of northern Tuareg women: the *tekamist*, a large wide shirt of cotton, identical in form and cut with a man's shirt; the *asegbes*, a large piece of cotton used for a skirt or a petticoat, fixed tightly around the waist merely by folding it at the upper edge; and the *tikest*, a large piece of cotton worn as a shawl over the shoulders and head, covering the head scarf. In addition to the head scarf, which women frequently wear rolled up on top of the head, women of the Kel Ewey and Kel Ferwan groups in the Aïr region wear three main garments: *aftek*, a very short shirt of poncho-like cut akin to the shirt worn by Hausa-speaking women of Agadez, who use the words *liga* or *tagua* for this garment; *teri*, a large piece of cotton

6.4

Dress with fringe (*tbetrine*)

Fatimata ult Arelli
Tuareg, Dag Rali
Tamanrasset, Algeria
Leather, pigment
165 x 89 x 4 cm
Musée du Quai Branly
71.1941.19.1625

Journeying through the Sahara
from 1818 to 1820, G. F. Lyon
commented on the leather clothing
worn by the Tuareg. "A leather
kaftan is also much worn, of their
own manufacture, as are leather
shirts of the skins of antelopes, very
neatly sewed and well prepared"
(1821, 110). Leather dresses or
shirts were common in the Ahaggar
region at the beginning of the last
century. Today, however, they have
been replaced by clothing made of
imported cotton.

6.5
This woman and young girl dress in
the long, dark robes typical of rural
Tuareg.

*Photograph by Thomas K. Seligman, Timia,
Niger, 1988.*

6.6

The woman holding a child wears a typical embroidered blouse but uses modern "wax" print cloth for her wrapper-skirt. Her friend wears a dark wrapper more typical of rural Tuareg.

Photograph by Thomas K. Seligman, Azel, Niger, 1988.

6.7

Chemo Saidi, a *tenet* (female artisan), wears a "wax" wrapper, modern-style blouse, and a gauze-like head wrap. She also wears a type of amulet known as a *tcherot* and is fashioning a cord for another one.

Photograph by Thomas K. Seligman, Agadez, Niger, 1980.

worn as a skirt wound around the waist in the same way as in the north; and *tesegbes*, a large piece of cotton used as a petticoat (Nicolaisen and Nicolaisen 1997, 369–71). There are several variants of a basic large and ample blouse. It can be embroidered, dark, or sometimes, as in Agadez, Niger, white, colored, or decorated with bands embroidered in red, green, or yellow.

In some other regions, such as the Ahaggar in southern Algeria and in parts of Mali, women wear a wrapper-skirt and another long piece of fabric draping over the head, rather than the separate head scarf. In the more pastoral, northern countryside, women sometimes wear a large hat plaited from date palm leaves and known as *tele*, a word which also denotes "shade." These hats are obtained from sedentary agriculturalists. Ida and Johannes Nicolaisen believe they were introduced to the Tuareg by Arabs and Arabic-speaking Haratin agriculturalists, who came to Ahaggar about a hundred years ago (1997, 361).

More recently, the cloths worn by the Tuareg have been industrially manufactured. Colors are thus becoming brighter and more diverse. Even in the countryside, some younger men now wear red, purple, and green veils, and some women wear wrapper-skirts of urban African "Dutch waxes" they call *wakkas* (fig. 6.7). Fabrics and styles from other parts of West Africa and Europe, available in the towns at large markets, are increasingly popular among younger and more urban Tuareg. Functionaries tend to wear the more urban African and European clothing styles, alternating them or combining them in the same ensemble. Most Tuareg, however, still reside in rural communities, where many continue to wear the conventional Tuareg dress.

Both women and men usually wear sandals. A popular type of sandal in the Aïr region of Niger is called *iratimen* (*takalmi* in Hausa). These have a very large rounded sole of untanned cowhide. The top of the sandal, which is generally red with black decorations, is sewn onto the sole. These sandals are made by Agadezian artisans (fig. 6.8).[1]

Tuareg Women's and Men's Dress and Cultural Values: Religion and Aesthetics

In early written descriptions of Tuareg dress, it was predominantly men's clothing and the *tagulmust* that received attention from explorers, traders, missionaries, travelers, and colonial administrators (Duveyrier 1864; Rodd 1926). Tuareg men, who tended to venture farther afield in raiding and trading, initially had closer encounters with outsiders than did Tuareg women, who, though not secluded, tended to remain in camps and villages. Most women felt timid toward outsiders, and their men protected them from contact with threatening aggressors such as soldiers and raiders.

Recently in the popular media, as well as scholarly literature, there has been much attention devoted to the topic of Islamic dress and in particular the dress of Muslim women (Abu-Lughod 2002). It is misleading, however, to lump diverse clothing under the rubric of "Islamic dress" and to ascribe highly political and religious meanings to such dress, projecting onto it Euro-American and Judeo-Christian categories and assumptions regarding gender and religion. Tuareg dress must be examined from a multiplicity of perspectives with attention to more contextual local meanings.

The connections among Tuareg dress; religious and other mores; and sex, age, and class are complex. Local cultural values shape interpretations of "official" religion in significant ways. Several characteristics distinguish Tuareg gender roles and women's and

6.8

Sandals (*tadakat*)

Emoud Gouga
Tuareg, Kel Aïr
Agadez, Niger
Leather, pigment
33.5 x 14.4 x 6.25 cm
Private Collection

These elaborate sandals take two days of continuous work to make.

6.9

The marabout El Hadj Ilias wearing an indigo *tagulmust* writes Koranic passages in ink on a board. Ultimately the ink will be washed off with water (see fig. c.5), which may be drunk by another person as a form of protection. Marabouts typically wear conservative dress even in cities.

Photograph by Thomas K. Seligman, Niamey, Niger, 1997.

men's dress from those of neighboring Muslim societies. Of note, among the Tuareg, both women and men inherit and manage property, and social interaction between men and women is relatively open and free. This stands in contrast to some neighboring Muslim societies, for example, the Hausa, Kunta Arabs, and the Moors, whose local cultural interpretations of Islam place greater restrictions on the conduct of women. Secondly, although dress is important to both sexes in Tuareg society, it is not (at least thus far) the focus of heated political or religious debate among most people.

As observed, Tuareg men, not women, veil the face. Men begin to wear the *tagulmust* upon initiation, and it communicates that they are henceforth of marriageable age. Women begin to wear the head scarf or headcloth upon marriage. While the latter is not as obligatory or as formalized as the men's face-veil, it is an important marker of a married woman's status and in some contexts—as with the *tagulmust*—it is given a "religious" meaning: one cannot pray without wearing these headdresses, and as a married adult of childbearing age, one's clothing must be modest.

Islamic reform movements, such as the Izala sect, have made some inroads in parts of Niger and Mali. In Hausa regions and some multiethnic towns of Niger, Izala members have attacked women for not wearing dress conforming to what they define as "Islamic" standards of modesty. As of this writing, however, these movements have not yet exerted much influence among the Tuareg, and many women and men describe themselves as "liberal" concerning religion. One man in northern Mali commented that, if attacked by religious reformists, "women here would destroy their reputations," referring to the long-standing power of Tuareg women to deliver critical commentary through verbal art performance.

In those Tuareg groups where the influence of Islamic scholars (*ineslemen*, or marabouts) and of clans called Icheriffen, who claim descent from the Prophet Muhammad, is strong, Islam is made to coincide more closely with local cultural values. Explicit connections are drawn between being Muslim and enveloping oneself modestly in voluminous clothing, and closer head covering for both sexes is encouraged. A few men in these clans indicated that one reason they wear the face-veil is "in order to resemble the Prophet, who wore a turban" (Rasmussen 1997b, 41; fig. 6.9). Some Tuareg women who are born into *ineslemen* clans or who marry Tuareg marabouts or Arabs tend to dress more in accordance with Arab-influenced interpretations of Islam. In the Kidal region of Mali, for example, some Tuareg women married to Kunta Arab marabouts wear more modest robes and drape their head scarves or shawls more closely around their faces in a manner resembling the *hijab* (a transcultural form of Islamic dress), although most do not veil the face. In this region the large cotton shawl that women wear over their head and shoulders has social functions and meanings similar to the head scarf or headcloth that women wear in other regions such as the Aïr.

I gained many insights into this type of garment and its headdress when I purchased two such ensembles (*tesoghelnet*) in the Kidal region, one as a gift for my field hostess and one for myself. These were sold as long, rectangular cloths, later sewn at two corners. Their indigo dye comes off on the skin, and when I was about to wash my own cloth, friends stopped me and urged me only to rinse it gently; for this hue is valued positively in Tuareg aesthetics and is also believed to protect the wearer from sunburn and skin

6.10

As these men, each of whom wears
a dark *tagulmust*, walk across a dry
plain, their ample, light-colored
robes billow about them.

*Photograph by Kristyne Loughran, near
In Gall, Niger, 1990.*

infections. When my field hostess and her sister dressed me in the *tesoghelnet* for the
first time, they murmured "Bissmillihhah" to obtain *al baraka* (blessing). They warned
me that if one allows the ensemble's headdress (*erkerkey*) to fall off before dusk arrives,
"spirits enter your head and cause illness." They also instructed that, "married women
must cover their head with the *erkerkey* part of this; they should be more modest." The
erkerkey can turn into a cloak or head scarf/shawl, depending upon social context. It
must be raised so that it covers more of the face to convey respect toward important persons and at rites of passage and times of prayer. Women showed me how to wrap it and
how to sit (ideally cross-legged) in it. They also demonstrated how to walk very slowly.
They advised me to raise the *erkerkey* on my head when I visited the mayor, traditional
chiefs, marabouts, and the elderly nomadic women outside the village. At a regional
cooperative meeting, women rearranged my *tesoghelnet* in this more restrictive style
with its *erkerkey* enveloping more of my face. This is the style favored by Kunta Arabs
who serve as marabouts to the local Tuareg nobles in that region of Mali. Thus this dress
suggests a compromise solution to the problem of female modesty, between the more
restrictive *hijab* head covering that hugs the face and is worn by wives of marabouts in
that region and the preference of other Tuareg married women for its more abbreviated
form, worn over the hair.

In some other *ineslemen* groups, such as among the Iwellemmeden of the Azawagh
region in Niger, there are further dress restrictions. Women hide their faces before
men of equal or higher status, particularly potential marriage partners. In many regions
women receive their headdress upon initiation, or as noted above, more informally upon
reaching marriageable age. Following the initiation ceremony conferring the headdress,
the initiate cannot remove it for seven days in order to protect herself from threatening
spirits. Women in this community also conceal their bodies by wrapping large mats
around themselves while traveling on foot and sitting beneath a large palanquin while

Nobles pose in their finest attire, each wearing a complex *tagulmust* of indigo with added bands of cloth wrapped over it.

Photograph by Col. Bernard, early twentieth century. Musée du Quai Branly, Photothèque.

traveling on camelback (Walentowitz 2002, 47). Yet the women's own explanation of this custom hints of flirtation, rather than the ideal of modesty. They say that "the more layers a woman envelopes herself in, the more men want to unveil!" (Walentowitz 2002, 48). The Iwellemmeden *ineslemen* women's veiling practices are, however, atypical. In all groups, modesty is the ideal for both sexes, yet there is flexibility even in this. Clothing and headdress are never static or rigidly fixed, and women and men alike subtly adjust clothes and veiling in flirtation and courtship situations.

Facile generalizations or causal connections between Islam, in the sense of Koranic injunctions, and women's and men's dress should thus be avoided. Local Tuareg cultural values, aesthetics, and sociability between the sexes also shape the form and meanings of dress. Many Tuareg find voluminous clothing to be more beautiful. Women and men positively value billowing, flowing sleeves and robes that freely sway or fall over the shoulder, since these motions are considered aesthetically appealing, resembling a "tree branch swaying in the wind," and also because they are considered flirtatious (Rasmussen 1995, 58; fig. 6.10). Many—in particular, rural nobles, marabouts, and elders—also believe that voluminous clothing that covers the head and orifices protects from malevolent external influences, such as evil spirits, and misfortune. Finally, voluminous clothing also protects from the sun, sand, and dust in the harsh Saharan climate. These complex associations suggest that Tuareg clothing, like any other cultural trait, cannot be analyzed in isolation or explained in terms of a single set of social relations. Dress and gender are part of the total sociocultural system.

Another important local cultural value that dress conveys, particularly among nobles, is honor or dignity (Claudot-Hawad 1993). In the precolonial social order, the wearing and use of voluminous robes; men's face-veils; accessories such as the sword, silver amulets, and jewelry; and the use of the white camel were governed by "sumptuary laws," dress codes restricted to nobles (fig. 6.11). Even in the past, however these laws were negotiable. A slave who through noble or courageous acts had demonstrated the sensibility and dignity associated with nobility would have to be liberated. Henceforth, he or she would be able to wear these noble insignia (Claudot-Hawad 1993, 14).

Also relevant to Tuareg dress and gender are cultural concepts of person and body. As in many African societies, the head is taken to be the location of personal will and intelligence (Biebuyck and Van den Abeele 1984; Rasmussen 1991). The orifices, particularly the nose and mouth, are believed vulnerable to pollution, through malevolent forces both human and superhuman, such as jealousy and the evil eye. Individuals are particularly vulnerable to these forces during times of transition. Thus the newlywed couple or a new mother and her infant need the ritual protection to be found through seclusion inside the tent and the wearing of a concealing headdress, clothing, and religious amulets.

For men, particularly nobles, dress styles emphasize the head, height, and long lines, reflecting the positive valuing of endurance and toughness in the old warrior-dominated society. Rural Tuareg men are still generally lean and muscular from a life spent roaming in the desert (Nicolaisen and Nicolaisen 1997, 48). By contrast, styles for women tend to emphasize layering and bulk, reflecting the positive valuing of fatness as a sign of feminine beauty. If they have the economic means, women attempt to avoid physical exertion and consume large quantities of milk and meat in order to fatten themselves. In the past, adolescent girls were fattened in a ritual called *adanay*, in which they were fed vast quantities of milk (Rasmussen 1997b). Nowadays, however, this ideal is difficult to maintain. The abolition of domestic slave labor has compelled women to perform arduous physical labor such as transporting water from the well, gathering firewood, and processing grain. In addition, droughts and decimation of livestock have caused shortages of milk and meat.

Equally important to the total effect of dress are gait, posture, and gestures, all intended to express qualities of elegance, refinement, and strength. There are specific gestures associated with the men's veil, relating to the warrior code of honor (fig. 6.12). If honor is threatened, for example, the first reaction will be to adjust the veil upward, over the nostrils and the end of the nose; this signals reserve and distance (Claudot-Hawad 1993, 39). This is the appropriate response to the advent of a rival, as well as the presence of women. It is also sometimes a sign of politeness. Wearing the veil very high and veiling almost all the face for a longer period, however, is considered a sign of mourning or sadness. Elderly men are often seen wearing the *tagulmust* in this way. The expression *tezef uden* (to bare the face) denotes raising the veil above the forehead, leaving a part of the hair visible. *Esertek* means dropping the lower portion of the veil and placing oneself at ease. This is often done while at home with family or with friends of the same age group; here, the veil is arranged so as to expose the nose but is left covering the mouth; at most, it may be allowed to slide under the lower lip or chin, but one still holds it tight. Usually, it is considered impolite even in this context to allow it to fall beneath the beard. Some *inadan* (smiths or artisans) and members of the formerly enslaved group do this, but never nobles. Different social contexts may modify the

6.12

This man visiting a regional market wears a shimmering indigo *tagulmust* in a manner demonstrating reserve and politeness.

Photograph by Thomas K. Seligman, Ayourou, Niger, 1980.

meaning or sense of this gesture, however. Thus a smith sometimes allows his veil to fall thus in order to denounce a situation where he has been dishonored and to assert his rights if he does not receive his due compensation of meat after a sacrifice (Claudot-Hawad 1993, 41; see also chapter 2 of this volume).

Tuareg Dress and Gender in Transitions over the Life Course

Sex, gender, and age are interacting forces. Dress and headdress styles announce changes in status over the course of a life. At the name day conferring human social identity, held approximately one week following birth, the baby's hair is shaved in order to sever its ties from the spirit world (Casajus 1987b; Rasmussen 1997b). Until weaned (at approximately three years), very young children often go around naked with the exception of amulets worn around their necks protecting them from being pulled back into the spirit world. They may also be covered with an ample blouse formed from a rectangle of cotton with an opening for the head. Sometimes, a firstborn male child wears a special hairstyle consisting of a small tuft of hair on top of the head (fig. 6.13). Most youths in their teens dress in long gowns, but until they marry, they tend to keep their heads uncovered. Youths who are enrolled in secular schools, established first by the French colonial administration and later by the independent nation-states, wear uniforms.

Adulthood is culturally defined as occurring for both sexes upon marriage. For men and women alike, headdress is central to married adult status. Men generally begin to wear the *tagulmust* at approximately the age eighteen, signifying their readiness to marry. Men also don wide trousers (*ekerbey*) at this time. Since married women must cover the nape of the neck and the hair, they change their hairstyle and begin to wear the head scarf/shawl upon their marriages, which is given either by the husband or the mother of the bride. This may envelop the entire body, draped toga-like (as in Ahaggar, Tademaket, and Ajjer), or it may only perch on top of the head (as in Aïr and Tagaraygarayt). It is usually made of cotton tinted indigo (fig. 6.14). The women's head scarf (called *erkerkey* in Ahaggar, *adalil* or *diko* in Aïr, and

afteg in the Mount Bagzan area) does not usually cover the face, but a woman holds its corner over her mouth in some situations, such as during Islamic rituals and rites of passage, in the presence of her father-in-law, and when confronted with potentially dangerous or polluting situations such as illness or healing. As women grow older, they tend to raise this corner of the head scarf/shawl higher more often, though never in the manner of the more elaborate and more permanently veiling turban worn by men (Rasmussen 1991).

Over a lifetime, as individuals age and undergo rites of passage, female and male headdresses figure in symbolic analogies, rituals where they are first worn, and marriage (Rasmussen 1997b, 43–44). The ritual for first taking up the *tagulmust* is known as *amangadezar*. At this rite, a marabout reads Koranic verses and spits ritually into a special indigo cloth as a benediction to convey *al baraka*, in order to "calm the heart." This act serves as a kind of protective amulet against misfortune and spirits believed to threaten during transitions (Rasmussen 1997b, 46). After this, the marabout places the veil on the man's head. The newly veiled man goes for seven days without removing his *tagulmust*, which could engender danger of spirit attacks. This seven-day period is called *issayat na nagade* (seven days of veiling). After this, the man can marry. A few younger men no longer undergo this formal ritual, but most still wear the *tagulmust*.

One context in which a woman covers her entire head occurs while in trance during spirit possession (Rasmussen 1995, 38). The headdress of the possessed woman differs from the man's turban/face-veil in substantial ways, however. It is not limited to covering the face but drapes "tent-like" over the entire head. It is designated by its own name, *ijewaren*. During the possession ritual, a white band is attached over the *ijewaren* by a girlfriend or female relative soon after the possessed woman, who initially lies prone beneath a blanket, has risen to a sitting position and as she begins to perform the trance dance to the music of chorus and drummers. The possessed woman's headband closely resembles that worn by a young bride during seclusion in her mother's tent. In form, it is also similar to a popular leather tassel hair ornament, which is often decorated with cowrie shells symbolizing fertility (Rasmussen 1995, 38). This ritual veiling of the woman in trance has very complex symbolism within the context of possession. In some respects, it inverts her daily form of dress; in other respects, it alludes to her wedding attire and thus transforms her status.

The wearing of the *tagulmust* is traditionally most strictly practiced by nobles, although it has been dropped by some male youths in large towns. It nonetheless remains a pervasive symbol worn by nearly all Tuareg men, albeit in different styles according to region, age, social stratum, and situation (fig. 6.15). Older nobles in rural areas tend to wear the face-veil highest, covering nose and mouth in most public situations. It is associated with mature male gender-role identity, which has complex meanings, and it signifies modesty, value, or reserve, particularly important in the presence of parents-in-law (Murphy 1967; Casajus 1987b; Rasmussen 1997b). A proverb states that the veil and the trousers are brothers. I observed that the veil can also be used flirtatiously and is considered artistic, somewhat like a hairstyle for men (Rasmussen 1991; 1997b). Men indicate that they "feel more attractive "wearing the face-veil. Wearing the veil and styling it are referred to as *anagad*. There exist additional terms to designate the over two hundred styles of draping the *tagulmust*. The lowest portion of the veil is the most mobile of its three sections and most important in terms of modesty. The men's veil serves a social function (Murphy 1964; Nicolaisen and Nicolaisen 1997, 49), and in rural communities, a man who is of married or of marriageable age always covers his mouth, nose, and brows in the presence of his parents-in-law (in particular his mother-in-law) and outside visitors.

Thus a man's face-veil and woman's headdress have similar social functions and meanings as central symbols announcing transformed social status over the course of a lifetime (fig. 6.16). Nowadays, mostly elderly, rural, and noble Tuareg men tend to attach greater importance to face veiling than do Tuareg of other social origins. Once

6.13 (OPPOSITE, TOP)

The child standing at the left wears a distinctive tufted hairstyle, signifying that he is a firstborn male. He also wears a protective amulet.

Photograph by Thomas K. Seligman, Dagaba, Niger, 1980.

6.14 (OPPOSITE, BOTTOM)

This woman wears an indigo head wrap and a silver earring in the form of the cross of Agadez.

Photograph by Thomas K. Seligman, Agadez, Niger, 1988.

6.15 (ABOVE)

This scribe wears voluminous robes and a *tagulmust* with only a narrow opening across the eyes.

Photograph by Fievet, Tamanrasset, Algeria, date unknown. Musée du Quai Branly, Photothèque, c.63.338.

6.16

Man and woman in characteristic festive attire.

Photograph by Kristyne Loughran, Agadez, Niger, 1991.

their children marry, older men tend to veil the face more closely. Yet the central government of Niger requires all men to remove this veil for their national identification photograph; causing some older, more conservative and modest men considerable embarrassment (Rasmussen 2001). Other men, particularly youths, those from the formerly enslaved group, and artisans, wear the veil only in specific circumstances, such as a wedding. Some young men—for example, Tuareg expatriates in Europe—who feel freer in their gender mores but wish to assert their cultural identity, now wear the men's turban only around the neck (*tagulmust tat iri*) in relaxed situations among their own age cohorts or peers. Yet when they return to the countryside to visit relatives, they usually don more traditional dress and head coverings to express respect toward elders, parents-in-law, and marabouts.

For both women and men throughout their lives the headdress and honor are directly linked. This association is not static, and it changes according to social category and transformation of status. People of both sexes are generally expected to show greater formal respect to elders, especially to those of the opposite sex, and to parents-in-law. They are also expected to display greater dignity and reserve as they themselves age. These principles of conduct are indicated through clothing, as when women and men wear increasingly more modest dress and headdress styling as they grow older (Rasmussen 1997b, 19).

Women's and Men's Dress in Wider Social Dynamics: Tradition and Change

In Tuareg society today differences in social standing are based in part on the older system of hereditary descent and occupational specialty, and in part on differential access to basic resources such as livestock herds, weapons and military dominance, oasis land, trading networks, and wage labor. The precolonial social system—comprised of nobles, vassals, smith/artisans, and descendants of client and servile peoples (see chapter 1 of this volume)—remains salient in the countryside, but roles and relations between the social strata are changing. Formerly, nobles controlled large herds of livestock, organized the caravans, and had a monopoly on weapons and domestic slave labor. This arrangement was abolished by the French colonial administration early in the twentieth century. Droughts, French colonial and independent nation-state policies promoting sedentarization, and the decline—though not demise—of caravan trade, have resulted in the impoverishment of many nobles and the rise of alternate trading forms such as by trucking and other travel by itinerant merchants. Many *inadan*, for example, are now traveling and selling jewelry abroad.

New socioeconomic classes are emerging from these upheavals, and opportunities have been unevenly distributed throughout the social order. Initially, nobles resisted forced enrollment in secular schools, which they perceived as a threat to their culture. They reacted by sending the children of their former slaves to these schools. Ironically, therefore, until recently, persons of lower status in the old system have benefited more from education and jobs in the modern infrastructure (Dayak 1992; Rasmussen 1997a). Persons of low or ambiguous status were also, until recently, more willing than nobles to take up manual and technical labor, for example, tailoring and oasis gardening.

Thus although clothing serves as a subtle index of stratification (Kuper 1973, 353), its meanings become complex, ambiguous, and disputed in times of social turmoil. Even in the precolonial system, as shown above, the sumptuary laws of class-based dress codes were in fact negotiable. Yet many clothing styles and materials in rural communities remain strongly associated with different clans, social strata, and occupations. Spirit possession songs that I collected in 1983 mocked some descendants of slaves for wearing belts of palm fibers in contrast to other, "more noble," groups who wore belts of fine cloth (Rasmussen 1995, 26–27). In principle, only *inadan* can wear a garment inside-out. If others do this, an *enad* performs a brief mumming or mocking rite, and the wearer must pay a small fine. Also, many rural nobles believe that, if one wears a stained garment, *inadan* will suspect that the wearer has eaten food and not shared it with them (an obligation in the client-patron relationship that exists between rural nobles and artisans), so they can take the garment or charge a fine. These clothing-related beliefs reveal underlying economic tensions in the noble-smith relationship.[2] Islamic scholars tend to dress in more voluminous robes, which are often Arab influenced, such as the burnous prevalent in North Africa. Diviners or mediums also dress distinctively. I noticed (Rasmussen 2001, 117) that during divination rituals when they throw cowrie shells, these specialists wear deep blue, a color associated with the spirits, apply henna to their hands and feet, use non-Islamic amulets, such as a small ring of copper on the finger (copper is believed to coagulate blood and heal wounds), and carry a mirror (believed to symbolize powers of "seeing" by divination).

6.17
El Hadj Saidi Oumba in his workshop in Niamey, Niger, wears a checked head scarf over a white skullcap, both of which indicate he has made a hadj, or pilgrimage, to Mecca.
Photograph by Thomas K. Seligman, Niamey, Niger, 2001.

A number of wider forces—namely, the flight of refugees, the nationalist/separatist rebellion; the peace accords between rebels and central governments, which were followed by tourism in Tuareg regions; and assertions by some Tuareg leaders and intellectuals of cultural revitalization and nationalism transcending local kin and social stratum identity—have all produced increasing self-consciousness concerning cultural identity and have directly and indirectly influenced dress (see chapter 3 of this volume). These processes are exemplified by another style of veil called *anagad wan fellaga* (veiling of the rebels), adopted by some rebels in the 1990s. This veil cloth is rolled haphazardly about the head and covers equally the lower face, but without respecting the traditional three movable parts of the *tagulmust*. This style is also associated with bandits and pillaging. The rebel fighters who adopted it in the 1990s often opposed not only the central state government but also what they viewed as the "stagnation" of their own society (Claudot-Hawad 1993, 43). Rebel leaders called on the Tuareg to widen their affiliations beyond ties to local kin and social strata (Rasmussen 2001). Male rebels expressed these ideals in their own dress choosing, regardless of social origins, to dress similarly in military camouflage uniforms and a green face-veil, a color adopted from the Western Saharan (Saharoui) Polisario Front (see fig. 3.9).

More sedentarized lifestyles have increased the enrollment of girls in secular schools. This coupled with predominantly male labor migration to more distant places has impacted gender constructs and relations between the sexes. These changes are reflected in some clothing trends. Many young women around Mount Bagzan in Aïr have been exposed to new products and monetization, and they now prefer gold to the traditional silver jewelry, and wear more urban "Dutch Wax" clothing, though in combination with, rather than replacing, older dress.

6.18

From left to right: El Faki, Ousmane, and Al Hassan Saidi, in the Oumba boutique. El Faki and Al Hassan wear Western clothing. Ousmane wears a suit typical of West African businessmen. Both Ousmane and Al Hassan have traveled to Europe to sell jewelry.

Photograph by Thomas K. Seligman, Niamey, Niger, 2004.

Some Tuareg men wear imported clothing and headdress (fig. 6.18). In the Aïr region of northern Niger, former slaves tended to adopt European clothing such as denim jackets and jeans sooner than other Tuareg, although nowadays younger men of diverse social origins are taking up these items of dress. Adolescents in the large towns of Niger and Mali wear baseball caps, although marabouts disapprove of them because their brims allegedly prevent the wearers from praying. Saidi Oumba (see chapter 8 of this volume) who recently completed the hadj, or pilgrimage to Mecca, wears the Arabic checked headdress in a draped Tuareg style (fig. 6.17). A few non-Tuareg men also wear the *tagulmust*. At a meeting in Djanet, Algeria, to mediate the armed conflict between Tuareg rebels and the central governments of Mali and Niger, Libyan leader Muammar el-Qaddafi wore the veil for political effect. A few European men married to Tuareg women similarly have donned the *tagulmust* in efforts to integrate into the community. In multiethnic towns, some men of mixed Songhai and Tuareg descent also wear the turban/face-veil, albeit in less formalized style than many rural Tuareg men.

Some clothing is increasingly deployed by women and men not solely for aesthetic purposes but also for making political statements. In the Aïr some political parties have selected the embroidery motifs on women's clothing depicting features of the natural environment significant in myth and cosmology (stars, flowers, millet stalks, sun, moon, and jewelry pendants) as emblems of Tuareg cultural identity and "authenticity." Several of these designs were prominently displayed on large banners at a rally. In the Malian countryside, during recent elections, some adolescent girls wore T-shirts with a photo of a Tuareg candidate for deputy. During the 1990–1996 armed rebellion, some women used clothes for resistance. One old woman, for example, confronted soldiers with a gun hidden in her clothing.

Despite considerable hardship in the wake of drought, war, and unemployment, which has resulted from restructuring policies of the World Bank and International Monetary Fund in Africa, some Tuareg are benefiting from an influx of aid programs and tourism into their region since the peace pacts of 1995 and 1996. In some sedentarized centers, international non-governmental organization (NGO) cooperatives train

6.19
Man on camel wearing indigo *tagulmust* and gown and black cotton pants with yellow machine-made embroidery on the lower leg.
Photograph by Thomas K. Seligman, Talak, Niger, 2001.

women in manual skills once shunned by female members of the noble class. At one cooperative in Kidal, Mali, as women sewed on machines donated by Luxembourg, a woman joked about working "like a Haratin [or Bella] slave," but others said, "No, this is different, it is sewing." Other local residents are able to benefit from transnational couture. In 1998 there was a fashion show in Tiguidit in the Sahara. This event, organized by Alphadi, a designer from Niger, featured models wearing ostrich feather designs and received some attention in the international media.[5]

6.20

Head wrap for a man (*tagulmust*)

Hausa
Kano, Nigeria
Cotton, indigo
742 x 75 cm
UCLA Fowler Museum
x88.1420

Head wraps for men and women are made of *aleshu* cloth, which is highly prized for its deep blue color and shiny patina. The cloth is manufactured in Kura, near Kano, Nigeria, and is made of narrow strips that are sewn together. The quality and value of a *tagulmust* are related to the number of bands of which it is made. Different numbers of bands are sold in long narrow packages, folded into thin pleats. The *tagulmust* is wound around the head and face, often leaving only the eyes exposed. The draping entails a series of winding motions. The first turn creates the part of the veil that covers the mouth, the second turn covers the face and the last several turns go around the head to create the turban.

During feasts, men sometimes augment their *tagulmust* by wearing a white one underneath. The *tagulmust* is distinctive of Tuareg men and donning the veil marks the passage into adulthood. It protects honor, indicates rank, and symbolizes reserve and respect. The indigo dye used on the *tagulmust* easily rubs off on the skin of the wearer, which is why the Tuareg have often been referred to as the "Blue People."

Conclusion

What then is at stake in terms of Tuareg dress in diverse social contexts and over time? Tuareg women's and men's dress styles illustrate the complexity of influences on clothing in culture and society (fig. 6.19). Clothing is not simply a creation of an individual expressing his or her own aesthetic choice but an index of social, economic, and political direction (Kuper 1973, 365). Yet there is no neat correlation between dress style and social distinction, nor is there a clear-cut boundary between "traditional" and "modern." There are many ways that dress communicates the cultural values and social identity of the persons wearing it. The strict, homogenized uniforms required of schoolchildren by the French colonial administrators in their nomadic boarding schools undoubtedly served as continual reminders to Tuareg children—many of whom were marched at gunpoint by soldiers to these schools during the first half of the twentieth century—of the discipline of these new sites of cultural control. Similarly, the more recent requirement that Tuareg men remove the veil for the national identification photo cards reminds them of the power of the state (fig. 6.20).

In radically different social settings, evidencing conflicting and sometimes contradictory influences, symbols of dress have diverse and ambiguous meanings. The deliberate use of dress to make political statements at rallies expresses one meaning. The apparent compromises made in women's dress in Tuareg communities with more "Islamic" and "Arabic" influences express additional, more subtle meanings. Many younger men and those dwelling in the cities are showing more and more of their faces. By contrast, a few women in some sedentarized and urban communities are beginning to veil the face. It is uncertain whether these external styles correlate with revisions of traditional relations between the sexes, with religious devotion, or notions of "modernity." Other stylistic combinations, for example, the latest "fashion" or fad of European clothing worn by a youthful Tuareg, may have little symbolic import for the wearer, but may be given highly charged significance by others.

Clothing is not merely a passive reflection or mirror image of social relations or cultural values; it is one of the many ways in which social dynamics are continually negotiated and re-created over time. Dress reveals that cultural "authenticity" is constantly changing, a fluid and debated process rather than a fixed or agreed-upon entity (Stocking 1985; Clifford 1988). The designation of beliefs and practices as "tradition(al)" does not imply they are static, undisputed, or unchanging; rather, they are conventional, long-standing, or customary and tend to be prevalent or widespread in a society. Traditional or "customary" dress, like any other cultural belief or practice, is not always rigidly opposed to the "modern," nor is "tradition(al)" always associated exclusively with rural. Many invitations to "modern" formal government receptions in African towns encourage guests to wear *le costume national*, which refers to what outsiders would consider "traditional" or customary dress. Yet neither is the "modern" associated exclusively with urban settings, as shown in the increasing popularity of non-Tuareg African and Western clothing in the countryside. In sum, dress does not consist of a unitary or singular object but rather an assemblage of items (headdress, clothing, and accessories)—new and old—that are creatively combined and recombined in diverse ways.

☉

PERSONAL BEAUTIFICATION AND GROOMING

The Tuareg are a very elegant people and spend considerable time on their appearance and grooming. They use large amounts of cream or grease on their skin to protect it from the dry climate. The indigo, which rubs off on their faces from close contact with the *tagulmust* (the man's face-veil) or with women's head scarves, is thought of as beautification and protection against the sun.

Both men and women spend hours dressing their hair. Young boys' heads are shaven except for a central crest. As they become adolescents and receive their first sword (*takuba*) and stone arm bracelet, they begin to wear braids. Women braid and dress their hair a couple of times a month. It is a time-consuming process as the hair must first be untangled with hair knives or pins, then washed and oiled before it is parted and separated into strands. Hair is either braided into a few large plaits or many small ones.

Men and women use kohl or antimony—which they keep in beautifully decorated leather bags—around their eyes, eyebrows, and eyelashes as a protection against diseases of the eye. Fingernails and toenails are kept short, and young women today use imported nail polish. Hands and feet are decorated with henna. Some women blacken their gums and lips with indigo. Women also tint their skin with ocher mudpacks and paint geometrical designs on their cheeks and foreheads for festivals and feasts. Men often carry engraved tweezers and scissor sets in their wallets. The Tuareg enjoy sweet smelling incense, and women believe that sweet smells keep the evil spirits known as Kel Esuf away. Both men and women love perfume and use it lavishly.

In 1550 Leo Africanus described Tuareg women as being very corpulent with round hips, large breasts, and very small waists. Among the Tuareg, canons of physical beauty emphasize length, delicacy, and bearing. These ideals differ slightly between men and women. From a man's perspective a beautiful woman should be of medium height, have thick straight hair, large eyes, a medium-size mouth, very white teeth, blackened gums, slender hands and feet decorated with henna, and soft skin. Corpulence reflects well-being and is appreciated by men. Today, however, there are few women of leisure, and young women do not like the "fattening" process their mothers endured. They are also attracted to global trends toward a long lean figure. Tuareg women, on the other hand, believe men should be tall, have slender hands and feet, and demonstrate a proud bearing. A corpulent man is seen as powerful and well-to-do.

K.L.

F.1

Wallet (*enafad*)

Hawa Ibu Ousman
Tuareg, Kel Ewey
Aïr, Niger
Leather, brass, glue, pigment
140.1 x 22.3 cm (with strap)
Cantor Arts Center
1997.49

Wallets like this one, intended to be worn around the neck, are common in many Saharan regions, although the designs and colors vary. They are composed of a small bag with several compartments that can be encased by another bag that slides over it along the leather cords.

F.2

Wallet (*enefel n' tan 'tot*)

Tuareg, Kel Icheriffen
Asongo, Mali
Leather, pigment
39.5 x 7.7 x 1 cm
Musée du Quai Branly
71.1941.19.1245

F.3

Wallet (*enefel n' tan 'tot*)

Tuareg, Kel Icheriffen
Daoussahak, Mali
Leather, pigment
40 x 10 x 3 cm
Musée du Quai Branly
71.1941.19.1253

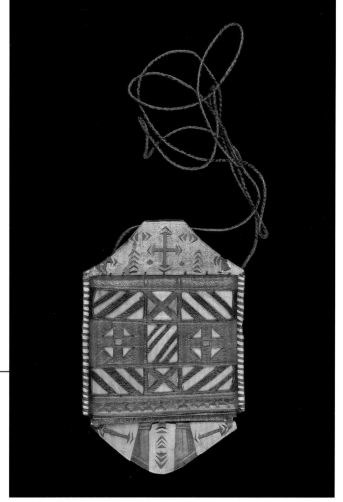

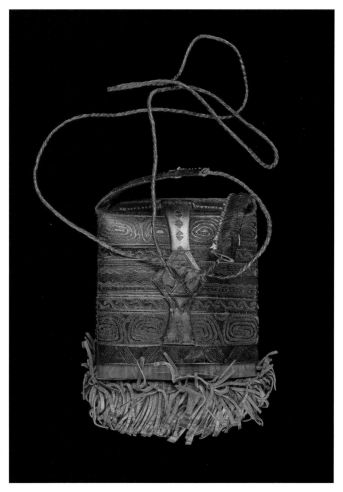

F.4 (OPPOSITE, LEFT)

Wallet (*enefel*)

Tuareg
Timbuktu, Mali
Leather, pigment
33 x 7 x 1.8 cm
Musée du Quai Branly
71.1941.19.653

F.5 (OPPOSITE, RIGHT)

Wallet (*enafad*)

Tuareg, Kel Aïr
Niger
Leather, pigment
58.4 x 20.3 cm
Cantor Arts Center
2001.177

F.6 (ABOVE, LEFT)

Wallet (*ettabu*)

Tuareg
Aouderas, Niger
Leather, shells, coins
73.7 x 10 x 2.54 cm
Private Collection

F.7 (ABOVE, RIGHT)

Wallet (*tarallabt*)

Tuareg
Adrar des Ifoghas, Mali
Leather, pigment
20 x 9 cm
Musée d'ethnographie, Neuchâtel
III.A.462

F.8

Hair Knife (*tasozolit*)

Tuareg, Kel Rela
Tamanrasset, Algeria
Steel, copper
21.5 x 4.4 x 0.6 cm
Musée du Quai Branly
71.1941.19.177

F.9

Conical container (*bata*)

Mala Mohamed and Fatima
Tuareg, Kel Aïr
Agadez, Niger
Leather, pigment
H: 13.3 cm; Diam: 11.5 cm
UCLA Fowler Museum
x88.1456

Bata boxes originated in Agadez, and the Tuareg use them to store incense, makeup, creams, or precious items such as jewelry. *Tinadan* (female artisans) cut small pieces of leather to soak until they are gelatinous and then form them over a clay mold to dry. When the leather is dry, the *tinadan* roll long strips of wax, which are then applied to the box in the form of geometric designs. The box is then dyed in a deep red liquid derived from millet stalks. The area where the wax is placed receives no dye. After drying the wax is removed to reveal the pattern. The clay mold is then broken and discarded, and the box is ready for use.

Bag to hold kohl (*tafen'di*)

Tuareg, Kel Adrar
Mali
Leather, pigment
33.5 x 12 x 5.5 cm
Musée du Quai Branly
71.1941.19.72

F.11

Doll on camel jaw bone (*aknar*)

Tanesmit cult Bilbil
Tuareg, Kel Rela
Ahaggar, Algeria
Bone, cotton, wood
26 x 9 x 4 cm
Musée du Quai Branly
71.1941.19.115.1-2

Children often make dolls using
camel jaw bones. This example
represents a handsome Tuareg
warrior in full regalia. This doll was
made about 1940 by Tanesmit cult
Bilbil, a twelve-year-old Algerian
Tuareg girl.

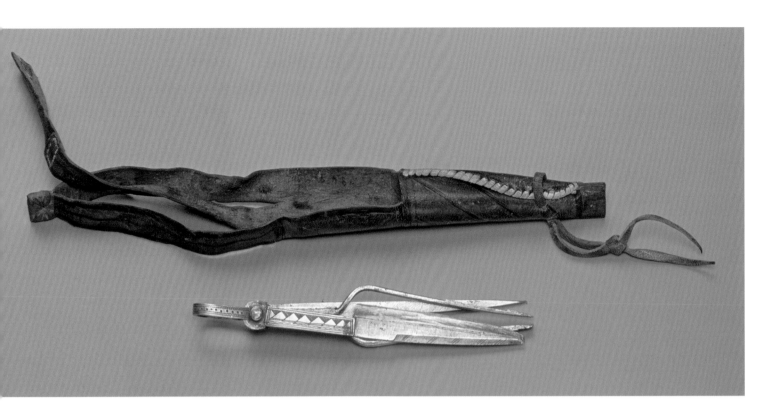

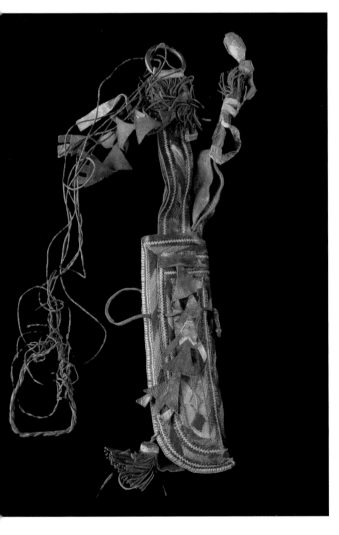

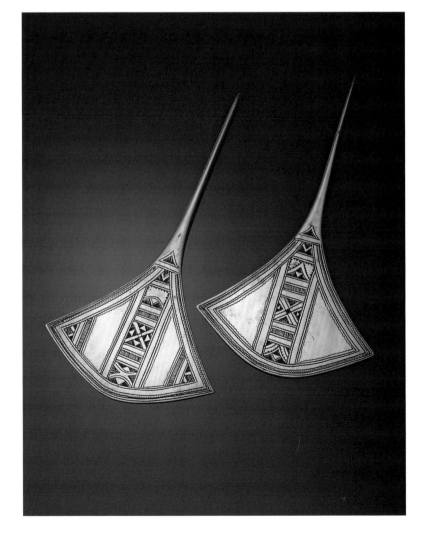

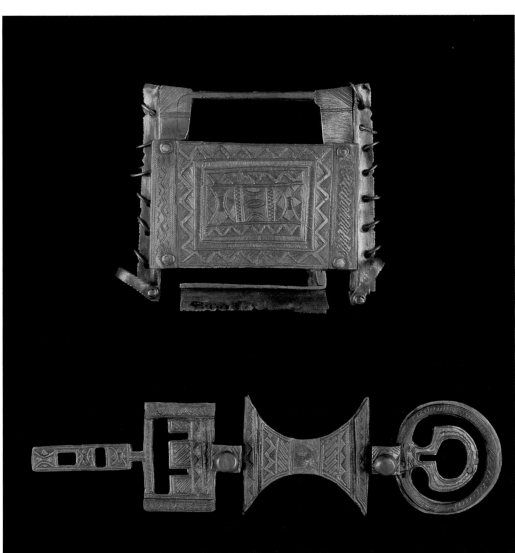

F.12 (OPPOSITE, TOP)

Knife, tweezers, and case (*ighemdan*)

Tuareg
Agadez, Niger
Metal, leather
L: 11 cm
Musée d'ethnographie, Neuchâtel
48.4.97. a -b

F.13 (OPPOSITE, BOTTOM LEFT)

Razor and case (*essemaad*)

Tuareg, Iwellemmeden
Gao, Mali
Leather, steel, copper, silk
32 x 6 x 3 cm
Musée du Quai Branly
71.1941.19.1302

F.14 (OPPOSITE, BOTTOM RIGHT)

Hairpins

Tuareg
Agadez, Niger
Silver
12.7 x 7 cm
Private Collection

F.15

Lock and Key (*tamask n'asrou*)

Abbas ag Inchoular
Tuareg
Adrar des Ifoghas, Mali
Bronze, copper, aluminum, steel
11.5 x 5 cm
Musée d'ethnographie, Neuchâtel
49.2.13.a-b

F.16

Lock and Key (*tamask n'asrou*)

Tuareg
Goundam, Mali
Bronze, copper, aluminum, steel
20.3 x 15.5 x 3 cm
Musée du Quai Branly
71.1941.19.761.1-2

Rectangular locks are used to secure
leather bags containing precious
items. They are made of iron and
decorated with copper, brass, and
tin overlays. The individual lock
mechanism is complicated and
can only be opened with the key
made specifically for it. Some locks
require several keys to open them.
The locking mechanism is placed in
the metal casing and consists of a
system of springs that are released
when the key, or *asrou,* presses them
together. Women sometimes attach
the larger, more ornate keys to the
corners of their head veils as weights.

7

TUAREG WOMEN AND THEIR JEWELRY

Kristyne Loughran

Tuareg women consider their jewelry to embody their aesthetic and cultural ideals, represent standards of taste, and convey social status and prestige. These precious objects are
commissioned for personal use, and women feel that they symbolize the more private
aspects of their lives. The individual pieces can be tokens of affection and friendship,
part of the bridewealth, or sentimental heirlooms passed from one generation to another.
Furthermore, when they are made of certain materials or in particular shapes, such as
the triangle, they can offer protection against evil.

In this essay I will discuss classical jewelry styles and types, the cultural contexts
from which they emerge, and their regional variations. The views of Tuareg women
on their classical jewelry pieces and their interaction with modernity and fashion will
also be examined. Tuareg women are very fashion conscious and take great interest in
the jewelry forms being produced in neighboring countries and abroad. Their opinions
about their jewelry clarify their artistic and aesthetic criteria and in turn reveal their
approach to change. In the past twenty years, many Tuareg women have redefined their
taste and cultural ideals. Although they still wear silver jewelry, which represents their
Tuareg identity, they now believe gold jewelry is just as important: not only because it
represents a stable economic investment but also because it is a sign of the times. Gold
has become a prestigious social insignia and is now considered fashionable (fig. 7.1).

Classical Jewelry

There is a general consensus that the ancestors of the Tuareg were North African Sanhaja
Berber peoples who migrated south in successive waves from Libya and Algeria. Classical Tuareg jewelry thus shares similarities with Roman, Carthaginian, and Christian
prototypes (Eudel 1902, 235) and also reflects Berber and Islamic stylistic traditions. As
a group, the Tuareg have always attracted attention, and travelers, archaeologists, and
anthropologists have consistently made note of Tuareg jewelry styles in their writings.[1]
Many of the forms they described in the past still exist today, though some of the objects
have become rare or are no longer used.[2] In the 1930s and 1940s European museums
started collecting Tuareg art, and the earliest extant jewelry pieces in these Western
institutions date from the late 1800s and early 1900s. These museum collections have
gained increased significance due to the drastic changes the Tuareg experienced in the
1970s and 1980s as a result of devastating droughts and political unrest. Many groups
who had been nomadic became sedentary at this juncture, settling in urban centers and
towns. In many instances jewelry was considered disposable wealth, and women had to
part with their treasures to support their families during these difficult times.

7.1

Tuareg women attend a wedding
wearing ample amounts of jewelry,
indigo head wraps, and decorated
blouses. They are watching as the
groom has his hands and feet dyed
with henna. The woman at right
wears a new style necklace known
as *celebre.*

*Photograph by Thomas K. Seligman, Agadez,
Niger, 1988.*

7.2

**Head ornament
(*tcherot* or *tereout tan 'eraf*)**

Tuareg, Kel Ewey
Timia, Niger
Silver
30.5 x 19 cm
UCLA Fowler Museum
x88.1406

7.3

The tall men's head ornament
(*takoumbout*) shown here was worn
by the Kel Ajjer of Algeria durng
the Islamic feast of the Sebiba.

*Photographer and date unkown, Algeria.
Musée du Quai Branly, Photothèque,
D.34.4298.238.*

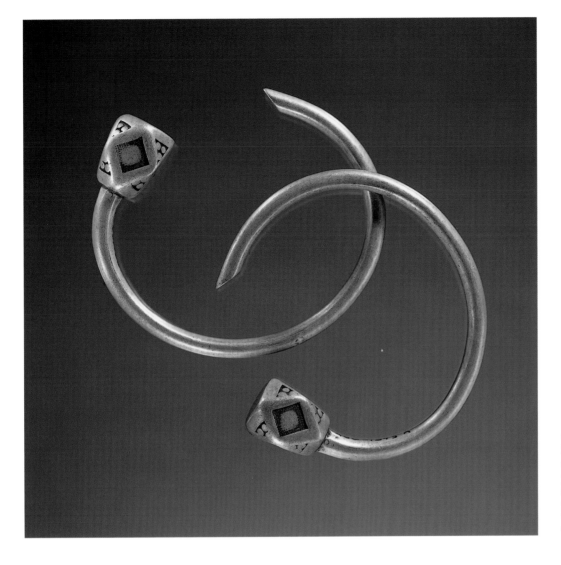

7.4
Earrings (*tizabaten*)
Tuareg, Kel Aïr
Niger
Silver
7 x 6.8 cm
UCLA Fowler Museum
x88.1393a,b

Visually striking for its clean lines, for the delicacy of its engraved decorations, and for the consistency of its geometrical shapes, Tuareg classical jewelry exists in myriad forms and is worn to emphasize the head, neck, and arms. Women wear head ornaments, earrings, necklaces, amulets, bracelets, rings, and counterweights that they attach to their head scarves. Men wear amulets, bracelets, and rings. The objects are relatively large and are often formed of rectangles, squares, tubes, and triangles. Unlike pieces worn by other Berber groups, they do not include large amber or coral beads or colorful enameling. By comparison, in fact, Tuareg pieces are relatively sober and appear as an accumulation of similar shapes and designs.

Most Tuareg jewelry is made of silver, red copper, brass, lead, tin, or aluminum. Other materials such as leather, faceted glass, agate, ivory, and shell or stone beads are also used. Silver pieces are often reserved for formal occasions, while brass or copper jewelry is worn daily. Jewelry forms are forged and cast using the lost-wax process then polished with sand and engraved, incised, or decorated with geometrical motifs in repoussé. They are the work of *inadan* (smiths or artists) who are found in all Tuareg groups.[3]

Tuareg women wear ornaments at the back of their head, at their temples attached in their hair or braids, and sometimes in the middle of their foreheads. These usually take the form of rectangular, triangular, or square cases decorated with repoussé motifs and little triangular baubles (fig. 7.2). They sometimes contain Koranic passages. Men wear turban amulets, which are often attached to a long strip of blue cloth that is then wound around the veil, or *tagulmust*. Some of these amulets are embellished with inset

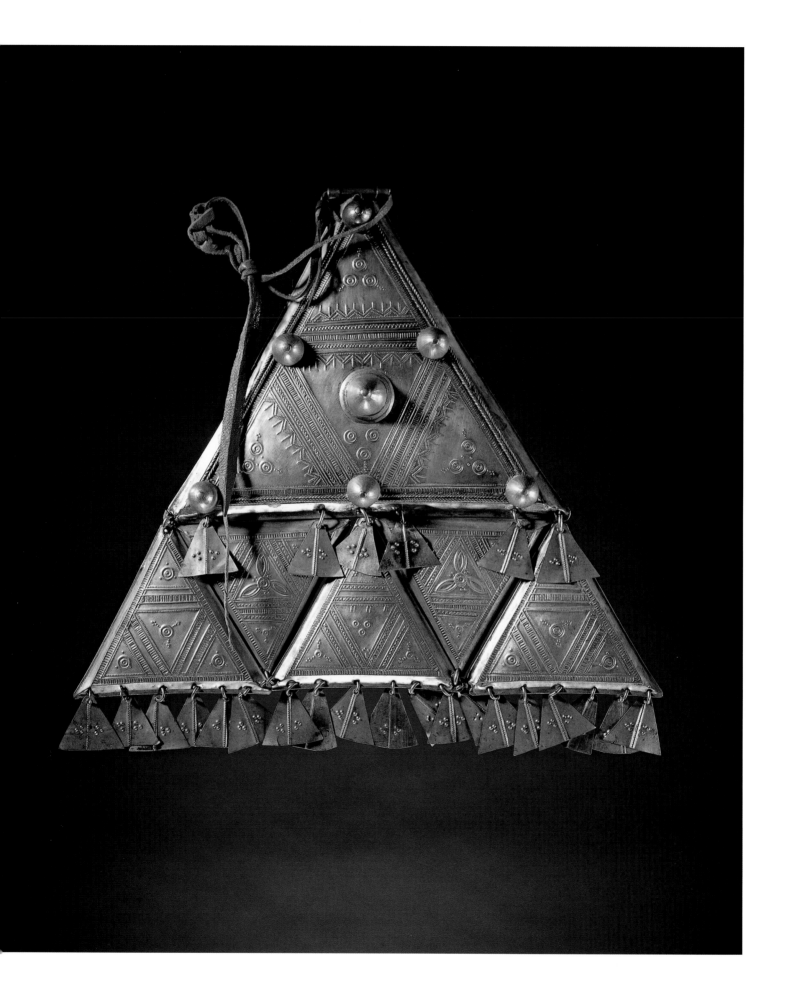

LOUGHRAN

mirrors and are principally used for purposes of decoration. Young men in Agadez wear tubular-shaped amulets, or *korkoro*, for feasts. The *takoumbout* headdress is unique in the repertoire and is worn by Kel Ajjer men in Djanet for the feast of the Sebiba. It consists of a tall red hat decorated with ostrich feathers and silver amulet cases (fig. 7.3).

Women's earrings, or *tizabaten*, consist of round hoops decorated with incised motifs and are mostly worn at the earlobe (fig. 7.4). Examples featuring polyhedral end knobs are striking due to their size and weight. They are worn around the ear and suspended from the hair because they are so very heavy. Another type, the *tsagur* is made of a strand of glass beads that ends in a boat-shaped bead or a triangular *chatchat* pendant. Married women wear these on the upper section of the right ear.

Amulets, or *tcherot*, exist in many different forms and shapes and are worn by men and women. Like the head ornaments described above, these cases are rectangular, square, triangular, or concave. Many are decorated with repoussé or engraved designs. Mixing different metals or using leather creates color contrast in these pieces. Some are flat, while others, resembling pyramidal constructions, are made with two to five levels. They are usually suspended from the neck on braided leather strands with tassels. *Tcherot* are sometimes filled with sand or with papers bearing Koranic inscriptions and texts or magical letters prepared by religious leaders (*ineslemen*). The *tereout tan idmarden* (fig. 7.5) is considered one of the most important pieces of jewelry worn by brides in the Ahaggar region of Algeria. It is made of several triangular cases, which are attached to one another, and is decorated with triangular baubles on the bottom section. It can be thirty-six centimeters in length and is embellished with triangular motifs and large ball nails. *Khomessa* amulets (figs. 7.6, 7.7) are also unique to the Tuareg and are composed of multiple diamond shapes of silver, camel bone, or ivory, which are attached to one another then fixed onto a leather base.

Pendants and beads are used to make necklaces worn by women. Two favored bead types are the tubular *ezmaman* and the faceted, square *negneg*. There are many pendant styles. The most popular are the *egrou* (which means "toad" and is used to make the *tadnet* necklace; fig. 7.8), the *n'gadoun* or *lahia*, the *chatchat*, and the *talhakimt* or *tanfuk*, which has a triangular shape and is usually made of agate or carnelian (see fig. 9.10). The pendant sometimes has a pierced circle or a ring-shaped top portion to facilitate its use on a necklace or its attachment to the hair. The *talhakimt* is also used to make the cross of In Gall. Cross forms or *tenaghalt* (meaning "that which is made by fusion") are one of the best-known pendant types (Casajus 1987a, 298). They are primarily used as pendant forms for necklaces. In 1991 there were twenty-one known cross forms named after geographical regions (fig. 7.9).[4] Necklaces are worn singly on a daily basis and in multiples for feasts and holidays. They can be composed of a variety of silver, glass, or stone beads, shells, and pendants strung on finely braided leather or cotton cords. Necklaces are sometimes named after the beads or pendants with which they are made, such as the *ezmaman* or *chatchat* (fig. 7.10).

7.5 (OPPOSITE)

Pectoral pendant
(***tcherot* or *tereout tan idmarden***)

Tuareg, Kel Ahaggar
Ahaggar, Algeria
Silver, leather
32 x 23.3 cm
UCLA Fowler Museum
x88.1385

7.6 (ABOVE)

Amulet (*khomessa*)

Madi Fode and Hawa Albaka
Tuareg, Kel Ewey
Niger
Pendant: 9.2 x 7.9 cm;
L (of necklace): 53 cm
Silver, leather
Cantor Arts Center
1997.50.a-b

7.7

Amulet (*khomessa*)

Tuareg
Gao, Mali
Leather, bone
Pendant: 6 x 7 cm;
L (of necklace): 18 cm
UCLA Fowler Museum
x88.1460

The use of *khomessa* amulets is
widespread in Algeria, Niger, and
Mali. Whereas examples made with
bone or ivory are more common in
Mali, silver *khomessa* predominate
in Niger and Algeria. They are
manufactured by attaching between
five and thirteen diamond-shaped
elements together and then affixing
them to a leather or silver base.
These amulets do not contain verses
of the Koran. Their power derives
from the word *khomessa*, which is
related to the Arabic *hamsa*, or the
number five. It symbolizes the hand
of Fatima, a potent amulet against
the evil eye.

7.8

Necklace (*tadnet*)

Tuareg, Kel Aïr
Niger
Silver, glass, cord
Pendant: 8.3 x 8 cm;
L (of necklace): 32 cm
UCLA Fowler Museum
x88.1444

Tadnet necklaces are given to the
bride by her husband at the time
of marriage and are from the Aïr
region of Niger. They are distinguished by the central pendant,
which is called *egrou* (meaning
"toad"), and by the long tubular
ezmaman beads and black beads
used for the necklace itself.

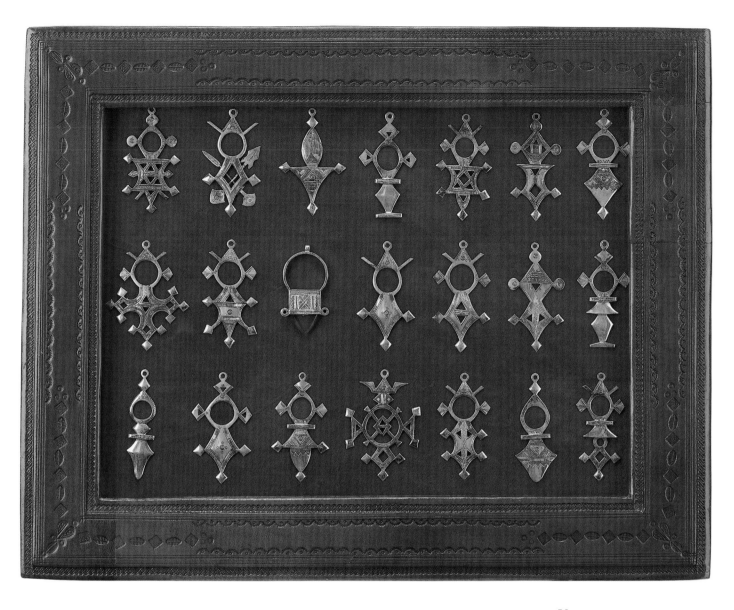

7.9

**Twenty-one silver crosses
in a tooled leather frame**

Ousmane Saidi
Tuareg, Kel Ewey
Niamey, Niger
Silver, leather, wood, glass
32 x 39.7 x 1.3 cm
Private Collection

The crosses displayed were made
in 2004 by Ousmane Saidi, and
the frame was made by a Malian
Tuareg living in Niamey, Niger,
who specializes in tooled leather
items.

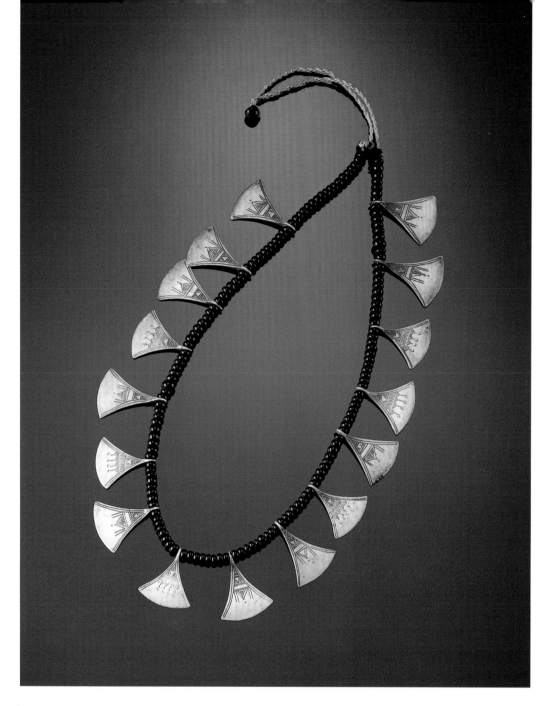

7.10

Necklace (*chatchat*)

Tuareg, Kel Aïr
Niger
Silver, glass, cord
Each pendant: 2.2 x 1.9 cm
Cantor Arts Center
2001.194

This necklace is called a *chatchat*
after the small triangular pendants
that adorn it. Some scholars have
suggested that the pendants might
represent little dolls. *Chatchat*
necklaces, which are also made of
gypsum, are among the first items
of jewelry given to young girls.

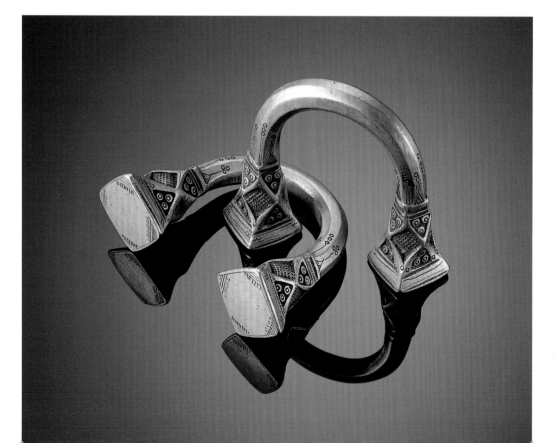

7.11

Bracelets (*elkiss*, pl. *elkizan*)

Mohammed Mohammed
Tuareg, Kel Geres
Niger
Silver
a. 6 x 8 cm; b. 6.1 x 7.8 cm
Cantor Arts Center
1997.41.a-b

a. Ring (*tisek*)
Tuareg
Timbuktu, Mali
Silver
Diam: 2.2 cm
UCLA Fowler Museum
x88.1459

b. Ring (*tisek*)
Tuareg, Kel Aïr
Agadez, Niger
Silver, solder
Diam: 4.5 cm
UCLA Fowler Museum
x88.1449

Rings that rattle are used by women
during festivals.

c. Ring (*tisek*)
Tuareg
Timbuktu, Mali
Silver
Diam: 3 cm
UCLA Fowler Museum
x88.1462

7.13

Veil weight (*asrou n' swoul*)

Tuareg
Niger
Silver, leather
32 x 5.5 cm
UCLA Fowler Museum
x88.1445

Bracelets are almost always worn in pairs, and with the exception of the *elkiss* bracelets (fig. 7.11), they are lightweight and made of sheet silver.[5] *Samboro* bracelets are flat circular metal bands that close with a hinge and are decorated with repoussé bosses and engraved patterns (see fig. 7.15). *Takafat* bracelets are decorated with engraved lines and triangles and are favored by older women. In earlier times, men wore stone bracelets known as *iwuki* on the upper arm or at the elbow, but these are rare today.

Men's and women's rings, or *tisek*, are similar in form. They are worn daily, are usually heavy, and are forged in solid silver (fig. 7.12a–c). During festivals and weddings, women sometimes wear domed rings with little seeds in them that rattle. Women also wear counterweights over their shoulders and attached to the corners of their head scarves (fig. 7.13). These are forged and display intricate openwork designs. They are considered typically Tuareg.

7.14

Pectoral pendant
(*tcherot* or *tereout tan idmarden*)

Tuareg
Tamanrasset, Algeria
Silver, leather
23.5 x 24.5 x 1.4 cm
Musée du Quai Branly
70.2001.28.24

7.15

Bracelet (*samboro*)

Tuareg, Kel Aïr
Niger
Silver
W: 2.6 cm; Diam: 6 cm
UCLA Fowler Museum
X88.14.02

Regional Variations

Though Tuareg jewelry forms are often described as a generic whole in the literature, variations occur from one region to another. These take the form of different object types and comparable objects worn in different ways. The Darfur Tuareg, for example, feel that the *talhakimt* pendant should be worn with two crosses as part of an elaborate necklace made of beads and metal pendants, whereas western groups wear the *talhakimt* in their hair.

The northern style is found in the regions of the Ahaggar and the Tassili-n-Ajjer Mountains in Algeria (see map, fig 1.9). It is characterized by cumulative constructions and by the clean lines of the jewelry, which emphasize its mass (fig. 7.14). Women in this area also wear large amounts of jewelry, and it is generally remarkable for its repoussé decorations and additive elements (such as ball studs), which relate to North African jewelry forms. A woman originally from the Aïr region in Niger remarked, "This style is too heavy: they wear too much. Men in Djanet wear triangles. In Niger, only women wear triangles" (personal communication, Niamey).[6]

The eastern style found in the Aïr region in Niger (see map, fig. 1.9) is more restrained. Women tend to wear the same kinds of objects as in the north but fewer

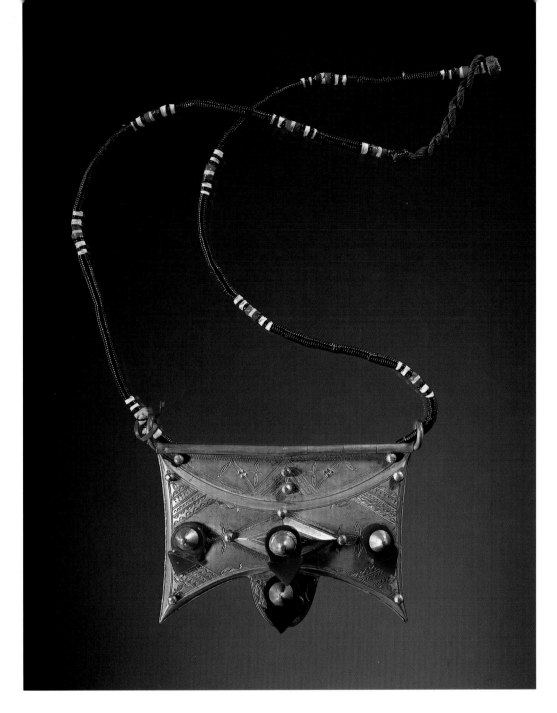

7.16

Amulet (*tcherot*)

Tuareg
Timbuktu, Mali
Silver, glass, stone, plastic
Pendant: 7.4 x 11.1 cm;
L (of necklace): 27 cm
UCLA Fowler Museum
x88.1465a,b

Amulets exist in many different shapes and forms and are worn by men and women. They are constructed of silver, brass, copper, or leather; the backs of metal amulets are often made of aluminum or tin from discarded cans. While some amulets are flat, others are augmented with two to five levels, forming a pyramid-like construction. These amulets are profusely decorated with incised and repoussé geometrical motifs. Some pieces also incorporate mirrors, which are thought to protect against the evil eye. Amulets can be worn around the upper arm, but most often they are worn around the neck, suspended from braided leather strands, which are sometimes decorated with tassels. They are usually filled with papers bearing Koranic inscriptions and texts or magical letters and numbers prepared by marabouts as protection for the wearer.

This amulet, or *tcherot*, from Timbuktu displays the mixing of aesthetic styles that has resulted from the Tuareg coming into contact with the Moors and the other peoples in the caravans that come to Timbuktu. These styles blend curved, concave, and oval forms and combine materials such as stone, metal, leather, and plastic to create color contrasts. This particular amulet is embellished with engraved motifs but is also decorated with *tanfuk* pendants and is suspended from a cord decorated with colorful plastic segments.

of them. Individual objects are emphasized, and there are a great variety of them from which to choose. Engraved and punched decorations accentuate rounded shapes and symmetrical lines, which in turn reflect light and shadow. Silver and copper are mixed to create color contrasts, and the repoussé technique is not widespread. Many smiths refer to the eastern style as *façon arabe* (in the Arabic manner).

The western style is found in the Adrar des Ifoghas region in Mali (see map, fig. 1.9). It is characterized by curved, concave, and oval forms and elaborate combinations of different types of materials (fig. 7.16). Refined engraving patterns recall Moorish motifs, and the frequent mixing of metals with leather to create cutout overlays is also reminiscent of Moorish jewelry (Göttler 1989, 221). Women in this region also make use of colored beads and leather amulets. The western style reflects contacts with neighboring groups.

The southern jewelry style occurs in the areas south of the Aïr region (see map, fig. 1.9). This style is noteworthy for its synthesis of Tuareg and foreign forms. Pieces are worn singly or combined with one another (fig. 7.17). The jewelry forms are curved and display very intricate decorations. Silver, copper, brass, leather, and beads are the preferred materials, and plastic and colored-glass beads are also often used.

7.17

Necklace made of crosses of Zinder

Tuareg
Niger
Silver, cord
Diam: 16.2 cm
Cantor Arts Center
2003.27

Necklaces made with the cross of
Zinder are especially prestigious
because Tuareg women once used
this type of cross as a form of currency. The ring form of the cross
with its conical protrusion symbolizes millet, a staple food in Niger.

Trade

Jewelry items are small, easily transportable, and can be changed, modified, and adapted
with relatively little effort. Long-standing trade networks and migration patterns in
West Africa and across the Sahara reflect centuries of contact and exchange and explain
why comparable jewelry shapes and decorations appear simultaneously in different
cultures. Many of the metals (e.g., silver, copper, and iron) used to make Tuareg jewelry
were brought by caravan traders from the north and from Sahelian regions. In the 1600s
glass, agate, and carnelian beads made in India were traded by Arab merchants. In the
1900s the agate bead trade was exploited by German and Czechoslovakian factories.
Today the market includes colored-glass and plastic beads, which are imported from
Europe. The Tuareg have always been responsive to foreign jewelry styles. This is visible
in earring and pendant forms borrowed from the rich variety of Hausa shapes (Creyaufmüller 1983, 18) or the affinities with Moorish jewelry. Over time, Tuareg objects have
also been adopted by neighboring groups who have adapted them to fulfill their own
aesthetic criteria and tastes. An object that seems to be Tuareg may in fact have been
reworked for a Fulbe or Moorish client or vice versa.

The classical jewelry repertoire has remained remarkably stable over time, but add-
ing, reworking, adapting, and transposing forms has occurred to satisfy the aesthetic
norms of individual groups (Frank 1988, 112). Trade also highlights the resourcefulness
and flexibility of individuals (merchants and *inadan* alike) faced with diverse aesthetic
systems and demands. This ongoing relationship between artisans, clients, and traders
has greatly enriched the range of Tuareg jewelry forms over the years.

Women and Their Jewelry

The Tuareg have always inspired a healthy amount of curiosity. This is in part due to their lifestyle in a very difficult environment, but it is also a result of their appearance. Poised, attractive, and elegant, the Tuareg project a culturally learned and emphasized style (fig. 7.18). Tuareg from all social classes have very clear ideas about how they should look and present themselves. Men and women move slowly and gracefully, their garments swaying gently around them. Women's clothing is always being rearranged—especially shirts and headcloths—and is thus in continuous motion.[7] Traditional clothing is usually sober and navy blue, black, or white accentuated by the shimmering blue turbans made of *aleshu* cloth.[8]

Jewelry is considered fundamental. It is integral to dress and presentation and being Tuareg. As with clothing, it must move and shine to adorn properly. Tuareg women would not consider themselves properly dressed if they were not wearing a bracelet, rings, and other pieces of jewelry, which they believe enhance their beauty while symbolizing their age and social position. Individual pieces are enriched with many dangles and little pendants, which make noise when women move. As one of my informants noted, "this noise is pleasing, it brings jewelry to life" (personal communication, Niamey).[9]

Generations of Jewelry Forms

As people reach different life stages, they are entitled to wear different pieces of adornment. Infants wear little leather amulets and bead necklaces around their necks or stomachs (fig. 7.19). After a boy reaches puberty, he is given a sword and starts to wear a stone bracelet and a ring. When he takes the veil, he begins to wear silver amulets (Rodd 1926, 289).[10] Turban amulets are used to decorate the veil and to protect the wearer. Men wear the same kinds of items throughout their lifetime.

7.18
Women departing a dance at a wedding wear necklaces, earrings, bracelets, and their finest clothing.

Photograph by Thomas K. Seligman, Agadez, Niger, 1988.

Women are given jewelry from the time they are little girls until they reach middle age. Girls are first given lightweight necklaces made of colored beads. These are considered appropriate for the young. Fatimata explained, "when a daughter is young, you should give her a necklace, something nice and pretty. When Aisha goes to a party, I put a necklace on her, and when she comes home, I take it off because she is little and that way she does not ruin it" (personal communication, Niamey; fig. 7.20). When they turn seven, girls wear small bead necklaces interspersed with little silver dangles known as *chatchat* or with agate or glass *tanfuk* pendants. As one person pointed out, "if they are rich and have many head of cattle, they start to spoil the girl early on" (personal communication, Agadez). Some start to wear little hoop earrings at this age as well, and only one ear is pierced at a time to allow for it to heal before the other is done.

At puberty, it is the "duty" of the parents to buy their daughters jewelry. At this stage, it is said that girls become "responsible" for their jewelry: they care for it, polish it, and do not lose it. They also wear heavier pieces. Gaisha, who lives in Agadez received such pieces of jewelry when she turned fifteen: "My father got me a necklace and *boucles* [from the French *boucles d'oreilles*, or 'earrings']. The necklace was made with *ezmaman* beads set in the shape of a triangle, it had no pendants. The earrings had pendants and three *ezmaman*. This was modern. I wore it everyday because I thought it was beautiful, and I did not want to leave it at home because I loved it so much" (personal communication,

7.19

Mother and child at the Cure Salée festival watch other Tuareg playing music. Note the necklace worn by the child.

Photograph by Kristyne Loughran, In Gall, Niger, 1990.

7.20

Fatimata and her daughter in festival attire. Fatimata wears gold jewelry and her daughter is attired in a Western-style dress.

Photograph by Kristyne Loughran, In Gall, Niger, 1990.

Agadez). Girls are also given large hoop earrings or the type with heavy polyhedral end knobs. A woman was quick to caution however, that "we should not wear these earrings until a certain age, they are too heavy (fig. 7.21). If a young girl wears heavy pieces, her ears get distended, this is not right" (personal communication, Niamey). Young women are also given bracelets and necklaces made with the crosses of Zinder or Agadez and begin to wear a type of silver amulet known as *tcherot*.

Adolescence is an important time in a young woman's life: she is old enough to marry and attends courtship gatherings. As with young people the world over, her gaze turns to the mirror: her demeanor, makeup, and hairstyle all become crucial to her, as do her clothing and jewelry (fig. 7.22). Elegance and large amounts of jewelry are synonymous with beauty. They are also the keys to popularity and courtship. Bernus remarks that when young people start dating, a young man sometimes takes a girl's amulet, ring, or necklace and wears it in public. These tokens are called *ikkusan* and are loaned for a short period of time. During guessing games, if a young woman does not know the answer, she must give a token (tobacco or a piece of jewelry), called *arewud*, which is returned the next day (Bernus 1981, 157). She wears the *adalil* (headcloth), and dresses her hair in a multitude of little braids knotted at the nape of her neck, a style known as the *akankan*.[11] This hair knot is often decorated with a triangular pendant called *tan eraf tan tamtut*, which hangs down the back, swaying from side to side as she moves.

7.21

After washing her hair with water and oils, this young woman has it plaited in a style of her own choosing. Her large earrings are supported by a braid of hair.

Photograph by Thomas K. Seligman, Agadez, Niger, 1998.

7.22

A young woman with kohl-dyed lips and eyes wears gold earrings and a *chatchat* necklace.

Photograph by Kristyne Loughran, In Gall, Niger, 1990.

When a woman marries, she receives more gifts of jewelry from her mother and from her husband. Wedding necklaces are usually made of *negneg* and black beads and silver pendants (fig. 7.23). Her mother gives the bride some of her own jewelry, whereas her husband commissions new pieces. Casajus recounts that the groom often gives another gift in addition to the *taggalt* (bridewealth), which is called the *tisakhsar*. This consists of various items of clothing and gold or silver necklaces (*ezmaman*), a bracelet (*alkez*) or a silver ring (*tasendert*), and heavy silver earrings (Casajus 1987b, 213).[12] Ornaments given at marriage also signify property and status. When I attended a wedding in Agadez, the bride-to-be eagerly showed me the jewelry she had been given, and scholars have also noted that these gifts are sometimes hung for public display (Gabus 1982, 344; Rasmussen 1987, 10). After marriage women sometimes sell animals to buy jewelry, or they receive additional presents from their husbands.

When a woman has children of her own, she begins to give jewelry to her daughters. Among certain groups in the event of a divorce, women wear a white knotted cord around their necks and arms to indicate this status. After three months have elapsed, the cord is cut off and they may appear in public and remarry.[13] In later years, a woman slowly starts to divest herself of her jewelry. Many women pass their jewelry down to their children or grandchildren. There is much sentimental value attached to jewelry, and mother-daughter relationships are very strong among the Tuareg. Still later, women revert to wearing the bead necklaces they first wore as little girls or a simple band with very sharp edges and engraved motifs known as *takafat*. When a woman dies, her jewelry is distributed among her children.

Social Aspects of Jewelry

Jewelry holds a prominent place within the social practices of the Tuareg and consistently emerges as an important marker in the lives of men and women. It fulfills aesthetic, ritual, and psychological functions. It is highly charged with personal and spiritual meanings and is emblematic of public and sociopolitical affiliations. It is used to indicate life stages and social rank. It is also steeped in artistic intent and process.

7.23

Necklace (*tadnet*)

Tuareg, Kel Aïr
Niger
Silver, glass, cord
Pendant: 9.5 x 8 cm;
L (of necklace): 47 cm
Private Collection

The Tuareg believe in the evil eye and mouth, or *tehot*,[14] and this belief dictates many facets of their social behavior and influences their interactions with others. People are reserved about their possessions, especially their jewelry, and during my research, women only showed me their jewelry once they had gotten to know me fairly well. One day, while visiting Gaisha, a woman I knew, her friend Awa arrived, covered in gold jewelry. Gaisha was surprised and asked her if she was going to a feast or gathering. After a while, they started teasing one another about their jewelry. Gaisha told me her friend was very wealthy because she had so much gold on, while she was only wearing a glass bead necklace! The other woman countered by saying that Gaisha had plenty of gold herself. The exchange was quick, light, and humorous, indicating that each woman knew exactly what the other had. Women often compare each other's possessions, and jewelry occasionally fosters competitiveness and longing. This might explain, in part, why women are secretive about their possessions.

The noble classes primarily wear silver and gold jewelry, and members of the former servile classes favor copper, bronze, and silver alloys and necklaces made of colored beads. Bella women,[15] for example, decorate their hair with agate, glass, or brass pendants. They wear multicolored glass necklaces and silver pendants as well. They tend to wear more jewelry than the members of the noble classes, both on a daily basis and for festivals. One day while showing a woman photographs of Tuareg jewelry, I asked her if she ever wore bracelets made of colored beads. She immediately responded: "Oh no, we should not wear colored glass, the Bella do" (personal communication, Niamey).

Sedentarization and the new lifestyles it has brought about have changed these social parameters. In the same way that women and men now wear colorful clothing (fig. 7.24), others commission jewelry once reserved for the noble classes. Liliane, a member of the noble class, noted: "You see, today, they have more income, and they can buy silver jewelry and wear bracelets like we do" (personal communication, Niamey). Contrasts between pieces may, of course, be evident in the value of the materials used, the weight of the metal, and the quality of the workmanship. The amount of jewelry commissioned today, however, is more a factor of increased financial means than social status (Creyaufmüller 1983, 60).

Jewelry forms sometimes become political emblems or are created to commemorate an important individual. During the French colonial period for example, the cross of Agadez was used as a prominent motif for pins that were worn on berets, shirts, etc., by members of the *méhariste* military corps (Boucher 1982). More recently, the *croix de Mano* was produced in memory of Mano Dayak (see figs. 3.7, 3.8), the founder of the Temoust Liberation Front, who died in an airplane crash in the Aïr Mountains in December 1995 (Thomas Seligman, personal communication, 1997). While some scholars have addressed the symbolism of certain jewelry shapes and forms, such as the cross of Agadez, and other objects,[16] this is a complex matter that merits more systematic and in-depth study.

Decorative designs can be thought of as ideograms or pictograms and often represent natural elements such as the sun (a circle) or stars (asterisks; Gabus 1982, 146–51).

7.24
Leila wearing a rolled headcloth, a gown of imported fabric, and gold necklaces (one a *chatchat*) and earrings.
Photograph by Kristyne Loughran, In Gall, Niger, 1990.

Jewelry is also the material manifestation of ideals of beauty and is sometimes used as a metaphor for a woman's beauty in traditional poems and songs, as demonstrated in an example of each given below

> Allili today is adorning herself,
> She is beautiful,
> She is wearing a *Tasseralt*
> Which throws a thousand murderous rays.
> My friends and I are overwhelmed
> And about to breathe our last breath
> And death is prowling around us.
> [Tamzali 1984, 88]

> The moment he saw her,
> He re-arranged his veil,
> He stopped, forgetting the road,
> Until his friends became surprised.

> They understood, of course.
> And told him he must be patient....

> Before seeing her face,
> He saw her rings, her *tizabatines*,
> Her necklace of amulets.
> He was sick with love....
> [Tamzali 1984, 106]

As noted earlier, many jewelry forms are considered amulets or are believed to have intrinsic protective properties. The distinction between Tuareg jewelry used only for the purpose of adornment and Tuareg amuletic pieces used for personal protection yet made in the form of adornment is almost imperceptible, and differentiation is rarely made between the two. Amulets derive their power from being close to the skin and are worn on the person, put on animals, or hung in tents. The Tuareg consider the triangle an important amuletic form, and it is consistently repeated in decorative motifs and jewelry shapes.

Various materials are used for different purposes as well. According to Rasmussen (1987, 10) copper is used for rheumatism, and informants related to me that gold is sometimes mixed with silver to prevent depression. Items such as shells and agates are thought to have protective values as well. Shells are used to make *khomessa* amulets,[17] employed in divination, worn in the hair, and considered fertility charms when the underside shows (Rasmusen 1987, 14).[18] Agates are connected with blood and thus associated with life.[19] Iron is considered the most potent metal of all and is used as a protection against the Kel Esuf, a type of malevolent spirit,[20] in times of transition and during curing rituals (Rasmusen 1994, 75).

Silver and Gold: Continuity and Change
Much of the literature on Tuareg jewelry is rather emphatic about the use of silver as opposed to gold. In the mid-1800s, Barth mentions giving some silver to a Tuareg chief, who was "very glad to have obtained a sufficient quantity of this much esteemed metal for adorning his beloved wife" ([1857] 1965, 3: 340). In 1902, however, Eudel mentions the jewelry worn in the Sahara by Tuareg women, stating that "rich women cover their arms with gold, which they sometimes alternate with others."[21]

Classical jewelry pieces are made of Maria Theresa thalers or French francs and are much heavier than those being manufactured in the cities today. The Tuareg favor thaler

7.25

A new mother participates in a ceremony held in her home wherein her child receives his name. This will be followed by an evening of feasting and dancing. The mother wears gold jewelry for this special occasion.

Photograph by Kristyne Loughran, Niamey, Niger, 1991.

silver in particular and speak of it as being warm and as shedding light. When the engraving wears off a piece of jewelry women sometimes take the piece to the family *enad* to have it remade. A friend explained that she still considers the pieces "old" because they are made by the same smith (or his son or grandson) and are identical in both form and decoration. The notion of age is quite relative. When people discussed old designs and forms, they mentioned these were "beautiful" and the engraving was more detailed and careful. Tuareg patrons care that pieces be fashioned as they were in the past. Juwa, Moussa Albaka's mother, told me, "This is our tradition. We have always worn silver and we like it this way" (personal communication, Agadez).

With the exception of jewelry they commission for themselves, my informants noted that contemporary jewelry is often produced for commercial markets, and the quality of the materials has become inferior. For example elephant or hippopotamus teeth were once used to make the *elgettera* necklace, and ivory or shell were used for to make *khomessa* amulets.[22] Today, plastic or other synthetic materials are being used. While Tuareg patrons think these new items are "pretty," they also note they are made for people who "would not understand the difference and would not know what Tuareg jewelry should look like." Sterling silver, a fairly recent addition, has become fashionable in urban centers and is viewed as being very cold.

In the past twenty years there has been a steady acceptance of gold jewelry forms as a result of social, economic, and political changes. What becomes apparent is that the classical pieces are kept and passed down from mother to daughter, and these are the repositories of cultural ideals and aesthetics; whereas the wearing of lighter silver forms and the increasing interest in gold jewelry forms is the result of an interest in fashion (fig. 7.25). Contemporary wearing patterns affect the jewelry forms being used and the way women perceive themselves and think about jewelry.

Some gold items have names indicating their place of origin, thus Saudi necklaces are either referred to as *collier d'Arabie* or *collier femme arabe*, and others are given names in Tamasheq, such as the *tadnet oragh* necklace. The wearing of gold jewelry

7.26

Agak Mohamed, an *enad,* in his
workshop at the National Museum
of Niger.

*Photograph by Kristyne Loughran, Niamey,
Niger, 1991.*

forms by Tuareg women indicates what some authors refer to as a sense of national identity. The Tuareg in fact have always considered themselves one people and have always
referred to one another by regional names such as Kel Ahaggar, Kel Geres, and so forth.
The idea of referring to themselves as Tuareg from Niger, from Algeria, or from Mali
has little historical relevance for them. The use of colored head scarves instead of the
adalil and gold jewelry instead of silver pieces indicates that some Tuareg are integrat-
ing themselves into a national identity (that of Mali, Algeria, or Niger; Claudot-Hawad
1993, 112).

Some gold pieces are similar to, though smaller than, classical silver examples, and
the notion of an object being a gold reproduction or copy does not create a dilemma.
During one of our many discussions in Niamey, a friend burst out, after listening to my
endless prodding on the differences between silver and gold: "You've got to stop. Gold,
silver, it doesn't matter. This is called a *tadnet* necklace, which is a real Tamasheq word.
Tadnet oragh, *oragh* means gold. What matters is the jewelry. I like my jewelry. I want
jewelry. It means I am beautiful" (personal communication, Niamey). Agak Mohamed,
the master smith at the National Museum in Niamey, simply laughed and said: "The
women. They talk. They have always loved gold" (personal communication, Niamey;
fig. 7.26).

Wearing Jewelry: Daily and Festival Attire

The aesthetic of dress among the Tuareg is based on a delicate balance between sobriety
and propriety on the one hand and opulence and conspicuous display on the other. Daily
wear is characterized by sobriety. Women consistently stressed to me that jewelry worn
daily should be lightweight, not too showy, bulky, or cumbersome. They typically wear
small, delicate necklaces, a bracelet, and some rings. Necklaces are prominent because
women believe they are meant to wear something around their necks.

In urban centers women prefer light hoop earrings, bracelets, and necklaces made
of gold to the heavier silver pieces. Gaisha explained, "In the city, you can give your

7.27
A man and a woman dance at a wedding. This dancing of couples together is referred to as the "man and woman's dance."
Photograph by Thomas K. Seligman, Agadez, Niger, 1988.

daughter a gold necklace, a small one, or some gold earrings. Many girls wear gold early now. Those who cannot afford it wear silver. Those who cannot afford anything, ask their friends to give them a bead each to make a necklace. I grew up in the city. Gold had already started" (personal communication, Agadez).

During festivals, people are always in a flurry of activity. They meet with friends and family members, exchange news, change their clothing ensembles, go to a camel race, change their clothing again to meet a possible suitor.[23] Individuals dress up in their most beautiful apparel and jewelry for these occasions (fig. 7.27). Not to wear jewelry at a feast is considered shameful. Liliane noted "you are not supposed to attend the Cure Salée festival[24] if you are not well dressed and covered with jewelry. If a girl has no jewelry to wear, she borrows it, with the understanding that it must be 'repaid by dawn'" (personal communication, Niamey). A week before a feast women clean their jewelry with salt and lemon (or Omo soap and lemon [Tom Seligman, personal communication, 2004]) so that it shines. Women commented that in the past they usually wore three necklaces, two bracelets, earrings, and rings. Haisha related, "They wore crosses, necklaces with the *ezmaman* beads, this is fine, the *tcherot* for the *akankan* hairstyle, and it is supposed to reach the middle of the back. It was not the quantity but wearing the right kinds of things is important. Normally, you should wear jewelry this way" (personal communication, Niamey). Liliane noted that this is when she chooses to wear her classical silver jewelry because it gives her a sense of pride in her Tuareg identity.

One woman, whose jewelry collection I had seen, told me she had loaned her "other" pieces to "the girls" (meaning her daughters, nieces, and daughters-in-law), so the pieces would not be "locked away." She stressed that what was really important to her was that all the jewelry be worn. Married women are more conservative. They emphasized that one should never be too showy, one should never exaggerate. "You should wear a lot of different pieces, yes, but to wear too much is shameful," Jorna said. "Today women wear too much: it hits their chest. These women want to be noticed, *les tape-à-l'oeil* [lit., those who hit the eye], they are looking for men, they want to marry and want to be seen. This is a new mentality. Before you boasted with how much livestock you had camels, sheep, and donkeys" (personal communication, Niamey).

When the feast is over, and when the dust has settled, pieces are carefully wrapped in cloth and put away in beautiful leather bags. At the Cure Salée, I admit I stood out quite sadly in my dusty skirts, tangled hair, and little wedding band. Women friends, who changed three to four times a day were forever asking me when I was going to change into my party clothes and take out "my gold" or whether I wanted to borrow some of theirs! Though the emphasis on adornment is obviously more the woman's domain than the man's, men changed their clothing ensembles almost as often as women did and decorated their turbans with silver amulets.[25]

Fashion and Change

As I mentioned earlier, the Tuareg are a very elegant people. They appreciate beauty and their self-image is very important to them. They take time with their appearance and make sure that such a "look" is "just so." From the motions made with their turbans and veils, to the little *agolo* (orphan) braid worn by women across their foreheads, however, there is also much playfulness involved. The wearing of beautiful jewelry forms—be they classical or modern, in silver or in gold—the significance accorded the proper metals and manufacturing techniques, and dignified social comportment emerge as meaningful aspects when one considers Tuareg ideals of beauty and taste.

The relevance of fashion and the response of women to it (be it positive or negative) are important. Corpulence is no longer a sign of beauty among the younger generations because the models and actresses they see in foreign fashion magazines all have slender bodies. With regard to jewelry, women do not always wear their classical jewelry forms. They are interested in new fashions and the new objects being produced. The younger generations insist that their main focus is gold, and they are driven by these new trends. Older women are just as fashion conscious and eager to see, judge, and acquire new pieces. Their attitudes, however, stem from a different perspective because they already own several pieces of classical jewelry. In places such as Agadez, women have been watching "the outsider" (desert tourists, Paris-Dakar assistants, aid workers, Peace Corps volunteers, etc.) for a long time. In November 1998 they also witnessed Alphadi's fashion, extravaganza,[26] which brought them up-to-date on the latest European high fashions at the time. In Niamey, Senegalese jewelers make copies of European pieces and those from neighboring countries. In addition when family members and friends travel or work abroad, they return with jewelry bought in Saudi Arabia. Some also bring gold coins, and one young woman told me that some bring jewelry catalogs. Women are dynamic and instrumental in endorsing change at local and national levels.

Today, whether a woman prefers silver to gold becomes a matter of personal taste, the influence of fashion, and her financial means. Young women already know what they like because they see what their friends wear, and they have more choices. Gaisha explained: "I have some silver pieces. My mother gave them to me. But I like gold much more because it shines. My mother and her friends, they wore the silver. Our generations and the younger ones like gold. Only gold" (personal communication, Agadez). Gulla, Abdulahi's wife, noted: "Silver is too white, it does not shine as much, and you must clean it all the time. You do not clean gold" (personal communication, Niamey).

A young woman in Agadez took great pleasure in showing me a European jewelry catalog called *Rosabelor*[27] and pointing out chain-link bracelets, drop earrings, rings set with zirconia, and a necklace with a central round pendant. What interested her the most were the *parures*, or ensembles: the matching earrings, bracelets, necklaces, and rings. In 1991 most women wanted "ensembles." Classical jewelry forms are considered ensembles, and certain pieces are meant to be worn with others, but they do not match.[28] Azara related: "When there is a feast, I wear the pure gold *ezmaman*, I really like gold coin necklaces too, and I wear more than one. I also have a coin bracelet and coin earrings" (personal communication, Agadez).

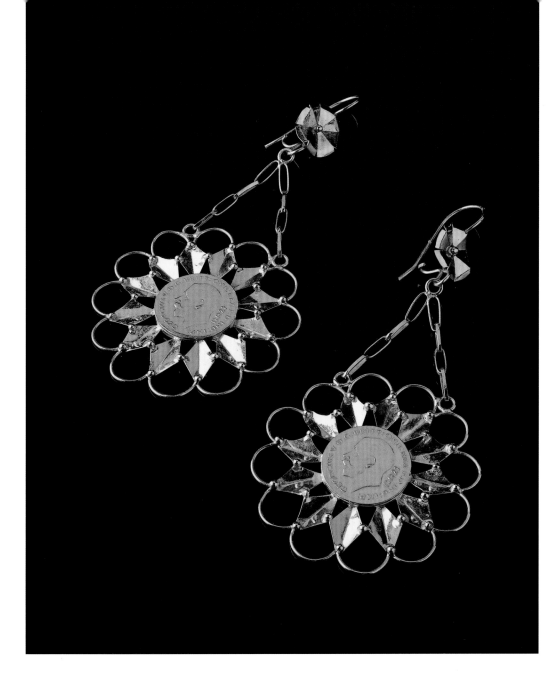

7.28

Earrings (*agalé* or *broderie*)

Salah Saidi
Tuareg, Kel Ewey
Agadez, Niger
Gold
Each: 7 x 4.5 cm
Cantor Arts Center
2001.203.a-b

Gold is not commonly used to manufacture classical jewelry styles. Silver has always been the preferred metal both for its clarity and because it is thought to attract *al baraka,* or blessings. Gold became fashionable in the 1960s when Tuareg men started working in Libya, and today it is often imported from Saudi Arabia in the form of jewelry or coins, which are then melted down. Tuareg women who work and earn wages are eager to invest in gold jewelry because it has a better resale potential than silver does. More and more *inadan* are thus training to work with this precious metal to create designs that appeal to a Tuareg clientele.

The earrings shown here, designed by Salah Saidi, are extremely popular and are called *agalé* or *broderie* (the French term for "embroidery"). This type of earring is often made with a central gold coin (either imported or made by smiths themselves) and decorated with a delicately scalloped gold wire design.

A popular ensemble at the time was made of gold coins imported from Saudi Arabia and called *broderie* (from the French word for "embroidery"). The name comes from the delicate scalloped gold wire surrounding the coins (fig. 7.28). Faceted red stones, which look like garnets or rubies, were popular as well. Fatimata remarked: "The red stones give shape to the necklace. They seem precious, they are pretty and they always keep their color. They also look good with gold. With new jewelry, we like stones....
I know they are valuable. If we get silver pieces made by our smiths, we like the black or blue stones better. This is as it should be" (personal communication, Niamey).

Women are very candid and open about the process of change. In the past, they accepted what men gave them and considered it precious. Many of them related that today they would rather choose their own jewelry. They go to town and see what is being made, and they decide what they want. Fatimata added: "My husband has bought a lot of jewelry for me, and I like his taste. He wants me to wear the things he chooses. He also allows me to get things I like, that is the way it is now. My father would not have thought this way" (personal communication, Niamey). Wearing jewelry gives women a sense of place: "If I go to the market, it does not matter what I wear. If I go out to a feast or a reception, I must look a certain way. Even at home, I am always careful because you never know who you will see, who will visit. I like to look correct" (personal communication, Niamey).

The Element of Choice

Women who cannot afford to buy pure gold jewelry purchase items made of alloy. Many smiths remarked that those women who could not afford to melt down their pieces were the keepers of the older pieces. If women work, they use their salaries to purchase their personal items, to help their mothers, and to buy their jewelry. One woman told me her necklace was twenty-four karat gold and was worth 500,000 CFA (approximately US$2,000 in 1991), or the equivalent of five goats. "My husband can buy things for me, but if I work, I can buy them too. My jewelry is my bank. I like having the jewelry. But I also know that I can make it work" (personal communication, Niamey).

Women have recognized and appreciated the value of their jewelry for a long time. The French scholar Henri Lhote remarked that the necklaces made of crosses of Zinder, which women once wore in multitudes (some had eight to ten crosses on one necklace), were often considered their banks. One person remarked: "I can tell if a person is rich from the kind of metal they are wearing, not by the jewelry." Women consider Senegalese traders and jewelers expensive and prefer to obtain gold coins from Saudi Arabia or from Libya when family members return. These are then melted down and reworked into the fashionable items the Tuareg women want. Women view gold as a form of investment, and value is based on weight and the type of gold used (twenty-four or eighteen karat).

Most women turn to the family *enad* when commissioning jewelry or go to specialists like Ahanti[29] for gold items. Some women reported that a smith had worked for their family for many years, and Liliane explained the patronage system this way: "His family have been our *inadan* for years. I can ask for things I want, and then I will decide what to give him as a present. It looks like a present, but in fact, it is a payment" (personal communication, Niamey). The *enad* told me he could never accept money from Liliane for his services, because this would be disrespectful. Women waste little time choosing classical jewelry items. They know the forms, and there is very little hesitation or discussion during the choosing process. Women know exactly what they want and smiths related they were also exacting in regard to the production of traditional pieces.

When ordering a modern item, women enjoy working out designs with the smith, or they redesign an older piece. Gaisha remarked: "I know what piece I want. I may have seen it on someone, maybe I invent it" (personal communication, Agadez). If the smith does not know how to make the piece or cannot make it a certain way, then the original model is modified or the woman chooses another. While in Agadez, Ahanti showed me line drawings of gold jewelry that he had made so that his clients could choose from them. During one of my visits, I met a woman from Côte d'Ivoire in his workshop who had ordered a number of gold Tuareg ensembles, stating she would never be able to find them in Abidjan.

Some of the pieces women find in foreign catalogs can be reproduced and others cannot. Women were quick to point out, for example, the pieces that were machine made. Gaisha liked the rings but said, "I cannot have them copied, because we cannot find the stones here." She went on to comment: "I have always gone to the same smith. I have known him since before, when he still worked in silver. He made my first necklace. He used to live in Arlit. I do not ask him to weigh the jewelry pieces, I ask him to weigh the gold. Then I choose a model, and I tell him what I want. A piece should weigh a certain amount. I also know that you lose a bit of gold when you pour it" (personal communication, Agadez). Abdulahi, a smith in Niamey, related that he was beginning to make gold jewelry because there was such a high demand for it. He also stated, however, that the work was "difficult," and he felt reluctant because the material was considered precious. This situation is not unusual and has created conflicts for many *inadan* now working in Niamey who are not trained goldsmiths.

7.29

A woman wearing a *tcherot* amulet.
Photograph by Thomas K. Seligman, Agadez, Niger, 1980.

The Tuareg Aesthetic

The Tuareg aesthetic has its roots in the proper shapes and forms. Great value and prestige are attached to the care and technical expertise with which pieces are created and embellished, as well as to the materials with which they are made. Formally, Tuareg jewelry is distinguished by design continuity, the attention paid to surface ornamentation, and the endless combination of geometric patterns. Decorative patterns consist of single and parallel lines, squares, diamonds, triangles, stars, and circles. These patterns highlight a design system that follows internal sequences and rhythms and evokes the world of the miniature.[30] Designs also reinforce the formal outlines of the jewelry shapes and enhance their symmetry and width. They are arranged in a premeditated fashion to create proper proportions and balance between contrasts. Silver is appreciated for its "clarity," because it is a luminous substance and acquires a tactile quality and texture through patina. Silver reflects light and enhances small engraving patterns. The addition of other metals (such as copper, brass, or leather) creates pleasing color contrasts and also adds texture to the pieces.

The *enad* must know "all the work" to have a good reputation. Tuareg patrons (and especially members of the noble classes) must know how to judge the workmanship, the quality of the designs, and the value of the materials used to manufacture jewelry. Informants were always pleased to see the photographs I had of the "older" pieces.[31] They looked at the objects very carefully, and many times lengthy discussions ensued. When I showed photographs of men and women from Djanet in Algeria, for example, people from the Aïr region felt these jewelry items were too heavy and exaggerated. Men were especially puzzled by the *takoumbout* headdress, worn by men at the annual feast of Sebiba. Some men had never seen such headdresses before and thought they were "strange." Women remarked, "you hide your personality and your beauty if you cover yourself too much." Liliane simply laughed when she looked at these photographs, noting with curiosity that what she wore at the back of her head on the *akankan* hairstyle, these people wore at the temples. They did not particularly admire or like the arabesques or the filigree work and much preferred the austerity and the simplicity of the Tuareg lines. When looking at the jewelry photographs, some people did not agree on the provenance, others discussed materials, and some remembered items their family members once wore. When defining the aesthetic of the pieces or the criteria applied to modes of manufacture, individuals often agreed. Familiarity with jewelry forms and demonstrated expertise in the matter were a point of honor, and this knowledge conferred prestige.

Tuareg women and the *inadan* share these ideals of beauty (fig. 7.29). Their approaches, however, stem from distinct perspectives. The smith takes great pride in knowing how to manufacture the jewelry and in work well done. Men and women are proud to know "all the work" and are also proud of their ability to recognize the materials used and the quality. Patrons have an intimate and direct relationship with the pieces they have commissioned because they wear them, and individuals who see them know what they are looking at. Jewelry must be worn to be effective. Tuareg women often related that their jewelry enhanced the body rather than just covering it and that the quality of individual pieces was more important than the quantity worn. In a way,

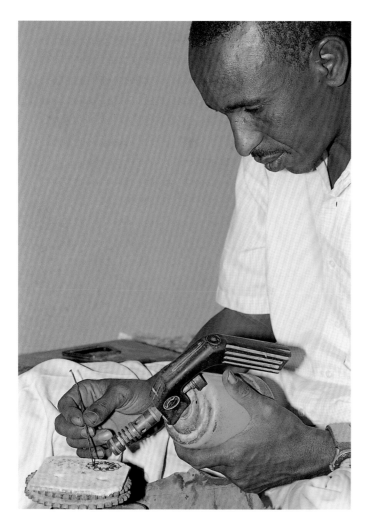

7.30

Salah Saidi making gold *agalé* or *broderie* earrings (see fig. 7.28).

Photograph by Thomas K. Seligman, Agadez, Niger, 2004.

patrons use this wearable art to project the appropriate image with deliberate flare. Smiths are profoundly aware that this is as it should be. One day, after a long discussion Moussa Albaka's brother, Khamadan, turned to me and said, "Women want beautiful things, jewelry should be beautiful, but jewelry also has to walk with a woman" (personal communication, Niamey).

Conclusion

Over the years I've pondered the issue of jewelry as an art form and believe—like the Tuareg women I spoke with—that it truly becomes artful when it is worn. Women use jewelry to project their self-image and taste and their ideas about beauty, prestige, and wealth. The way it is worn is unique to each woman and radiates something of her character and individuality. On another level, jewelry has personal meanings known only to the wearer: a souvenir—laden with memories—a token from an admirer, a good luck charm. The feelings and desires that are associated with jewelry are universal.

In the past, Tuareg social customs dictated that jewelry should be part of the dowry, precious heirlooms, or gifts from friends, family, or spouses. It was not considered socially acceptable to buy one's own jewelry. Only few women could buy themselves pieces simply because they "wanted" them. These parameters have changed now that women have entered the workforce. Sometimes, and in order to be in step with fashion and the times, women have older pieces melted down to make new models or have a piece they like copied in another material. When a new fashion is introduced, women who can't afford the expensive originals buy copies. There are also women who shun fashion dictates purposefully to make a social statement. Jewelry belongs to the woman who owns it and is hers to keep and to dispose of as she wishes. Jewelry empowers.

When I was at the Cure Salée in 1991 I was surprised at the amount of gold jewelry I saw Tuareg women wearing. After reading books by Jean Gabus, Gerhard Göttler, and other scholars who have written on the subject, this was not what I had expected. People cautioned me that the *citadines* (city dwellers) favored gold (fig. 7.30). I realized that my focus, which had been directed primarily toward classical jewelry styles, would have to expand. The canons related to Tuareg jewelry in the literature needed to be enriched. I had to address modernity and fashion and Tuareg approaches to their changing world. The women I had the pleasure of meeting and speaking with while I was in Niger are very generous, curious, and outspoken. It is my belief that Tuareg women will continue to embrace change in the years to come, all the while keeping their classical forms for the young, thus offering them a solid foundation from which to grow.

⊡

DOES IT HAVE TO BE BEAUTIFUL TO EMPOWER?

Amulets are personal and private—worn to protect against evil, to attract good fortune, and to heal. When they are worn directly against the skin, they gradually become smooth to the touch and acquire a patina. Those made of precious metals, such as silver, also serve to display wealth and prestige. Amulets empower and are a tangible representation of the strength of individual hopes and desires in the face of often harsh everyday realities.

Tuareg amulets are striking for their myriad forms, their diverse materials, their exquisite workmanship, and the secret knowledge they embody. Container amulets hold verses and prayers from the Koran prepared by Islamic religious leaders. Stones and metal thought to contain special powers are also used as amulets.

G.1

Amulet (*tcherot*)

Tuareg
Ahaggar, Algeria
Silver, tin, cotton
11.43 x 12.7 x 1.9 cm
Private Collection

To make an amulet, an *enad* must first hammer a piece of silver until it is thin. The piece is then filed to even out and soften the surface in preparation for engraving. Engraving requires skill and steady pressure. Tuareg methods of engraving are considered unique. The *enad* quickly rotates his wrist as he cuts a line with the engraving tool, hence the process is referred to as the "trembling hand technique." Additional decorations are created with punches. The back piece of the amulet is hammered very flat, and once the contents (which might include a prayer, magic numbers, or sand) have been added, it is folded over the front section. Because the amulet is hollow, punch designs must be made very carefully. Some smiths add decorative designs or signatures on the back of amulets, though this is not common.

The amulet shown here displays delicate engraved zigzag lines, little triangles, circles, oval forms, and triangular punched motifs. It also includes applied braided elements and ball studs, which resemble Mauritanian amulets. These similarities are probably the result of years of exchange and the transfer of techniques between nomadic peoples.

As with most Tuareg objects, amulets are distinguished by their design continuity and the wealth of decorative motifs used to enhance their various shapes. Silver amulet cases can be rectangular, square, tubular, or triangular. They are beautifully engraved, and their motifs are enhanced by the reflective quality of the silver. Leather examples, which are more often worn directly against the skin, are soft and embellished with punched designs and embroidered motifs. There is a general belief among the Tuareg that power objects such as amulets must be beautiful to be most effective.

K.L.

G.2

Turban amulet
(*tcherot* or *tereout* or *korkoro*)

Saidi Oumba
Tuareg, Kel Ewey
Agadez, Niger
Silver
14 x 3.8 x 2 cm
Private Collection

G.3

A Tuareg man wears an amulet at the side of his *tagulmust,* or face-veil and turban.

Photograph by Thomas K. Seligman, Agadez, Niger, 1980.

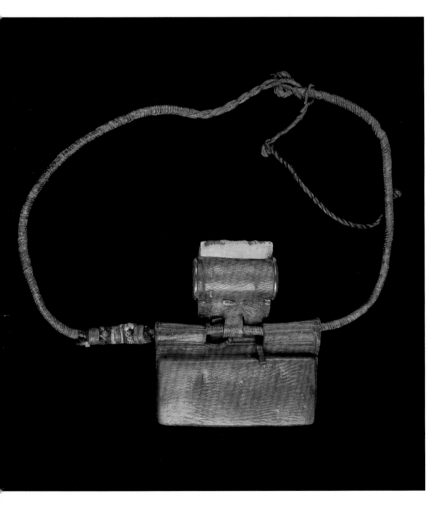

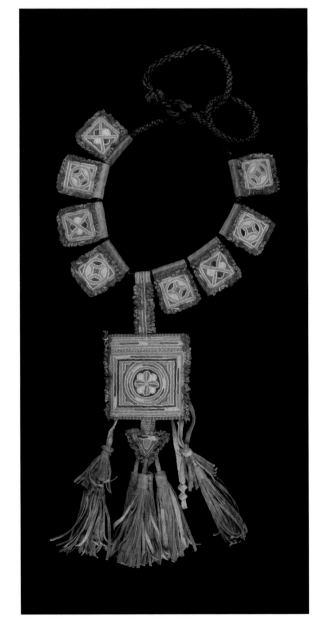

G.4 (OPPOSITE, TOP)

Amulet (*tereout 'n 'alem*)

Tuareg
Ahaggar, Algeria
Leather
Amulet: 6 x 6 x 2.2 cm;
Ornament: 4 x 2.5 cm
Cantor Arts Center
1998.38

G.5 (OPPOSITE, BOTTOM LEFT)

Amulet (*assesrade*)

Tuareg, Tenguerendieff
Goundam, Mali
Leather, pigment
8 x 12 x 3 cm
Musée du Quai Branly
71.1941.19.739

G.6 (OPPOSITE, BOTTOM RIGHT)

Amulet (*assesrade*)

Haratin (Tuareg)
Touat, Algeria
Leather, pigment
84 x 13.5 x 1.2 cm
Musée du Quai Branly
71.1933.78.10@1

This brightly embroidered wallet
has been augmented with little
amulet cases. It is from the oasis
of Touat, made by Haratins, who
are sedentary farmers. This object
is not typically Tuareg and displays
a North African influence. As with
other examples of Tuareg art, it
reveals how objects move across
cultural boundaries through contact
and trade.

G.7 (BELOW, LEFT)

Amulet (*tcherot* or *tereout*)

Tuareg, Iwellemmeden
Asongo, Mali
Leather, pigment
47 x 12.3 x 1.4 cm
Musée du Quai Branly
71.1941.19.1291

G.8 (BELOW, RIGHT)

Turban amulet (*tcherot* or *tereout*)

Ismael
Tuareg, Kel Rela
Tamanrasset, Algeria
Silver, tin, leather
11.6 x 7 x 0.6 cm
Musée du Quai Branly
71.1941.19.1643

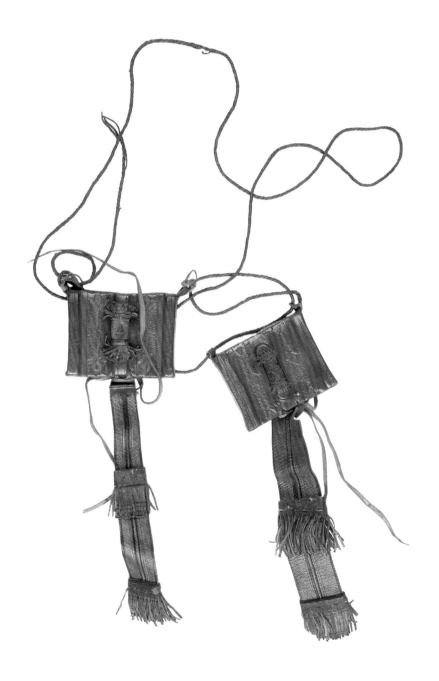

G.9
Amulet (*tcherot*)

Tuareg
Niger
Brass, leather
Pendant: 14 x 12.3 x 1.8 cm;
L (of necklace): 51 cm
Cantor Arts Center
2002.53

G.10
Amulets (*assesrade*)

Tuareg
Niger/Mali
Leather
Largest pendant: 7.6 x 6 cm
Cantor Arts Center
2001.172

198

G.11
Amulet (*tcherot*)

Tuareg, Kel Aïr
Niger
Silver, cord
Pendant: 8.6 x 8 cm;
L (of necklace): 35 cm
UCLA Fowler Museum
x88.1391

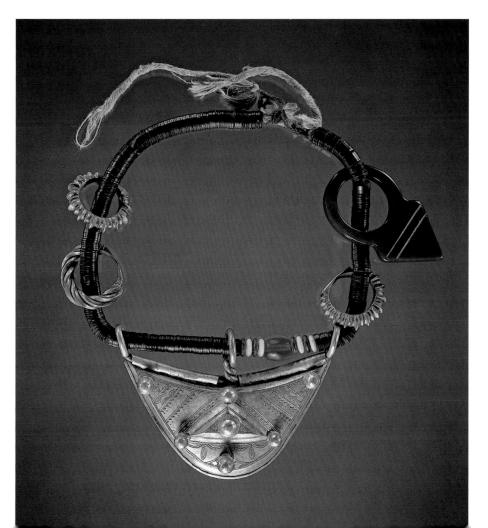

G.12
Amulet (*tcherot*)

Tuareg
Gao, Mali
Silver, plastic, cotton, glass
Pendant: 5.3 x 7.6 cm;
L (of necklace): 10.5 cm.
UCLA Fowler Museum
x88.1469

G.13

Amulet (*tcherot*)

Tuareg, Kel Aïr
Niger
Silver, copper, tin, leather
12 x 10.2 x 0.6 cm
Private Collection

G.14

**Pectoral pendant
(*tcherot* or *tereout tan idmarden*)**

Tuareg
Ahaggar, Algeria, or Aïr, Niger
Silver
19 x 19 cm
Musée d'ethnographie, Neuchâtel
47.1.39.a-d

This pendant, known as the *tereout
tan idmarden* is thought to be the
most important item worn by an
Ahaggar bride on her wedding day.
It is essentially a large triangle composed of smaller ones. Sometimes it
is suspended from a necklace form
known as *tasralt*. The triangle is
considered a potent amulet against
evil spirits and is a constant motif in
Tuareg art. This pendant embodies
many aspects of Tuareg artistry. It
displays technical expertise, attention to minute surface detail, and
consideration of internal decorative
sequences.

G.15 (OPPOSITE)

**Head ornament
(*tcherot* or *tereout tan 'eraf*)**

Tuareg
Ahaggar, Algeria
Silver, brass, copper, leather
26 x 18.7 cm
Cantor Arts Center
2001.185

This type of head ornament is also
referred to as an amulet: *tcherot* and
tereout both mean "amulet," and
tan 'eraf means "of the head." In
the region around Agadez, Niger,
women wear this type of amulet at
the back of their heads, attached to
their hair. Women in the Ahaggar
region, however, use this ornament
as a large pectoral amulet.

200

TUAREG JEWELRY

Tuareg jewelry is distinguished by the simplicity of its form, the attention paid to detail, and the decorative continuum on small intimate surfaces. Much of its appeal is rooted in the grammar of the miniature. Women and men both wear and appreciate classical jewelry forms. Daily usage is, however, restrained with individuals reserving their finest pieces for feasts and holidays.

Women wear head ornaments that emphasize their elegant hairstyles and sway when they walk. Their earrings range from heavy sculptural forms, such as the *tizabaten*, to delicate hoops worn on a daily basis. Necklaces and pendants, more than other pieces, symbolize age, wealth, and rank. They are worn singly on a daily basis and in multiples for feasts and celebrations. Bracelets and rings

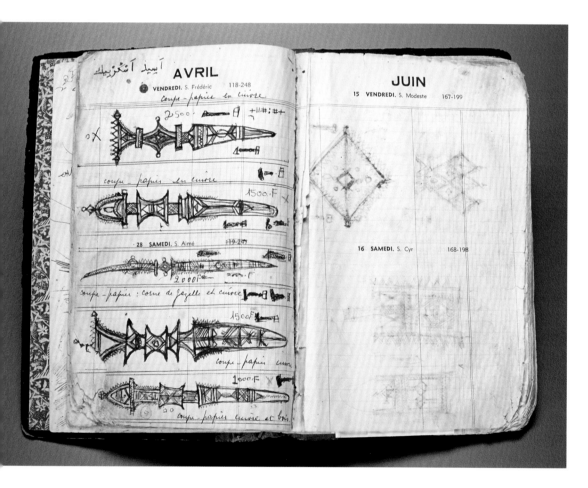

H.1

Catalog of designs

Abeidarere Ben Amareoide
Tuareg
Tamanrasset, Algeria
Paper, ink
24.5 x 15.5 cm
Musée d'ethnographie, Neuchâtel
71.2.9

It is unusual for the *inadan* to make drawings of the objects they create. Usually Tuareg clients know exactly what they need and want and don't really discuss the form or shape of the pieces they commission. They might simply ask for variations in size and materials. The early date of this book, a recycled diary for the year 1956, makes it a "curiosity," considering the Sahara was not yet a tourist destination. According to the Musée d'ethnographie's collection notes, it belonged to the "first" *enad* of the Ahaggar region, Abeidarere Ben Amareoide.

call attention to wrists and slender fingers. Veil weights are attached and thrown over the shoulder to keep a head covering in place. Men wear bracelets, rings, and amulets—the latter are worn around their necks and on the *tagulmust*, or face-veil and turban.

The aesthetic of Tuareg jewelry is based upon the use of proper materials, such as silver or leather, and the repetition of delicate geometric motifs in the same intricate structure. Angular shapes and forms predominate in sharp contrast with the curvilinear shapes favored by neighboring peoples. Design motifs include small circles, dots, parallel lines, and zigzags, all of which emphasize the outline of the pieces and reflect light as the wearer moves.

K.L.

H.2

Bracelet with Tifinar (*ahbeg* or *iwuki*)

Tuareg
Niger
Stone
W: 1.5 cm; Diam: 12 cm
UCLA Fowler Museum
X64.106

Stone bracelets or armlets like this one are rare today. Formerly they were given to young men along with a sword at a rite of passage. They were worn on the upper arm above the elbow, and one of the Tamasheq names for them, *iwuki,* means "upper arm." The bracelets were sometimes passed down from father to son. Some, like this example, were inscribed with signatures or short messages in Tifinar.

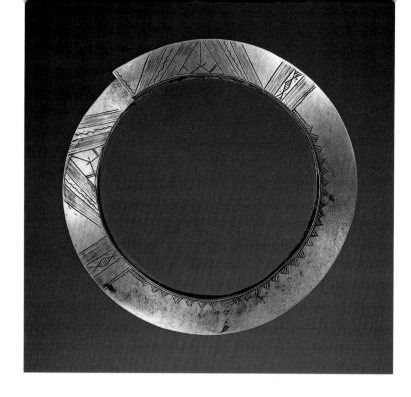

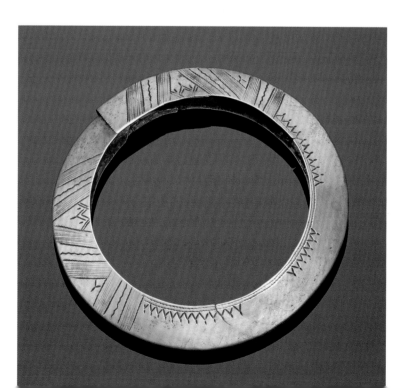

H.3

Bracelet (*takafat*)

Tuareg, Kel Aïr
Niger
Silver
W: 1.2 cm; Diam: 7.7 cm
UCLA Fowler Museum
x88.1457

H.4

Armlet (*ahbeg* or *iwuki*)

Tuareg
Niger
Slate, brass
Diam: 11.4 cm
Cantor Arts Center
2001.169

H.5

Bracelet (*takafat*)

Tuareg
Agadez, Niger
Silver
Diam: 7.2 cm
Musée d'ethnographie, Neuchâtel
47.1.33

H.6 (OPPOSITE, TOP LEFT)
Bracelets (*elkiss*, pl. *elkizan*)

Tuareg, Kel Aïr
Niger
Silver
Each: 6 x 6.5 cm
UCLA Fowler Museum
x88.1394a,b

H.7 (OPPOSITE, TOP RIGHT)
Bracelet (*elkiss*)

Tuareg, Kel Icheriffen
Gao, Mali
Aluminum
6.7 x 6.9 x 1.8 cm
Musée du Quai Branly
71.1941.19.554

H.8 (OPPOSITE, BOTTOM)
Bracelets (*samboro*)

Tuareg, Kel Aïr
Niger
Silver
W: 2 cm; Diam: 5.9 cm
UCLA Fowler Museum
x88.1418a,b

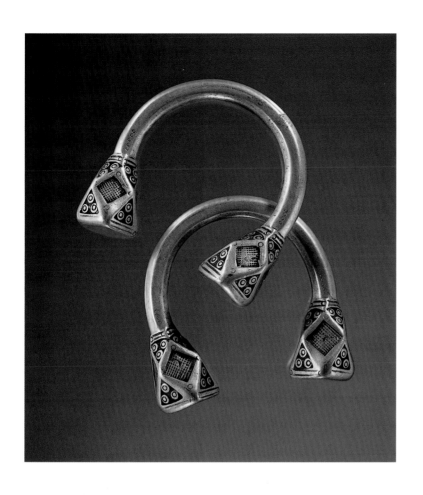

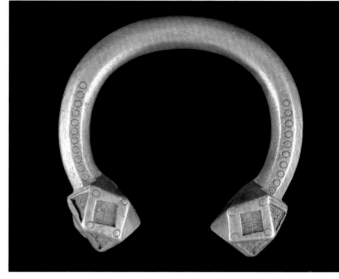

H.9

Bracelets (*elkiss,* pl. *elkizan*)

Tuareg, Kel Geres
Tahoua, Niger
Silver
Each: 7 x 10.1 cm
Cantor Arts Center
2001.198.a-b

These *elkiss* bracelets are often worn by women when they wear the heavy *tizabaten* earrings. Considered part of the bridewealth, they are made of solid silver and are extremely heavy. Women usually wear them in pairs, with the end knobs pointed toward the side of the wrist.

In addition to these prestigious silver bracelets, Tuareg women like to wear simple V-shaped bands with engraved motifs called *takafat* or flat bracelets with repoussé motifs known as *samboro.* Glass bracelets, or *tahoka,* were once common in Algeria and Niger, but it appears that today women prefer *dengela,* or beaded leather bracelets.

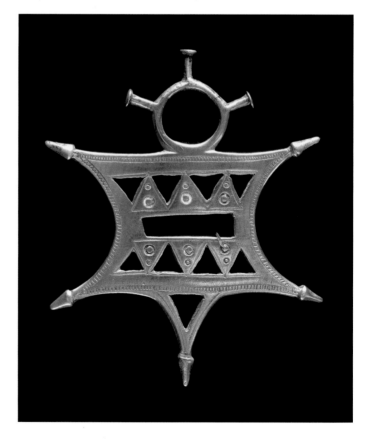

H.10

Man's Ring (*tisek*)

Tuareg
Niger
Silver
H: 1.9 cm; Diam: 2.5 cm
Cantor Arts Center
1997.38

H.11

Cross (*takararat*)

Tuareg, Iwellemmeden
Gao, Mali
Silver
7.6 x 6.3 x 0.4 cm
Musée du Quai Branly
471.191.19.1263

Veil weight (*asrou n' swoul*)

Tuareg, Kel Aïr
Niger
Silver, leather
19.7 x 5 x 0.3 cm
Private Collection

H.13

Earrings (*tizabaten*)

Aboubacar (Adi) Yahaya
Tuareg, Kel Geres
Niger
Silver
Diam (each): 3.2 cm
Cantor Arts Center
1997.46.a-b

Tizabaten earrings are distinctively Tuareg. The elongated polyhedral end knobs suggest they come from Tahoua, Niger, or surrounding areas. This earring style can be worn through the earlobe (but the earrings are sometimes addition-ally supported by a string attached to the hair) and can also be worn around the ear. *Tizabaten* are part of the bridewealth and are consid-ered too heavy to be worn by young girls. They are forged in solid silver. Other earring styles include varia-tions on hoops, which are much lighter and worn on a daily basis.

H.14

Earrings (*tizabaten*)

Tuareg
Niger
Aluminum, copper
Diam (each): 8.25 cm
Cantor Arts Center
2003.24.a-b

H.15 (OPPOSITE, TOP)

Necklace (*takassa*)

Tuareg, Kel Ewey
Niger
Silver, beads
Pendant: 6.7 x 3.5 cm;
L (necklace): 42.5 cm
Cantor Arts Center
1997.54

The central pendant is the *n'gadoun* or *lahia*.

H.16 (OPPOSITE, BOTTOM)

Necklace (*tasralt*)

Tuareg
Ahaggar, Algeria
Silver, glass, leather
Pendant: 7.5 x 9.2 cm;
L (of necklace): 37 cm
UCLA Fowler Museum
x88.1386

H.17

Necklace (*chatchat*)

Tuareg, Kel Aïr
Niger
Silver, agate beads
Largest pendant: 4.5 x 2.5 cm
Cantor Arts Center
2001.193

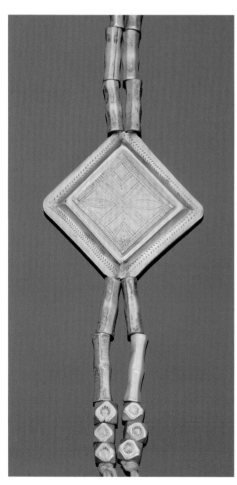

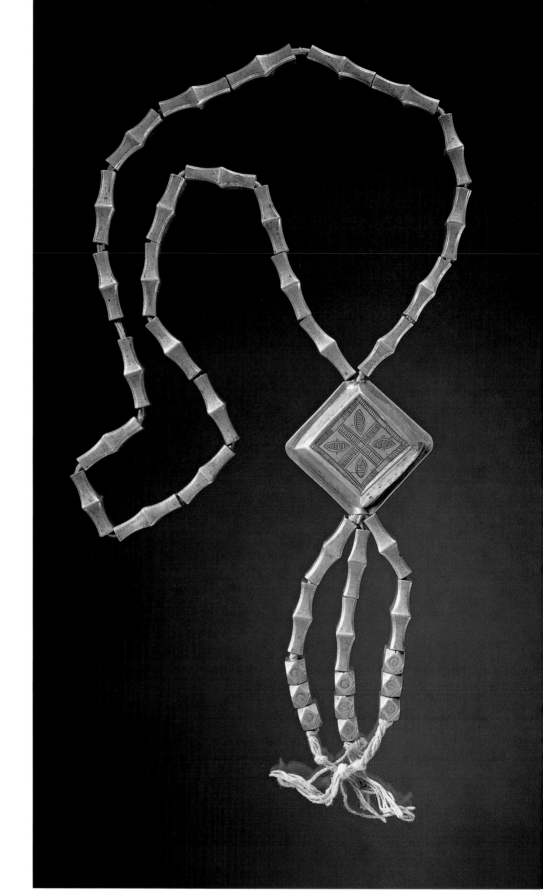

H.18 (OPPOSITE, LEFT)
Necklace (*taperkit*) (detail)

Tuareg, Iwellemmeden
Aïr, Niger
Silver
L: 37 cm
Musée d'ethnographie, Neuchâtel
47.1.35

H.19 (OPPOSITE, RIGHT)
Necklace (*taperkit*)

Tuareg, Kel Aïr
Niger
Silver
Diamond-shaped pendant:
5 x 5.2 cm; L (of necklace): 32.5 cm
UCLA Fowler Museum
x88.1447

H.20
Necklace (*taperkit*)

Tuareg, Kel Ewey
Niger
Silver
Pendant: 2.5 x 2.5 cm;
L (of necklace): 39.3 cm
Cantor Arts Center
1997.44

8

THE ART OF BEING TUAREG

Thomas K. Seligman

In 2001 in Agadez, Niger, Andi Ouhoulou compared two pairs of older, well-used silver earrings (*tizabaten*) made by an unknown artist (*enad*). She remarked that she preferred one pair because the silver was of better quality (probably sterling—.925); the engraved design was more regular, clearer, crisper, and more consistent; and the earrings had been gently softened by use and care.[1] It was not particularly surprising to me that the aesthetic criteria Andi employed resembled those embraced by others in her extended family and were generally shared among *inadan* of her generation (fig. 8.2).

Saidi Oumba, Andi's husband of over forty years, is well known in the Aïr[2] as one of the most talented and creative *inadan* in the region. His design skills and creative ideas for new jewelry, as well as for jewelry derived from old styles, equal his talent for working and engraving silver. His comments about leather bags made by Andi and other women artists (*tinadan*) or about older silver jewelry were essentially consistent with the criteria that guided Andi. Using words like *clear, bright, even, balanced*, and *appropriately organized* or *arranged*, Saidi has conveyed to me, over many years of interviews,[3] aesthetic sensibilities that mirror much of what Westerners have come to associate with "traditional" Tuareg aesthetics.

Andi and Saidi are "artful" Tuareg in their self-presentation; in the way they have educated and trained their nine children and numerous grandchildren; and in the creation and fabrication of works in silver, gold, wood, leather, and fiber. In fact for them, and for all *inadan*, art and life are inseparable. Andi and Saidi are also living examples of how *inadan* have dealt with the many changes that the Tuareg have undergone following the French colonial period.[4]

Since the late fifteenth century, when Bernadetto Dei, the first European to reach the fabled Tuareg city of Timbuktu, reported his findings, the nomadic Tuareg have been romanticized as a noble and proud people who mysteriously shroud themselves in indigo-dyed turbans, veils, and robes. This image of the aristocratic Tuareg, mounted on his large white camel (*mehari*) and carrying his ever-present sword (*takuba*), was irresistible to Europeans. That the Tuareg were also fierce warriors, who in the late nineteenth and early twentieth century defeated the advancing French colonial army on several occasions, added to their allure.

The *inadan*, a social class of smiths and leatherworkers who have always been considered marginal by the noble Tuareg (*imajeren*), nonetheless occupy an essential position within the group. They make virtually everything used by the Tuareg and act as intermediaries between and within the many noble groups. Marriage brokers, wedding organizers, musicians, poets, and ambassadors—their ambiguous social status results from their complex roles and capabilities.[5]

8.1
Saidi Oumba and Andi Ouhoulou in festive attire.
Photograph by Thomas K. Seligman, Agadez, Niger, 1988.

8.2

Andi Ouhoulou, her hair plaited, wears an embroidered blouse. The wall of the family compound behind her was decorated by drawing fingers through the wet mud to form wide arcs.

Photograph by Thomas K. Seligman, Agadez, Niger, 1980.

Another factor essential to understanding the arts of the Tuareg is the history of the anonymity of the individual *enad*. Since the late nineteenth century, the names of numerous nobles and leaders of different Tuareg confederations (Kel Ewey, Kel Ahaggar, etc.) have been recorded. In addition these leaders were often photographed by Europeans. The *inadan*, however, were seldom mentioned in the literature, much less identified by name; and in the few cases where they were mentioned, it was only in association with the nobles with whom they were affiliated. While the roles and the creations of the *inadan* were well documented, they themselves were seen simply as followers of tradition.[6] They were portrayed as having learned from their fathers and mothers, more or less continuing to do what their parents did generation after generation as they moved with the *imajeren* from one area of pasture to the next.

What is clear from my research with Saidi, Andi, and their family, however, is that they have been creatively and dynamically involved in the significant ongoing transformation of Tuareg culture. Few *inadan* today maintain a clear and specific relationship with pastoral nobles. In fact, due to profound changes caused by severe drought and the death of thousands of camels and goats; the introduction of a market and cash economy; roads and vehicles moving diverse peoples, goods, and new trade items more rapidly around the Sahara; the ongoing penetration of Islamic teachings and belief; and the imposition of rules from the central government of Niger in Niamey, as well as many other more subtle forces, most *inadan* are no longer pastoral and have settled in larger villages and towns as well as in Niamey itself. They are actively engaged in exchange relationships with other Africans and non-Africans and are major players in the cash economy of Niger, which is rapidly becoming globalized.[7] As a result, they are today often wealthier and more financially secure than the *imajeren*.

Saidi and the couple's sons—and to a lesser degree, Andi and their daughters—are engaged in the profound transformation underway in the Aïr.[8] They are affected by many new forces, while simultaneously acting as agents of change. Their lives and work reveal a dynamic relationship to their world that is based upon their creative interactions with and responses to change. The discussion that follows will focus on the artistic and commercial lives of Saidi, Andi, and their children as they engage with the many forces now at work in Tuareg society.

Saidi and Andi: The Early Years

Saidi Oumba was born between 1938 and 1940, the second child and first son of Oumba Mohammed and Fatima. Both of his parents were *inadan* in the Kel Ewey confederation in the Aïr region. Fatima was from the oasis town of Timia and Oumba from Iferouane. When Saidi was born, the couple were living and working in the village of Azel, a few miles north of Agadez. As a young boy, Saidi would help his father, who was a saddle-maker, bringing him the tools, pieces of wood, and leather necessary to make the Tuareg camel saddle (*tamzak*). At about five years of age, Saidi also began going to a Koranic school, where he learned Islamic prayer. As was customary among *inadan*, Saidi's father educated all his sons through a long informal apprenticeship, just as his mother did with her daughters. Along with social skills, the children were taught technical skills, design patterns, and the uses of objects that the *inadan* fabricated. By the time Saidi was beginning to learn to make wooden spoons and knives of iron, wood, and leather at age eight or nine, he and his older sister, Assalama, had three younger sisters and two younger brothers. Eventually, Oumba and Fatima would have ten children, many of whom are still alive and are active as *inadan* in the Aïr.

Saidi's apprenticeship with his father continued, and Saidi relates that he learned to hammer and file very well. He learned how to use the axe and adze and, under his father's direction, began to make camel saddles. He made small-scale saddles as souvenirs for French administrators and businessmen and regular riding saddles for Tuareg patrons. He would accompany his father on trips to Agadez and further south to Zinder to sell camel saddles in the city markets. In his early teens, Saidi remembers that he went to Timia to learn silverwork from his maternal grandfather, Dangarra, who, according to Saidi, was the most prominent *enad* of the time.[9] The first silver object Saidi learned to make was the cross of Agadez (*tenaghalt tan Agadez*). Just as he had developed skill with various tools, he also had to learn how to melt, cast, and work silver. Casting was done by carving the shape of the cross of Agadez into a piece of soft stone (usually talc). After the silver was melted in a clay crucible, it was poured into the mold, and after cooling, it was filed smooth and engraved. When Saidi had mastered these difficult techniques, he began to learn to make more complicated objects, such as earrings and bracelets, which require careful heating and hammering to form correctly without breaking.

8.3

Saidi Oumba making an amulet (*tcherot*).

Photograph by Thomas K. Seligman, Niamey, Niger, 1997.

8.4

Saidi Oumba (center), Andi Ouhoulou (left), and some of their family.

Photograph by Thomas K. Seligman, Agadez, Niger, 1980.

8.5

Entry to Saidi Oumba's workshop
and the family compound.

*Photograph by Thomas K. Seligman, Agadez,
Niger, 1980.*

Saidi recalls that the hardest pieces to learn how to
make (as his eyesight is failing, he no longer even tries)
were locks, knives made of silver with ebony inlaid in
the handle, camel saddles, and containers for amulets
(*tcherot*; fig. 8.3). After about five years of practice, he
relates that he was making a wider range of jewelry of
higher quality than his grandfather did. He had begun
to have some commercial success and was aware of the
nascent opportunities to sell to Europeans in Agadez. He
was becoming anxious to go out on his own as an *enad*.

Andi Ouhoulou was born about 1944 to Ouhoulou,
a silversmith, and Anudoufout, a leatherworker, in the
small Aïr village of Toudou. She was the sixth child in a
family of seven daughters and one son, Tchebe. Her early
childhood activities involved helping her mother and
sisters around the house and learning leatherwork from
them. She also briefly attended a local Koranic school run
by the village marabout.[10]

In about 1960 Andi was married to a cousin who divorced her after seven or eight
months and left her pregnant with a daughter, Chemo. Shortly thereafter, at the marriage
festivities of her brother, Tchebe, in Azel, she met Saidi, and they were soon married.
For the first several months they lived in a small straw house in Toudou, and each day
Saidi would ride his camel to Azel to continue working at the new forge of Dangarra.
When Andi delivered Chemo, Saidi regarded the child as his own. Saidi and Andi moved
to the edge of Agadez about this time and began to build their first mud brick house
and compound. Salah, their first son, was born there in 1964, and soon thereafter they
adopted Gonda, the son of one of Saidi's sisters. From 1966 through 1983 seven more
children would be born to the family (fig. 8.4).

In 1975 Saidi, Andi, and their children moved into their current compound in
Agadez (fig. 8.5). They were already making a good living as *inadan*, creating work on
commission for other Tuareg and selling to the increasing number of foreign workers
who had come to Agadez with aid agencies that were trying to help the Tuareg survive
the food crisis caused by the severe droughts of the early 1970s. Saidi was also active
in assisting other Tuareg to sell their old and newly made silver jewelry in this time of
economic stress.[11] To further his prospects, he provided old silver jewelry to be sold at a
boutique opened by a Frenchman.

Profound change was now a reality in Agadez. The town was growing rapidly and
diversifying in its ethnic makeup, and there were numerous challenges and opportunities. As *inadan* and parents of a growing family, Saidi and Andi followed their own
experiences and began to teach their sons and daughters the skills involved in working
in metal and leather (figs. 8.6-8.8). Along with technical skills, they also attempted to
pass on their knowledge of the names of the various designs and meanings of each. Saidi
and Andi spoke Tamasheq within the family, but they also began to speak more Hausa
with outsiders, as this was becoming the language most commonly used in Agadez. Saidi
also became more conversant in French.[12] The children were going to Koranic school,
and they were also being taught in French in the government school. As a result, they
were exposed to experiences and ideas that Saidi and Andi had never known given their
own rural upbringing.

I made my first trip to Agadez and the Aïr in 1971, following a two-year stint as a
Peace Corps volunteer in Liberia. It was on my brief stop in Agadez that I met Saidi.
Mano Dayak, who was involved in a nascent tourist business, introduced me to him.[13] As
my notes from that trip are lost, I have no specific records, but Saidi says he recalls our
meeting and having shown me his silverwork at the time.

8.6

Andi Ouhoulou and her daughter Atyi (now deceased) making a leather bag.

Photograph by Thomas K. Seligman, Agadez, Niger, 1980.

8.7

Saidi Oumba polishes silver with soap, water, and lemon juice as his daughter Atyi (now deceased) sits near him.

Photograph by Thomas K. Seligman, Agadez, Niger, 1981.

8.8

Saidi Oumba (left) and his sons Gonda (middle) and Salah (right).

Photograph by Thomas K. Seligman, Niamey, Niger, 1997.

217

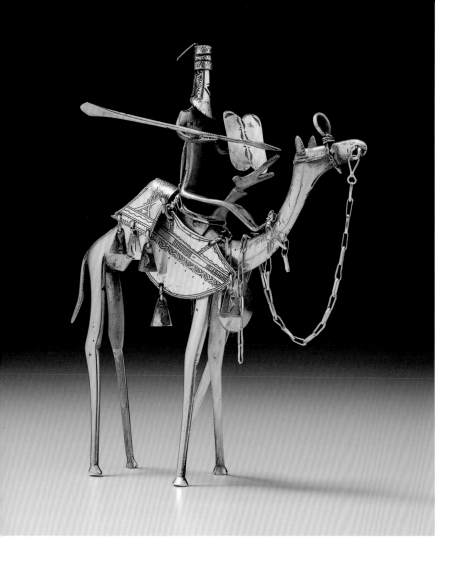

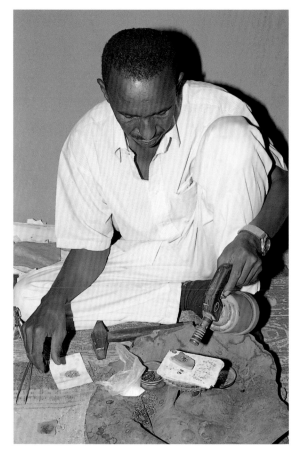

8.9

Camel and rider

Saidi Oumba
Tuareg, Kel Ewey
Agadez, Niger
Nickel silver
17.2 x 5.1 x 15.2 cm
Private Collection

Intended as a tourist object, this
sculpture is, nonetheless, beautifully
and carefully made. It portrays a
Tuareg warrior sitting on a camel
fitted with an elaborate saddle
(*tamzak*) that is draped with leather
bags. The warrior holds a spear in
one hand and a shield in the other.
The camel wears an *akeskabbu*, a
type of a bridle typically worn at
feasts. This object could be thought
of as representing the way in which
the Tuareg perceive themselves,
as it alludes to the values that have
always been central to their worldview: freedom, nobility, and courage.

8.10

Salah Saidi working in gold.

*Photograph by Thomas K. Seligman, Agadez,
Niger, 2004.*

The 1980s

I returned to Agadez in 1979 and 1980 and spent considerable time with Saidi, Andi,
and their growing family. I was interested in understanding what they were making, for
whom, and their methods of working. At this time, both Saidi and Andi had begun to
expand the nature of their work. Saidi had a photograph of a very complex silver sculpture of a Tuareg warrior mounted on a camel and equipped with a removable sword,
shield, and spear (fig. 8.9); this image had just been published as a full-color illustration
in the August 1979 issue of *National Geographic* (156, no. 2). Saidi claimed that he had
created this piece on speculation, hoping to sell it to someone in the ever-enlarging tourist market. He was successful in selling this sculpture to an American visitor who told
me many years later that he had actually commissioned the piece and helped design it.
Saidi devoted some of his increased resources from this sale to making gold jewelry in
hopes of obtaining greater wealth.

His shift to working part-time in gold is significant for several reasons. According
to traditional Tuareg belief, various metals have specific qualities. Silver, for instance,
is bright and pure, and iron is polluted and should not be touched. Brass and copper,
which can be worked with silver, are relatively pure, and they are often used to embellish
silver jewelry or as a less-costly substitute for silver.[14] Gold was believed to be a negative
metal by the Tuareg. Not only was it prohibitively expensive and unavailable locally, it
was understood to be polluting and dangerous. From the point of view of the *enad*, gold
is also much harder to work than silver, brass, or copper (fig. 8.10).

Saidi has never told me how he learned the techniques for working gold, but he has
remarked that because its price was known and was stable relative to silver, he thought
that a few Tuareg and other "Arabs"[15] from the north would commission gold jewelry.
He seemed not to be particularly concerned about the conventional taboos surrounding
gold, and he did get a few commissions. One of these, however, resulted in Saidi getting

into considerable trouble in 1980. He was arrested for allegedly stealing some of the gold given him by an Algerian woman to make into jewelry.[16]

Working gold may be seen as a significant change in Saidi's artistic and commercial practice, but it was not the only one. He and Andi joined a marketing cooperative run by Andi's older brother, Tchebe, and they now sold their goods through the cooperative, as well as from their family compound. Saidi's forge and workshop were in one of the front rooms of the family's compound, behind an exterior door and below a blue sign reading "Saidi Oumba, *forgeron*."[17] The other unmarked door in the front of the compound led into Andi's atelier, where she worked leather into bags commissioned by Tuareg patrons and into purses for sale at the cooperative. Andi was also a specialist in plaiting hair, which added to her income and kept her in close touch with her social network (fig. 8.11). In fact, both workshops often had men and women, Tuareg, Hausa, and tourists, coming and going for business or just to spend time in conversation. The children were often present, helping out by running errands, learning how to make things, and, in the case of the girls, preparing meals and tending to the home.

Saidi and Andi each responded to new market opportunities occasioned by the increasing "Hausazation"[18] of Agadez and by the increasing number of tourists who came to see the Aïr Mountains and the extraordinary dunes of the Ténéré Desert. Saidi adapted traditional Tuareg silver jewelry styles for outsiders. He developed a framed set of the twenty-one different crosses of the Aïr region (fig. 8.12 and see fig. 7.9). Each was cast in silver, filed and engraved, and mounted under glass with a typed identification label. Knowing of the growing interest in the very large silver earrings (*tizabaten*) and large silver bracelets (*elkizan*; sing., *elkiss*), he scaled them down to a size closer to the pierced earrings worn by outsiders and their smaller bracelets. Saidi also made objects such as locks and key rings that were beautifully worked and elaborately embellished with silver to serve as souvenirs of a visit to Tuareg lands (fig. 8.13).

8.11
Andi Ouhoulou plaiting her granddaughter Amina's hair.
Photograph by Thomas K. Seligman, Agadez, Niger, 2004.

8.12
Saidi Oumba holding a framed set of the twenty-one cross types. Saidi developed this particular means of presentation for sale to tourists.
Photograph by Thomas K. Seligman, Agadez, Niger, 1988.

8.13

Key ring with the cross of Agadez

Saidi Oumba
Tuareg, Kel Ewey
Niamey, Niger
Silver
Cross: 9.7 x 4 cm
UCLA Fowler Museum
X97.17.12

8.14

Andi Ouhoulou making a leather
bag.
*Photograph by Thomas K. Seligman, Agadez,
Niger, 1997.*

As the female artists (*tinadan*) are less exposed to tourists, and as leatherwork tends to take longer and is less profitable than working in silver, Andi's creative output responded to outside market forces in a more limited way. She added purses, handbags, and key chains to her repertoire of larger decorated bags used by the Tuareg (fig. 8.14). She experimented with some new materials, incorporating plastic strips and using colored marking pens to speed up production by diminishing the dyeing and cutting of the leather elements required for the traditional bags. She soon realized, however, that the color from the marking pens faded rapidly and that the plastics were unpopular with her customers, so she ceased using them.

By the mid-1980s, Saidi and Andi were both very focused on their production. They were making objects of the highest aesthetic quality using the best and most traditional materials (leather, vegetable dyes, high-quality silver, etc.). They invented or adopted new forms, especially in silver, but also sometimes in leather. They used new tools as they became available, such as inexpensive high-quality scissors to cut leather or gas torches to help work the silver. As a result of the prosperity they achieved through their hard work, they were able to add electricity and a faucet with running water from the city of Agadez to their compound, along with consumer items such as tape cassette players and electric fans. At this time their children were reaching marriageable age and becoming ready to move on with their own lives. Chemo, their oldest daughter, who had become a very accomplished leatherworker, married an *enad* cousin of Andi's, Mohamed Abou-bacar, in 1978.[19] After living with Chemo's parents for a couple of years and having two children, the young couple moved into their own compound in Agadez (fig. 8.15).

Salah, the oldest son, was going through his apprenticeship at the time that Saidi was experimenting with gold. After becoming very accomplished at working in wood and then silver, Salah left home in 1985 to work on his own in Arlit where he specialized in silver. As he told me in 1997, it was at that point that he knew he was a "real" *enad*.

After a short period of working in the artisans' workshop of the National Museum in Niamey with Agak Mohamed, he returned to Agadez in 1988 to begin learning goldwork with Saidi's cousin Mohammed Agaliton (fig. 8.16). He continues to work in Agadez at the Agaliton workshop and sometimes works with Saidi and his younger brothers, Gonda, Al Hassan, Ousmane, and El Faki.

While raising and training their children in Agadez, Saidi and Andi continued to maintain a degree of connection to their former noble patrons among the Kel Ewey. When rural Kel Ewey *imajeren* come to Agadez for business or medical attention at the hospital, they often stay at Saidi and Andi's compound. The couple also maintained close relationships with their brothers and sisters in Agadez and the Aïr, who also stay at their home when in Agadez. With the droughts of the 1970s and 1980s, much of the Tuareg social and political organization was damaged or destroyed along with the economy. Urban dwellers engaged in the new cash economy were becoming more successful, while the nobles and others dependent on animals or farming for their wealth lost everything. Some of these newly impoverished Tuareg went to refugee camps in Algeria and elsewhere, becoming dependent on government and foreign assistance. By contrast, the urbanized *inadan* were becoming increasingly successful. Their children were going to school and were fluent in several languages, including French. They were a part of a generation of younger Tuareg undergoing profound change. This generation, which included the children of Saidi and Andi, was less fluent in Tamasheq and was unexposed to or inexperienced with the traditional Tuareg pastoral life. Even more important, none of these children had or have today any sense of obligation to the Kel Ewey nobles who had been the patrons of their parents. The children do not know Tenet, the so-called secret language of the *inadan*. Thus, while they are closely involved with their parents, Saidi and Andi's children are becoming citizens of Niger and are involved in an increasingly global economy.

8.15
Chemo Saidi wearing an embroidered blouse and gold jewelry.
Photograph by Thomas K. Seligman, Agadez, Niger, 2001.

8.16
Salah Saidi (right) examining silver jewelry with a friend.
Photograph by Thomas K. Seligman, Agadez, Niger, 1997.

MOTIF	LOUGHRAN NAME/MEANING	SAIDI OUMBA NAME/MEANING	SALAH SAIDI NAME/MEANING	AL HASSAN SAIDI NAME/MEANING	OUSMANE SAIDI NAME/MEANING
1.	trace of the jackal	trace of the jackal (*edrz n'gour*)	trace of the jackal	eye of the chameleon	did not know
2.	eye of the chameleon	eye of the chameleon (*tnchintouet*)	eye of the chameleon	eye of the chameleon	did not know
3.	teeth	teeth (*el caret*)	crooked road	teeth	sand dune
4.	fawn	fawn (*karadet*)	name of Tuareg wedding dance	did not know	did not know
5.	guinea fowl	guinea fowl (*talel*)	guinea fowl	did not know	did not know
6.	basket	moon (*telet*)	moon (*teldit*)	did not know	moon
7.	he is running	did not know	did not know	did not know	did not know
8.	comb	filed teeth (*tchen*)	teeth (*ichena*)	did not know	did not know
9.	moon	moon (*telet*)	moon	did not know	did not know
10.	star	star (*atari*)	star	star	cross of the south
11.	closed teeth	closed teeth (*amazao*)	did not know	like a mat	did not know
12.	scarab	did not know	did not know	did not know	did not know
13.	chameleon	chameleon	eye of the chameleon (see 2nd motif)	eye of the chameleon	did not know
14.	lines	lines (*karadet*)	cut sand dune (*atareg*)	toad or dune	did not know
15.	line	means nothing	did not know	did not know	did not know
16.	nothing (as trace of a bird)	where there is nothing (*amazoat*)	some kind of animal track	two stars	did not know
17.	lines	moon (see 9th motif for confusion)	did not know	calabash	did not know

8.17

Silver punch motif design correlations.

Designs, Meaning, and Memory

Before discussing the tumultuous 1990s in Niger, I would briefly like to examine the "traditional" knowledge of silver jewelry forms and their various design motifs that Saidi has and to compare it to that of his sons. There have been several notable studies of specific artistic and aesthetic changes in African art (Abiodun, Drewal, and Pemberton 1994; Cole 1982; D'Azevedo 1973; Drewal and Pemberton with Abiodun 1989; Fischer and Himmelheber 1984; Loughran 1996; McNaughton 1988; Thompson 1974; Vogel 1997). Of note, Kristyne Loughran made a very interesting analysis among the Tuareg, related to the understanding of design motifs and object types (Loughran 1996). Building on her work, I have focused specifically on the transmission of knowledge from Saidi to his three older *inadan* sons: Salah, Al Hassan, and Ousmane. Using photographs or actual objects, I developed a questionnaire and chart. I relied on Loughran's list of Tamasheq names for specific object types and the design motifs used to stamp silver. In 2001 I interviewed Saidi and his three sons separately on two occasions to determine correlation, difference, and retention or loss of specific knowledge related to these forms and designs. While not strictly scientific, this method was also useful in determining the proper and the common Tuareg name for specific object types or design patterns.

For example, the well-known large-loop silver earrings that end with a hexagon, which Loughran refers to as *tizabaten*, were referred to in exactly this manner by Saidi, Salah, Al Hassan, and Ousmane. Using thirty-six different object types, I found a high correlation between Saidi's knowledge and that of his sons. Among the four *inadan*, only 25 percent of the names had variant forms or differed from Loughran, and in only three instances did more than one *enad* give a name different from what Loughran has used. In two of these three instances, each *enad*'s name was not only different from Loughran's but from that of the other *inadan*. As these specific variations were based upon looking at a line drawing, a lack of clarity in the representation could explain the lack of consistent terminology.

A second set of questions addressed to Saidi, Salah, Al Hassan, and Ousmane focused on the naming of seventeen different punch design motifs used by *inadan* in silver jewelry (Loughran 1996, 586, fig. 17). Unlike the questions regarding the naming of object types, where results had been quite consistent, these questions revealed an overall lack of continuity of knowledge between Saidi and his three sons (fig. 8.17). Saidi's replies correlated with Loughran's 66 percent of the time, and in each instance where Saidi recognized the design motif, he also knew the Tuareg name in Tamasheq. The interpretations of Saidi's three sons correlated with his own in 32 percent of the examples. What was most interesting was that Salah, the oldest son, born in 1964, correlated with Saidi 50 percent of the time and with Loughran 39 percent of the time. On the other hand, the youngest, Ousmane (b. 1976), only correlated with Saidi or his older brother Salah in 11 percent of the examples, and in fact he could only name three of the design motifs. Al Hassan (b. 1975) correlated with Saidi in 28 percent of the examples but could not identify about half of the motifs, although he freely admitted that he used these designs even though he didn't know their meaning or name in Tamasheq.

This data suggests that as a result of the family's move to Agadez, where the male children encountered and engaged in an increasingly diverse and nontraditional Tuareg world, the knowledge of the "traditional" names used in silverwork was lost. While the sons have developed high levels of skill in silverwork, they did not learn or retain many of the meanings of the designs they were using. In effect, they use motifs in a pleasing relationship with each other without deeper knowledge of their historic relationships or meaning.[20] Members of the younger generation have continued their parents' pattern of developing new forms for new markets, while maintaining high-quality fabrication and good materials. Evidence for this will emerge more fully as I discuss the many changes caused by the rebellion of the Tuareg in Mali, Niger, and Algeria in the 1990s.

The 1990s

Tuareg society and ways of life have been threatened since the late nineteenth century when the French began their attempts to conquer the Sahara and lay a railroad from the Mediterranean to the Gulf of Guinea. There are numerous historical accounts of the Tuareg resistance, but ultimately the force of superior technology prevailed, or did it?

The French colonial era witnessed continued resistance as well as armed rebellions by groups of Tuareg. After independence and the creation of the Republic of Niger in 1960—followed by numerous elected or military governments—little changed for the Tuareg. The parched northern region of Niger, which is home to many of them, is much poorer economically and less developed than the south. The Hausa, Djerma, and other smaller ethnic groups, who dominate the more fertile, populous, and prosperous south, excluded the Tuareg from the government and positions of power.

While the Tuareg never violently rebelled against the central government until 1990, over the years they had led limited raids against military outposts, and there was increasing unrest in the north due to the perceived disinterest or hostility of the government. The Tuareg longed for their former freedom to move about as they wished, especially across the borders with Mali and Algeria, which had historically been nonexistent. The Tuareg in Niger, Mali, and Algeria had also suffered the devastation of their camel

8.18
Saidi Oumba and his Peugeot
outside his Chateau I workshop.
*Photograph by Thomas K. Seligman, Niamey,
Niger, 1997.*

and goat herds, and had experienced humiliation at the hands of government and foreign aid organizations that relocated many of them to refugee camps. The Islamization
of the region was also disruptive and disturbing to many Tuareg leaders, who clearly saw
this as a further erosion of their culture, language, economy, and freedom. At this time
Western-educated Tuareg in Europe (particularly France) were organizing politically
with the goal of establishing an autonomous Tuareg region and had garnered support
from some highly placed Europeans. The pressure mounted, so that young Tuareg,
frustrated by the treatment of and misery experienced by their families in the refugee
camps, declared a revolt at Tchin Tabaraden in May of 1990. The Niger army responded
with overwhelming violence and humiliated and massacred many Tuareg. This incident
cemented the Tuareg of Niger with those in Mali, who were already in rebellion against
their own government. Led by Mano Dayak, Rhissa ag Boula, and others, the Tuareg of
northern Niger were now relatively united with other Tuareg groups in the region with
the perceived goal of creating an autonomous Tuareg state in the Sahara.

The effect of the rebellion on Saidi, Andi, and their family was profound, as it was
on many other *inadan* and residents of Agadez. The north was effectively cut off from
most commercial activity. Many aid groups and all Peace Corps volunteers withdrew,
and tourists stopped coming. Saidi's business was collapsing; thus, as he had done in the
past, he made a decision to embark on a new path.

In 1991 Saidi and his oldest sons went to Niamey and set up one of the first Tuareg
inadan workshops in an area known as Chateau I, a neighborhood where many Westerners lived and worked (fig. 8.18). He made an agreement with the owners of a large
compound to build a small plywood house with an attached open-air, but roofed, workshop between the wall of the compound and the street. In what was hardly more than a
box, Saidi, Salah, Gonda, and Al Hassan started to create silver jewelry, attract customers,
and make their way commercially. To add to the family's income, Andi and her daughters
sent specialty foods and finished leather bags from Agadez to Niamey with friends who
occasionally traveled between the two cities. This move marked a major transition and
obvious dislocation for the family.

Until the move to Niamey, Al Hassan and Ousmane had been doing much of the
work in Saidi's forge in Agadez, and under his guidance, they were becoming very skillful. For them the move was exciting and a great opportunity. Ousmane was particularly
energetic commercially, and in 1992 he presented his work at the Salon International
Artisinat de Ouagadougou in neighboring Burkina Faso. He received a certificate or
diploma from this ten-day international fair, and he says it was then that he became a
"real" *enad* and subsequently joined his father and brothers in Niamey.

But more was at play within the family. Saidi understood Ousmane's temperament
and interest in engaging with the wider world. It would not be many more years before

8.19
Ousmane Saidi at a cultural fair in France.
Photographer unknown, 2004.

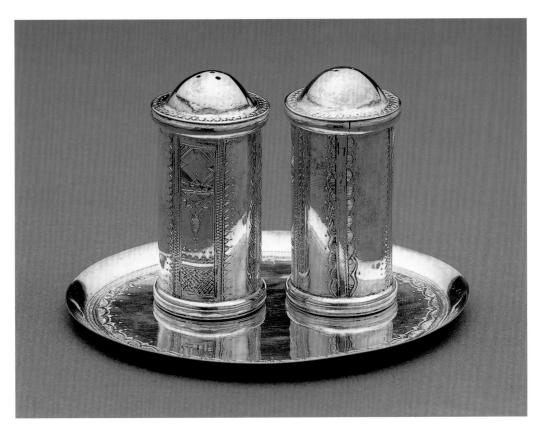

8.20
Salt and Pepper shakers and tray

Saidi Oumba
Tuareg, Kel Ewey
Niamey, Niger
Silver
Tray: 9.5 x 7.8 cm;
Shaker: H: 4.7 cm; Diam: 2.5 cm
UCLA Fowler Museum
X97.17.1a,b

Al Hassan and Ousmane traveled to France and Germany to display jewelry and leather from the workshop (figs. 8.19, 8.25). But before those trips could be undertaken, Saidi and his family had to rebuild their assets. Ever inventive and attentive to consumer input, Saidi and his sons developed all sorts of new items for sale to their essentially non-Tuareg market in Niamey. They continued to transform traditional motifs into new forms such as earrings, a letter opener with the cross of Agadez on its handle, and a chess set commissioned by the American ambassador and comprised of figures of Tuareg and animals of the desert. In fact, that particular ambassador became a patron of Saidi's and commissioned several items as gifts. The workshop made silver salt and pepper shakers (fig. 8.20), ebony and silver chopstick (or knife) rests, silver cases for Bic lighters and pens, barrettes, brooches, and many new types of bracelets. All of these were sold to Western and African customers.

8.21
Salah Saidi on his motorbike.
*Photograph by Thomas K. Seligman, Niamey,
Niger, 1997.*

Gradually, more and more *inadan* moved to Niamey from the north. Having relatives and friends in Niamey provided much-needed emotional support, but more producers of silver jewelry also meant greater competition. Throughout this period Saidi and his sons maintained excellent quality in their workmanship and high standards in their materials. They were not seduced into using silver diluted with other metals, and they did not descend to making low-quality, tourist items. They clearly and consciously believed that the way to succeed was to follow their training and apply their skill to the production of pieces of the highest quality.

Saidi ran the business, doing virtually all of the selling and other transactions, while Gonda, Al Hassan, Ousmane, and other younger apprentices that Saidi had taken in, were doing much of the silverwork. Saidi critiqued each person's work, pushing for improvement. He continued to make the most difficult pieces himself, such as the stepped silver amulet cases (*tcherot*) that contain Koranic prayers (see fig. 8.3). Saidi gave each son and apprentice money—a kind of allowance—as it was not based on any production output. They slept in the closed wooden room, where they stored their tools and silver for security, or on the floor of the open workshop.

Saidi was beginning to have serious problems with his eyes, which made it difficult for him to do any detailed work. He obtained a pair of used eyeglasses that helped somewhat, but this was the beginning of his transition to the role of a nonworking elder, as he turned more of the fabrication over to his sons. The family was prospering again and had saved enough for Saidi to make the Hadj, or pilgrimage, to Mecca in 1994, and for Andi to follow on her own pilgrimage in 1996. While neither was a devout Muslim, both thought this was an important undertaking. It deepened their commitment to Islamic principles, and since their pilgrimages, they each pray regularly. While the Hadj was important to both Saidi and Andi, it had no noticeable effect on their artistic production. In Saidi's case, it was also somewhat of a practical matter, as he understood that to be commercially successful in the increasingly strict Islamic capital city of Niamey, it would be useful to be known as "El Hadj Saidi Oumba," as the new sign on his shop proudly proclaimed.

8.22
Andi Ouhoulou and her grand-
daughter Amina working leather.
*Photograph by Thomas K. Seligman, Agadez,
Niger, 2004.*

The rebellion made it difficult for me to return regularly to Niger. There had been
a peace treaty signed in October 1994 known as the Peace Treaty between the Government of the Republic of Niger and the Coordinator of Armed Resistance. Unfortunately,
that treaty and several other attempts at a peace agreement were not successful, so that
when I went to Niger in 1997, Saidi was still in Niamey, although there was more movement of people between the north and south.

Saidi and his sons in Niamey had prospered. Saidi had made his Hadj and now had
an old well-used Mercedes-Benz, while his sons shared a motorbike (fig. 8.21). They
began to acquire some trappings of success, including new items from the consumer
markets in Niamey—stereos, a fan, a refrigerator, and new tools in the workshop, such
as an electric polisher. I discussed with Saidi the differences he experienced between living in Agadez and in Niamey. Saidi noted with real emotion the pain the separation had
caused the family with only males in Niamey. While he had been to Agadez several times
since moving to Niamey, he missed Andi and his other children and relatives. The living
situation in Niamey was difficult, as the house was small and located on a noisy, main
street. He clearly missed the quiet of his compound in Agadez. Niamey had different,
unpleasant smells and noises, and for him the sense of time and space was comparatively
compressed. Compensation was found in greater economic activity and potential. There
were many more clients, but they were more demanding and harder bargainers than the
Tuareg. Saidi remarked without nostalgia that the new items they made had nothing
to do with tradition and were only about new fashions. As previously noted, Saidi now
worked less and less on production, devoting his energy to managing and selling. The
cost of living in Niamey was much higher, and his sons had greater opportunity to shop,
watch TV, and generally adopt an urban consumer lifestyle. This, of course, created
some tension between the two generations, and in the eyes of his sons, Saidi was becoming a man of the past.

Saidi's personal transition was made evident when he told me some of the experiences he had during his Hadj. He was in Mecca and Medina for about one month, and
this was his first time away from his homeland. While the costs of making the Hadj were

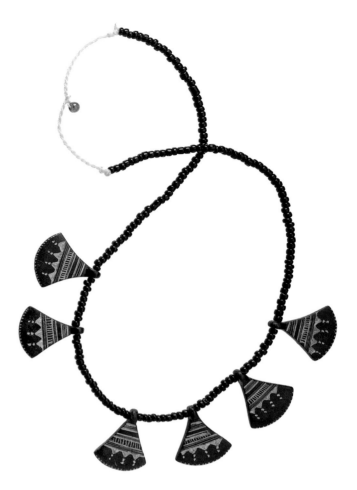

8.23

Hamidan Oumba (left) and other
members of his extended family
with their soapstone carvings.

*Photograph by Thomas K. Seligman, Azel,
Niger, 1988.*

8.24

Necklace (*chatchat*)

Souliman Oumba
Tuareg, Kel Ewey
Azel, Niger
Gypsum, cord
Pendants (each): 2.5 x 1.9 cm
Cantor Arts Center
2001.202.1

great, he felt that it had changed his life. He said that after his pilgrimage he thought
only of doing good things and being good to his family and others for Allah. He told me
he could die in peace as he had lived virtuously.

After spending some time in Niamey, we made our way to Agadez, driving on the
day the military convoy was patrolling the one road to the north. The trip was uneventful, other than a few breakdowns of Saidi's old Peugeot (he had sold the Mercedes, as it
was too costly to maintain), and we arrived at the compound in Agadez to a very warm
welcome. The whole family, with the exception of Al Hassan and Gonda, who had stayed
in Niamey to keep the workshop going, was gathered in Agadez, where much change
was evident. The rebellion was virtually over, and Agadez gave the impression that it was
starting to recover.

Andi, her daughters, and other female relatives were actively making leather goods
for a new cooperative in Agadez, as well as creating works on commission (fig. 8.22).
In the Aïr, Saidi's brothers Kaggo and Hamidan were again making camel saddles, as
the camel and goat herds had recovered following the last drought. Their families were
making sculpture and jewelry from soapstone, which they quarried in the Aïr Mountains
(figs. 8.23, 8.24). Their wives and daughters had developed techniques for making fiber
place mats and purses. All of these tourist items were being sold in neighboring countries and in western Europe, taken to market by one of the younger males in the family.
There were several new cooperatives being developed as many of the *inadan* who had
gone to Niamey were returning to the north.

Always ambitious, Ousmane, who now called himself Mania,[21] had obtained some
money from his father to start a small dry goods store in Agadez, which he operated
with little commercial success from 1995 to 1998. During this period, however, he
learned different aspects of business practice that he has since applied to the commercialization of the family's silver jewelry and leather products. Based upon his dry goods
shop experience, Mania hoped that by significantly increasing the family's production
he could enhance their economic prospects. Mania and Saidi, for example, received
a commission from an ex-Peace Corps volunteer to provide a thousand necklaces and

8.25
Al Hassan Saidi demonstrating silverwork in Germany.
Photographer unknown, 2000.

a thousand sets of earrings for sale in America via the Home Shopping Network. Although this experiment failed due to lapses in quality control and problems of delivery from Niger, it illustrates the kind of new opportunities that Mania was pursuing for the family. What he learned, however, was that the international market for silver jewelry demanded uniqueness and high quality, rather than mass production. What Saidi and his family did not yet know was that other silverworkers around the world (for example in Senegal, Bali, and Hong Kong) were making inexpensive replicas of Tuareg jewelry using industrial techniques unavailable to the Tuareg. And of course, there was continuing competition for clients among the many *inadan* families now in Agadez.[22]

Saidi, Andi, and their family have continued to aggressively explore broader commercial possibilities while keeping within their means. Al Hassan went to Ouagadougou to sell at its international fair in 1998, and having made friends with a young German who owns several jewelry stores, he then traveled to Germany and France to demonstrate jewelry making and to sell works made by his family (fig. 8.25). He took a similar trip in early 2000. Mania also traveled to Bobo-Dioulasso in Burkina Faso and Bamako in Mali, to sell the family's wares. He has also, due to the gracious hospitality of French friends of mine, been able to travel to France to market his work.

It is important to note that when Al Hassan, Mania, and many other Tuareg travel to Europe or America, they are very conscious about dressing as "classic" Tuareg. They typically wear a gown, jewelry, and the distinctive indigo turban/veil (*tagulmust*) that conform to the image of the noble desert warrior known in the West. They leave their blue jeans and T-shirts at home.

Because I have become a patron of Saidi and Andi in the course of acquiring works for several museum collections—most notably those of the de Young Museum in San Francisco, the UCLA Fowler Museum of Cultural History, and the Cantor Arts Center at Stanford University—the family expects me to support them in times of need. Occasionally an American friend returning from a visit to Niger will deliver a package of jewelry for me to buy. I have found it impossible to avoid engaging in these business transactions, as the family misunderstands when I am reluctant to do so. When the jewelry arrives,

8.26

Salah Saidi fitting small gold spheres on earrings for soldering.

Photograph by Thomas K. Seligman, Agadez, Niger, 2004.

8.27

Necklace (*celebre*)

Ousmane (Mania) Saidi
Tuareg, Kel Ewey
Agadez, Niger
Silver, glass
Largest pendant: 3.2 x 0.6 cm
Cantor Arts Center
2001.206

This necklace was designed in 2001 by Ousmane (Mania) Saidi who has named it *celebre* (the French term for "famous"). The modern pendant forms are interspersed with red beads to create a balanced oval shape. The artist has engraved classical Tuareg design motifs on the pendants, thus creating a link with earlier types of Tuareg jewelry.

8.28

Jean-Yves Brizot (center) with Hani (left) and Atobeul (right) at A l'Atelier.

Photograph by Thomas K. Seligman, Agadez, Niger, 2001.

I offer it to my family, friends, and work colleagues at the price established by Saidi and send the proceeds to him. The family also has this type of relationship with several other people in the West. It provides them with another market and another opportunity to prosper. The resources received from Western patrons are especially important for special occasions, such as the joint weddings of Salah and Mania, which took place in early 2001, or for needed medical care, for example, obtaining cataract surgery and proper prescription glasses for Saidi.

Salah has continued to work in gold, and since 1997 he has been back in Agadez. The return of many Tuareg to Agadez and the Aïr and the continued influx of Hausa and "Arabs" since the end of the rebellion have caused a significant change in tastes in jewelry. While gold jewelry is common in Niamey and in southern Algeria, it was formerly seldom seen in Agadez and never in the Aïr until the late 1990s. I saw almost no gold being worn in Agadez in 1997, but from 2001 to the present it has been plentiful and in demand. Salah has been very busy making a new style of gold earring that he claims to have invented, and it is now the most common earring seen in Agadez (fig. 8.26).

In addition to the exposure many younger urban Tuareg have had to other cultures, especially the Hausa, who like gold, other factors have contributed to the growing market for gold jewelry. Silver, traditionally the much-preferred metal, has become more difficult to obtain, and its price and purity have become difficult to ensure. Many *inadan* began to mix silver with other metals, making value more uncertain. Following the rebellion, however, the Niger Bureau of Mines opened an office in Agadez and provided a service to assay and certify gold. The international price of gold was also reported on a daily basis, giving it credibility. It is now in such popular demand by those living in an urban context that many risk their financial well-being to buy gold jewelry.

Gold is much more difficult to work than silver, but technological improvements have begun to make it easier. There is a roller press at the Agadez cooperative that allows *inadan* to flatten gold or silver into very thin, even sheets and to make wire. Digital scales have become available, along with calculators, allowing for a more precise determination of weight and value. Gas cylinders are now widespread, so that gas torches, which efficiently and evenly heat gold to the high temperatures required to melt and work it, can replace the charcoal of the forge. There is also a regular trade in gold coins coming from Saudi Arabia, making available a trusted source of raw material.

It seems that urban Tuareg do not care about traditional prohibitions against gold. Outside of Agadez, in the Aïr, however, gold jewelry is still seldom seen, and in 2001 there were no *inadan* said to be working gold aside from those few in Agadez and Niamey. An important marabout in the Aïr has reportedly officially condemned the wearing of gold. While Salah continues to work gold in the workshop of Mohammed Agaliton, he is seriously thinking of starting his own workshop and beginning to train young people, including his two sons. As gold jewelry is always made on commission, and as Salah has a local reputation as a talented designer of new models of jewelry (many of which derive from a *Spiegel Catalog* he has acquired), he is confident that in the future he will work primarily in gold.

Mania has a somewhat different view of the future. He is also able to work in gold, having learned from Salah, but he believes that gold causes problems because women seem to want it more and more, significantly stretching the finances of their families to afford it. He is concerned that gold is also another force causing the Tuareg ways to disappear. Mania continues to work in silver, creating new forms of necklaces, bracelets, and earrings for a local market that is now accustomed to and desirous of new styles, as well as for an international market that he keeps trying to develop and nurture. He has become well known for the "*celebre*" style necklace, sometimes sold with matching earrings (fig. 8.27). When he sells this new style, he consciously relates it to traditional Tuareg designs. He describes the necklace as being derivative of the Tuareg punch design motif known as "teeth of the camel." He also acknowledges privately that he "borrowed" the design from "Arabs" in the north that make it in gold. His views indicate that he is trying to be creative in response to changing and expanding consumer tastes, while at the same time rooting his creations in what he understands to be Tuareg traditions. What remains undetermined is whether this is just good marketing—something his family seems to have excelled at for generations—or reflects a deeper caring for traditions of the past.

By the end of 1999 much of the family was spending most of its time working in Agadez, while Saidi, Al Hassan, and Gonda ran the business in Niamey. Saidi still controlled the finances, a situation that was clearly beginning to annoy several of his sons who were looking to create their own independent workshops. Saidi was feeling these pressures and was also losing his eyesight. He was tiring of moving from Agadez to Niamey and back, yet he seemed very reluctant to surrender financial control.

Before discussing the new millennium and the period following the September 11, 2001, attacks on the United States, I want to mention another project that was developing in Agadez. Starting in 1993, Jean-Yves Brizot, a young Frenchman, and his Tuareg partner formed a guild of a few talented *inadan* to make silver jewelry for direct export to Europe and America (see chapter 10 of this volume). In the period when this guild was getting established, conflicts developed between the partners, and by 1999 Brizot had started a new guild he called A l'Atelier (fig. 8.28). He had obtained a remarkable commission from the French fashion house Hermès to make specific silver items for their handbags, belts, and necklaces. Brizot also had an American partner, Alison Mezey, and together they owned a business called Exote. Mezey designed jewelry items for Exote inspired by Tuareg forms that were manufactured and engraved by the twenty-two master *inadan* and their assistants in A l'Atelier. A l'Atelier was managed by Atobeul N'Gataw, a Tuareg but not an *enad*, while the workshop was directed by Hani, one of the master smiths.

Brizot, concerned about the designs for Hermès or for Exote being "borrowed" by other *inadan* in Agadez, which would have jeopardized his relationship with the French company, maintained a veil of secrecy surrounding A l'Atelier. All production was directly shipped to Hermès or Exote and was never seen in Agadez. Of course, word of the workshop spread, nonetheless, engendering curiosity and sometimes disdain on the part of other *inadan*. While neither Saidi nor his sons ever said anything to me specifically about the Brizot enterprise, I know they were trying to find out all they could in order to copy whatever seemed to them of value.

2000 to the Present: Uncertainty

The attacks on New York and Washington on September 11, 2001, were a shock to the world with repercussions that continue to affect Niger and the Tuareg region of the central Sahara. I had been planning for some months to return to Niger in September 2001 to further my research into Tuareg artistic production, as well as to make an extended trip with Tuareg and American friends to the Tenere Desert. As it worked out, I flew from San Francisco to Paris and on to Niamey on September 15, 2001, having had the good fortune to have my reservation on the first flight from San Francisco to Paris that was allowed to leave the United States following the attacks.

The situation in Niamey was confused, as there was great uncertainty about what had happened and whether Osama bin Laden had been the mastermind of the attacks. Most Tuareg I talked with, including Saidi and his sons, deplored the attack, and Saidi said to me, "a true Muslim would never do such a thing." As bin Laden had helped fund many Koranic schools and mosques in West Africa, including Niger, he was generally held in high regard. People were genuinely concerned and perplexed by the situation (fig. 8.29).

Saidi, now El Hadj, was particularly troubled as confirmation of the attacks had shaken his faith in other Muslims. While, as I have previously indicated, he is not in any way a rigid or strict Muslim, Saidi does believe in the virtuousness of Islam. He is also close to a number of Americans and was deeply troubled that America had been

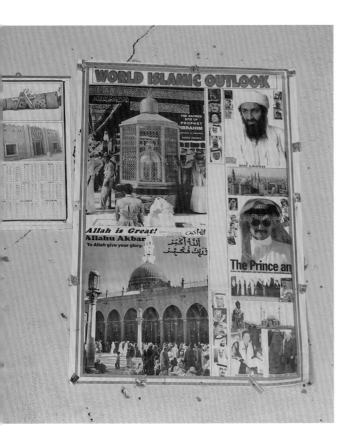

attacked. His sons in Niamey, Gonda, Al Hassan, and Mania, were not as dismayed and appeared to be more focused on developing business.

Although Saidi and his family do not describe their activities as such, I think their various enterprises display the characteristics of a "family business," including the strains of transition. By late 2001 it was clear to all that Saidi's eyesight had deteriorated to the extent that he could not work. He helped clean up in the Niamey workshop, made tea, socialized with clients and visitors, and did most of the actual bargaining that is part of any transaction. He still tried to examine and critique the work in progress, but this seemed to me a formality, a symbol intended to demonstrate that he was still active and able.

What concerned Saidi and others in the family (I do not know if Andi was part of this discussion or not) was not only moving Saidi back to Agadez but also the nature of the new mode of doing business they would have to develop. As Saidi was well known, keeping his name on the workshop and representing everything that issued from the workshop as having his approval (although this was not actually the case) made good business sense. In fact, however, Salah was effectively working on his own, and Al Hassan and Mania were really running the business in Niamey and making occasional forays into Europe. El Faki, now in his early twenties, was in Agadez literally sitting at the anvil and forge that Saidi had used for all the years before he moved to Niamey. He was making high-quality silver jewelry and contributing substantially to the finances of the Agadez household. Andi and several of her daughters and granddaughters were making beautiful leatherwork, which was selling well. Andi's cousin Tchebe Issoufu had developed Azamau, an aggressive new marketing cooperative, and was selling items created by the Oumba, Ouhoulou, and Tchebe families in Niamey and France.

The expense of running a larger enterprise that includes international travel as part of its marketing strategy became another family business issue. There was increasing competition from other marketing cooperatives, including A l'Atelier, in an indirect way, and the Koumama family, who had entered into a business arrangement with Ann Elston of California to promote and sell some of their work (figs. 8.30, 8.31).[23] Saidi and his

8.29

A poster titled "World Islamic Outlook" on a wall in the Agaliton workshop where Salah Saidi works.

Photograph by Thomas K. Seligman, Agadez, Niger, 2001.

8.30

Elhadji Koumama (right) and an assistant.

Photograph by Thomas K. Seligman, Agadez, Niger, 2004.

8.31

Elhadji Koumama (background)
and Ann Elston (right) in their
booth at the Union Street Fair.

*Photograph by Thomas K. Seligman, San
Francisco, California, 2004.*

family participate in several marketing opportunities, work hard, create high-quality
and creatively designed work for an ever-changing clientele, and are well off compared to
many Tuareg. The expectations and needs of Saidi and Andi's children and increasing
numbers of grandchildren, however, appear to be putting considerable strain on the family,
not only in terms of their traditions but also in relation to economic realities (fig. 8.32).

The war on terrorism in the wake of September 11, 2001, brought Niger under
severe scrutiny. It was widely reported that Saddam Hussein had obtained uranium from
Niger. While the information proved to be a total fabrication, it put great pressure on
the government of Niger. From late 2003, news sources reported that the United States
military special operations forces were engaged in training, arming, and fighting along-
side so-called antiterrorist military in Mali, Niger, and Algeria.[24] The expressed concern
was that remnants of Al Qaeda had set up camps in the central Sahara and might be
creating an Afghanistan-like terrorist training and planning center.

In February of 2004 the only Tuareg minister in the government of Niger, Rhissa ag
Boula, was arrested and charged with ordering the murder of a politician near Agadez.[25]
Ag Boula had been the leader of the largest armed faction of the Tuareg rebellion, and
as part of the peace agreement, which promised the Tuareg more jobs and opportunity,
he was appointed minister of tourism and artisans. He had been in government since
1997, having survived several reshuffles of the cabinet. After he resigned his position
to face his accusers, the ministry was disbanded. It is rumored that one or two other
Tuareg have been given government positions in an effort to assuage the Tuareg.

The immediate effects that the uncertain and unstable political situation in Niger
and the central Sahara will have on the Oumba family and other smiths remain unclear.
In general, the *inadan* continue their ambassadorial role, now helping to promote a
positive image of the Tuareg within and outside of the region. There has been a decline
in tourism, and there have been incidents of groups of tourists being robbed during
their trips through the desert, which will lead to further declines. Niger remains one of
the five poorest countries in the world according to the United Nations.[26] As the *inadan*
in the north depend on tourists for a significant portion of their sales, the near-term

8.32
Saidi Oumba.
Photograph by Thomas K. Seligman, Agadez, Niger, 2001.

outlook, is not good for the *inadan*, especially those like Saidi, who is now living full-time with Andi in Agadez. As opportunities of any type are very limited, most of Saidi and Andi's grandchildren are learning the skills necessary to become *inadan* while also attending school. I know of only one younger cousin who has become a schoolteacher. Everyone else continues to try to make his or her living as an *enad*.

There are some promising signs that may help Salah, Al Hassan, Mania, and El Faki become successful in their attempts to market to Europe and America. Unlike many Muslims and peoples from North Africa and the Middle East, the Tuareg continue to be positively stereotyped. Although some Tuareg in the Aïr have been labeled "bandits" or "rebels," they have not been labeled "terrorists" and still appear in popular magazines, newspapers, as well as on television and in films, as noble people trying to maintain their way of life in the Sahara. They are certainly still romanticized. If the Volkswagen Touareg SUV is able to "conquer the wilds" and the automotive consumer's imagination, perhaps the Tuareg themselves will be able to at least continue their struggle for the self-sufficiency and "freedom" they desire, while maintaining their language and culture.

Saidi's sons are not particularly concerned with the larger social and political agendas of Tuareg intellectuals and nobles. As *inadan*—who have always maintained a somewhat ambiguous social status—they have recently achieved a better standard of living than most other Tuareg. Thus, they are concerned with advancing their business and maintaining their lifestyle. Due to stricter visa requirements for visiting Europe and the United States, it is harder for Al Hassan and Mania to travel to the West; but somehow they manage and generally make each trip more profitable than the last. Always dressing as the "true" Tuareg, they engage clients and audiences at jewelry-making demonstrations and have made numerous friends and business connections that should continue to be productive as long as they are able to meet the expected quality standards. If these young men continue to remain creative and inventive with designs that are still unmistakably Tuareg, they and their extended family will probably thrive. They can take advantage of the developing global market to offset the probable downturns that the Saharan region

8.33

Saidi Oumba and Andi Ouhoulou
with one of Andi's newly made
leather bags.

*Photograph by Thomas K. Seligman, Agadez,
Niger, 2004.*

will face in the wake of the global war on terrorism, increasing population pressures, and environmental degradation as evidenced by the renewed drought and food shortages in 2005. Certainly, however, the family's prosperity and relatively strong reputation are far from guaranteed.

In describing the family of Andi Ouhoulou and Saidi Oumba, I have attempted to show some of the dynamics of change at play over three generations of Tuareg *inadan* of the Aïr (fig. 8.33). While there has been considerable effort by scholars to understand the changes and evolution of the art of Africa, as Mohamed ag Ewangaye so correctly points out in his essay (see chapter 3 of this volume), it is important to make these descriptions locally and specifically. The Ouhoulou and Oumba family cannot be understood as representative of all Tuareg *inadan* or even those of the Kel Ewey or the town of Agadez. Yet by describing some of the specific transitions of this family, set in the larger context of Agadez, the Aïr, Niger, and increasing globalization, perhaps the reader will gain a more concrete grasp of some of the central issues of concern to many Tuareg *inadan*.

Several of the essays in this volume address changes that confronted the Tuareg beginning in the late nineteenth century. Saidi and Andi's parents were very young at that time and were part of the generation that lived during the period of French conquest and colonization, resistance to that colonization, and the coming of independence. Saidi and Andi grew up as independence was sought and achieved, and they have witnessed the introduction of the global economy in the Aïr. Their children have studied at Koranic and government schools, have apprenticed and learned the skills to become *inadan*, and most of them now have children of their own.

I have always been interested in the characteristics of this family that have allowed them to succeed within their own society and now nationally and internationally. They have been taught and have attained excellent technical skills; they have focused on making high-quality works in silver, wood, and leather. From time to time one or more family members might have compromised workmanship in order to make works quickly or cheaply to sell to an unsuspecting tourist, but Saidi, Andi, and their older children, Chemo and Salah, have always corrected this misdirection. They recognized that a reputation for excellence is more valuable than a quick profit. Within a conservative framework, they have created stylistic and technical innovations, which they have tested in the marketplace, and when these were successful, they have pushed the new products forward commercially.

All of them believe that family concerns and harmony are of greatest importance, therefore business, which is a family concern, matters to all. They have all grown up in a business setting—one of making, marketing, selling, and sharing in the rewards. Profits go to feeding and clothing the family, providing housing and improvements of their living situation, and to the business through the acquisition of more leather or silver for subsequent projects. Consumer goods have been acquired during times of relative wealth, and seldom, over the generations, were there prolonged downturns in the family business. There was always stress, experienced particularly by Saidi who felt he was primarily responsible for the family's economic well-being, but this was not a major factor affecting family life.

The family has been flexible and adaptive to change. Saidi has learned French so that he can do business in the national arena and has had to move residences and workshops because of situations beyond his control. The family has sought out new clients, Tuareg, other Africans, and non-Africans. They have been creative and have seized opportunities at every turn. They have used the romantic image of the Tuareg in their marketing, and they are in fact very calculating in the use of their "Tuaregness." While, as noted, there are several significant issues now confronting them, I am hopeful that this creative and determined family will continue to be exemplars of the "artful" Tuareg.[27]

☑

UPON REQUEST

Commissions with Saidi Oumba and Andi Ouhoulou

The parents of Saidi Oumba and Andi Ouhoulou belonged to the last generation of *inadan* to live among the Kel Ewey and benefit from the complex relationship that formerly existed between Tuareg nobility (*imajeren*) and artists. Almost everything the *inadan* created was made at the request of the *imajeren* and was required for a specific purpose. Saidi and Andi are part of a transitional generation of *inadan* who years ago worked for nobles but have long since moved from their home villages to Agadez. Today most of the silver and leather objects Andi and Saidi make are intended for sale to unknown buyers. They do, however, continue to receive commissions from Tuareg, as well as from other Africans and outsiders.

1.1

Amulet (*tcherot*)

Saidi Oumba
Tuareg, Kel Ewey
Agadez, Niger
Silver, gold, leather, cord
L (cord with pendant): 62.2 cm;
W (of pendant): 10.2 cm;
D (of pendant): 1.9 cm
Private Collection

1.2 (OPPOSITE, LEFT)

Amulet (*tcherot*)

Saidi Oumba
Tuareg, Kel Ewey
Agadez, Niger
Silver, leather, thread
L (cord with pendant): 48.3 cm;
W (of pendant): 11.4 cm;
D (of pendant): 1.9 cm
Private Collection

1.3 (OPPOSITE, RIGHT)

Amulet (*tcherot*)

Salah Saidi
Tuareg, Kel Ewey
Azel, Niger
Silver, gold, leather, cord
L (cord with pendant): 62.2 cm;
W (of pendant): 10.2 cm;
D (of pendant): 1.9 cm
Private Collection

Over a period of years, I have commissioned three *tcherot* amulets from Saidi in order to determine how he makes them; how the amuletic insert—a paper prepared for me by a Muslim cleric, or marabout—is properly blessed and placed inside the *tcherot*; and how Saidi has taught silverwork to his sons. During the first commission of two *tcherot* in 1988, I learned from Saidi that this particular amulet is one of the most difficult silver objects to make as it requires a very deft touch to properly hammer the cover into stepped facets, to engrave the surfaces in a detailed and balanced manner, and to align and attach the back. As a demonstration of his skill and friendship, Saidi added a central cone of gold onto the front of the one *tcherot*, which was exquisitely fused into the surrounding silver (fig. 1.1).

1.4

Lock and Key (*tamask n'asrou*)

Saidi Oumba
Tuareg, Kel Ewey
Niamey, Niger
Silver, copper, steel
Lock: 8.9 x 10.2 cm;
Key: 10.5 x 3.2 cm
Cantor Arts Center
2001.201.a–c

1.5a–c

a. Letter opener
Saidi Oumba
Tuareg, Kel Ewey
Agadez, Niger
Silver
21 x 3.8 cm
Private Collection

b. Spoon with cross of Agadez
Saidi Oumba
Tuareg, Kel Ewey
Agadez, Niger
Silver
15.9 x 2.9 cm
Private Collection

c. Pen encased in silver
Saidi Oumba
Tuareg, Kel Ewey
Niamey, Niger
Silver, Bic ballpoint pen
L (with pen): 12.7 cm; Diam: 1.3 cm
Private Collection

1.6 (OPPOSITE, TOP)

Necklace and pendant

Saidi Oumba
Tuareg, Kel Ewey
Niamey, Niger
Silver, stone, glass
L (with pendant): 29.2 cm;
W (of pendant): 6.4 cm
Private Collection

1.7 (OPPOSITE, BOTTOM)

Earrings with cross of In Gall

Saidi Oumba
Tuareg, Kel Ewey
Agadez, Niger
Silver, glass
5.5 x 2 x 0.8 cm
UCLA Fowler Museum
x97.17.32a,b

240

As a result of the great skill and pride that Saidi demonstrated in fashioning these two *tcherot* for me in 1988 (figs. 1.1, 1.2), I commissioned another in 1997 when Saidi was living and working in Niamey. Although he had not made a "traditional" *tcherot* for nearly five years, he accepted my commission. It took him considerably longer to make this *tcherot* than the ones he made in 1988 as he was out of practice. It was difficult to retain the skill specific to making objects in the old style when his modern clientele preferred "new" styles. From the early 1990s Saidi and his sons had begun to design and make more contemporary jewelry and to accept commissions for previously unknown object types, such as knife and chopstick holders and rings to be placed around the necks of wine bottles to stop drips (of note, the Tuareg seldom use knives to eat and never use chopsticks or drink wine).

Andi never left Agadez for the capital city Niamey as Saidi did (see chapter 8 of this volume). She continues to make traditional style leather bags, wallets, and cushions on commission, as well as purses, key chains, and other Western-style accessories for sale via a local marketing cooperative. I commissioned Andi to make an *eljebira* bag in 1988 (fig. 1.9), which she executed beautifully. In early 2004, I mailed her a photograph I had taken of a bag hung on a man's camel during a wedding in 2001 and asked her to make me one like it. When I visited her in late 2004, the bag was finished—a beautiful interpretation of a very old and "traditional" style (fig. 1.8). The work took Andi about two months yet cost about the same as one of Saidi's *tcherot*, which require great skill but take no more than three to five days of work to complete.

This apparent disparity in the value of labor and time reflects the fact that silver, an imported commodity, is sold on the international market and can be priced accordingly. Leather, which is locally produced, tanned, and fabricated, generally remains rural and more localized to the Tuareg. Prices also differ considerably between the capital, Niamey, and Agadez, a twelve-hour drive away. Finally the disparity reflects inequities in the value placed on work done by men as opposed to that done by women in the modern market place.

T.K.S.

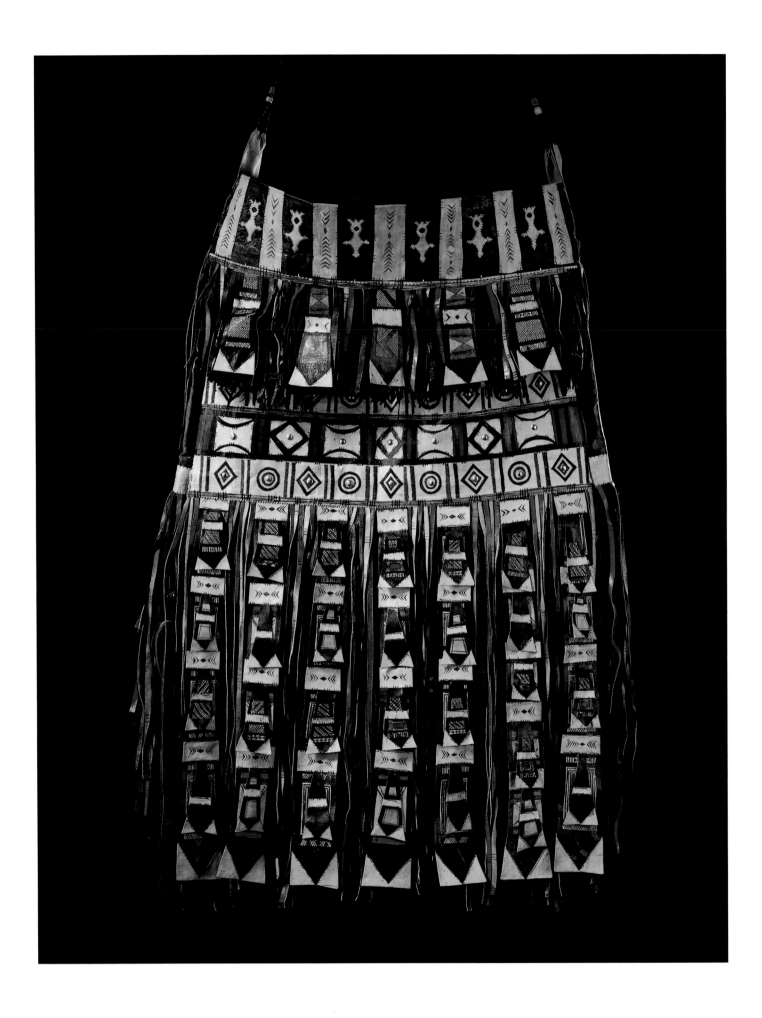

242

Bag (*taghrek*)

Andi Ouhoulou
Tuareg, Kel Ewey
Agadez, Niger
Leather, pigment, metal
102 x 61 x 5.1 cm
Private Collection

1.9

Bag (*eljebira*)

Andi Ouhoulou
Tuareg, Kel Ewey
Agadez, Niger
Leather, cloth, pigment
89 x 86.1 x 1.3 cm
Private Collection

1.10a,b

a. Hair clip
Saidi Oumba
Tuareg, Kel Ewey
Niamey, Niger
Silver, ebony
3.5 x 10.7 cm
UCLA Fowler Museum
X97.17.7

b. Hair clip
Saidi Oumba
Tuareg, Kel Ewey
Niamey, Niger
Silver, glass
3.5 x 10.7 cm
UCLA Fowler Museum
X97.17.6

1.11a,b

a. Lidded container
Saidi Oumba
Tuareg, Kel Ewey
Niamey, Niger
Silver
5.1 x 3.6 x 2.2 cm
UCLA Fowler Museum
X97.17.2a,b

b. Lidded container
Saidi Oumba
Tuareg, Kel Ewey
Niamey, Niger
Silver
5.1 x 3.6 x 2.2 cm
UCLA Fowler Museum
X97.17.3a,b

1.12a,b

a. Knife or chopstick rest
Saidi Oumba
Tuareg, Kel Ewey
Niamey, Niger
Ebony, silver
L: 7.6 cm
UCLA Fowler Museum
X97.17.41

b. Bottle ring
Saidi Oumba
Tuareg, Kel Ewey
Niamey, Niger
Silver, fabric
H: 1.6 cm: Diam: 4 cm
UCLA Fowler Museum
X97.17.43

1.13

Necklace (*houmeni*)

Saidi Oumba
Tuareg, Kel Ewey
Niamey, Niger
Silver, ebony, glass
Pendant: 10.4 x 10 cm;
L (of necklace): 53 cm
UCLA Fowler Museum
X97.17.18

I.14

Necklace (*n'ekade n'azrouf*)

Saidi Oumba
Tuareg, Kel Ewey
Niamey, Niger
Silver, stone, glass
Pendant: 6 x 4.2 cm;
L (of necklace): 49.3 cm
UCLA Fowler Museum
X97.17.15

I.15

Cross of Mano Dayak

Hamidan Oumba
Tuareg, Kel Ewey
Agadez, Niger
Silver, glass
Pendant: 7 x 3.3 cm;
L (of necklace): 51 cm
UCLA Fowler Museum
X97.17.37

The Tuareg Mano Dayak was born
in the Aïr region of Niger, near the
Tenere Desert. After studying in
France and in the United States, he
started a travel agency in Agadez.
He was instrumental in determining the various stopping places for
the Paris-Dakar Rally, created a
production of Antoine de Saint-
Exupéry's *Le Petit Prince* in the
Tenere Desert, and authored two
books: *Touareg: La tragédie* and *Je
suis né avec du sable dans les yeux*.
When the Tuareg uprisings com-
menced in the 1990s, Dayak became
politically involved in the Tuareg
cause. He died in a plane crash in
1995. This cross was created in 1996
to honor his memory.

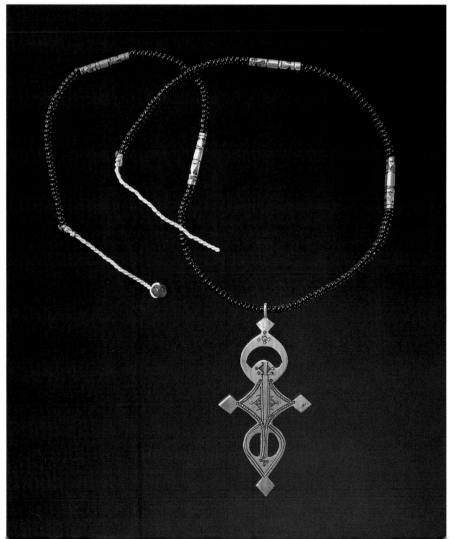

1.16a–d

a. Necklace with pendant
Souliman Oumba
Tuareg, Kel Ewey
Azel, Niger
Gypsum, leather
Pendant: 7.6 x 3.8 cm
Cantor Arts Center
2001.202.3

b. Necklace with cross of Agadez
Souliman Oumba
Tuareg, Kel Ewey
Azel, Niger
Gypsum, leather
Pendant: 6.7 x 2.9 cm
Cantor Arts Center
2001.202.2

c. Necklace with pendant
Souliman Oumba
Tuareg, Kel Ewey
Azel, Niger
Gypsum, leather
Pendant: 4.8 x 2.9 cm
Cantor Arts Center
2001.202.5

d. Necklace with pendant
Souliman Oumba
Tuareg, Kel Ewey
Azel, Niger
Gypsum, leather
Pendant: 5.7 x 4.5 cm
Cantor Arts Center
2001.202.4

1.17

Necklace (*chatchat*)

Sidi Oumba
Tuareg, Kel Ewey
Azel, Niger
Gypsum, cord
L (overall): 20.3 cm;
W (of pendants): 5.1 cm
Private Collection

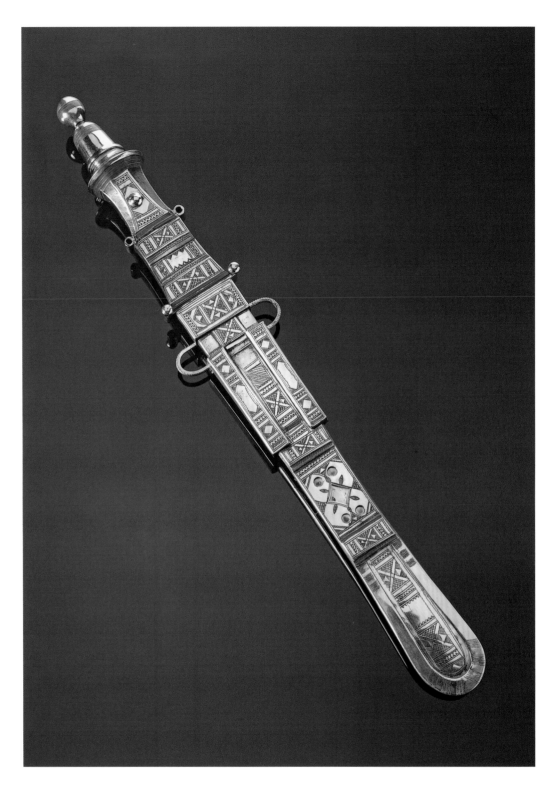

1.18
Knife and Sheath (*elmoshi*)

Saidi Oumba
Tuareg, Kel Ewey
Niamey, Niger
Steel, ebony, brass, silver
29.8 x 5.1 cm
Cantor Arts Center
2001.200.a-b

1.19a,b (OPPOSITE, TOP)

a. Container and lid
Sidi Oumba
Tuareg, Kel Ewey
Azel, Niger
Stone
Diam: 4.3 cm
Private Collection

b. Tortoise
Tuareg
Azel, Niger
Gypsum
2.5 x 7.6 x 5.1 cm
Private Collection

1.20 (OPPOSITE, BOTTOM LEFT)
Purse with cross of Mano Dayak

Tuareg
Agadez, Niger
Leather, pigment
58.4 x 24.9 cm
UCLA Fowler Museum
x97.17.38

1.21 (OPPOSITE, BOTTOM RIGHT)
Miniature camel saddle

Hamidan Oumba
Tuareg, Kel Ewey
Azel, Niger
Wood, leather, metal
27.9 x 25.4 x 11.4 cm
Private Collection

9

THE CROSS OF AGADEZ (*TENAGHALT TAN AGADEZ*)

Kristyne Loughran and Thomas K. Seligman

In Niamey, the capital of the Republic of Niger, the cross of Agadez is ubiquitous. One can purchase it in the form of a gold or silver pendant in many jewelry stores, and it is available for sale to visitors at the artisans' center at the National Museum. There are numerous subtle variations on its form, and it has been incorporated in many ingenious and often surprising contexts as well. The cross of Agadez has been used as a sculpture in traffic circles (fig. 9.2) and in public parks. It has been employed as an ornamental motif on wrought iron fences (fig. 9.3), used to decorate walls, appeared on billboards promoting the work of various jewelers, and been embossed on bars of soap (figs. 9.4, 9.5). Shirts, blouses, and aprons (fig. 9.6) are embellished with the motif, and leatherworkers create handsome boxes using the cross as a design. Some individuals are so taken with it that they use it on their letterhead, and others attach small crosses to their key rings. Formerly, twenty-three different crosses were recognized and reproduced in Niger, but presently *inadan* make only twenty-one (Saidi Oumba, personal communication, 1979). The cross of Agadez has consistently attracted attention and served as a source of inspiration. It has been reproduced, adapted, and reworked over time to address new concerns, fashions, and trends. The subject of numerous articles,[1] this particular cross has attracted more curiosity than any other Tuareg jewelry form.

Heinrich Barth, a German explorer in the employ of the British government, visited Agadez as part of his six-year journey through Africa (1849–1855). In his three-volume book, published in 1857, he briefly described Tuareg women as wearing silver jewelry. He also noted that during his stay in Agadez in 1850, considerable silverwork was being done. The first photograph to specifically document the cross of Agadez, however, was published by F. Foureau in 1905 in his book describing the famous Foureau-Lamy expedition across western Africa, which passed through the Tassili-n-Ajjer and the Aïr regions and later paved the way for the annexation of the Aïr by France (Mauny 1954, 70).

The cross of Agadez, unlike some of the other Tuareg cross types, is distinctly cruciform in shape and is relatively sober when compared to many of the other crosses. The top portion is a round or oval loop, which is sometimes decorated with two small lobes, occasionally referred to as "ears" in the literature (Gabus 1982, 442). The bottom section is a lozenge with concave sides ending in rounded or pointed knob ends. The flat areas of the cross are engraved with linear and circular motifs along the sides and at the center. As its name would indicate, it is thought to have originated in the large trading town of Agadez on the edge of the Sahara in the Aïr region of Niger. Its simplicity has made it a very popular form among foreigners, and this is probably what has spurred variations and novel uses. Agak Mohamed, the master smith at the National Museum in Niamey related: "There was a man, a doctor, who looked for older pieces. I was still a little boy;

9.1

Examples of each of the twenty-one "regional" Tuareg crosses

Silver
UCLA Fowler Museum
x88.1421–x88.1441

Beginning in the 1970s, Tuareg *inadan* began making "sets" of twenty-one crosses for sale to tourists and aid workers. The cross of Agadez is located in the center of the second row from the bottom. (These crosses are not in the exhibition.)

The crosses are (from left to right, top to bottom): In Gall, In Wagan, Martchaksa, Tchimoumenene, Madaoua, Aïr, Takarmenda, In Aranganak, Timia, Tahoua, Crip Crip, Tchin Tabaraden, Tilya, Iferouane, Taghmert, Agadez, Bagzan, Zinder, Karaga, Bilma, Abalak.

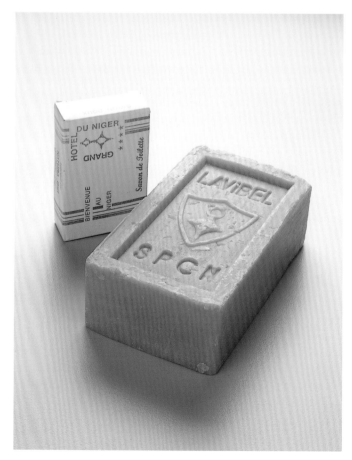

9.6

Apron with the cross of Agadez

Tuareg
Niamey, Niger
Cotton
61 x 102 cm
Private Collection

I didn't wear trousers yet. This man bought everything. People thought he was crazy because he only wanted older pieces" (personal communication, Niamey, 1991). The man to whom Agak refers was B. Dudot, who would publish several essays on the cross of Agadez between 1955 and 1970. According to French scholar Raymond Mauny: "The centers of production have been mainly the oases in the Aïr Mountains and surroundings such as Agadez, Iferouane, In Gall, Tahoua, and, since the 1950s, Dakar, Morocco, Algeria, and France" (1954, 72).

Another French scholar, Jean Gabus, discovered that numerous *inadan* in the Aïr and Tahoua regions of Niger identified a consistent morphology for the cross of Agadez (fig. 9.7). He has also suggested that assigning names of parts of the human body to different areas of the cross is standard practice among the *inadan*: "It stems from the need to humanize [their] work, and to find, in the tool [they] know well, a part of [themselves]" (Gabus 1982, 442). It also functions as a mnemonic device and is certainly not unique to the *inadan*; consider, for example, "table legs" and other expressions of the sort. Gabus relates this practice to the use of similar anthropomorphic terminology for the component parts of the pommel of the Tuareg camel saddle, and Nancy Mickelsen notes that the "same motif is found in a number of other Tuareg articles—the shield, the cross-hilted sword, the pommel of the camel saddle, the head piece, and the top of the spoon handle" (1976, 18).

Inadan create the cross using the lost-wax process (fig. 9.8). The form is first shaped out of wax, which is then covered in a fine clay that is allowed to dry. The wax is then melted out of the clay mold leaving a hollow impression into which molten silver is poured. After casting, the clay mold is broken and the formed silver is filed and further shaped. The *inadan* engraves the surface of the cross according to his own taste, and the designs used have no meaning of their own (fig. 9.9a–c).

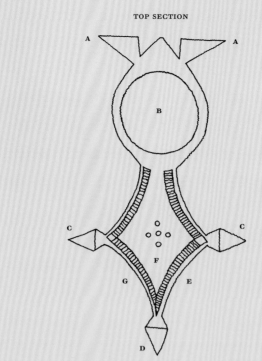

TOP SECTION

A   the ears
B   the opening
C   the shoulders
D   the head
E   the face
F   the eyes of the chameleon
G   the trace of the jackal

BOTTOM SECTION

VARIATIONS ON TOP SECTION

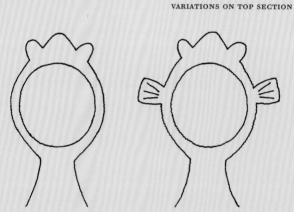

9.7

Drawing of the morphology of the cross of Agadez, after Gabus (1982, 442-43).

Illustration by Patrick Fitzgerald.

9.8

The son of Hamidan Oumba makes a wax model of a cross preparatory to casting.

Photograph by Thomas K. Seligmn, Niamey, Niger, 2004.

9.9a–c (OPPOSITE)

a. Cross of Agadez (*zakkat*)
Atenhanana Wadjo
Tuareg
Niger
Silver
9.2 x 5.7 cm
UCLA Fowler Museum
x88.1407

b. Partially engraved cross of Agadez (*zakkat*)
Atenhanana Wadjo
Tuareg
Niger
Silver
9.1 x 5.6 cm
UCLA Fowler Museum
x88.1408

c. Mold for cross (*telak*); rough cast of cross of Agadez (*zakkat*); and finished cross of Agadez
Saidi Oumba
Tuareg, Kel Ewey
Agadez, Niger
Mold: clay; Crosses: silver
Mold: 9.6 x 3.9 cm;
Rough cast 8.7 x 4 cm;
Finished cross: 7.5 x 4 cm
UCLA Fowler Museum
x88-1453a–c

254

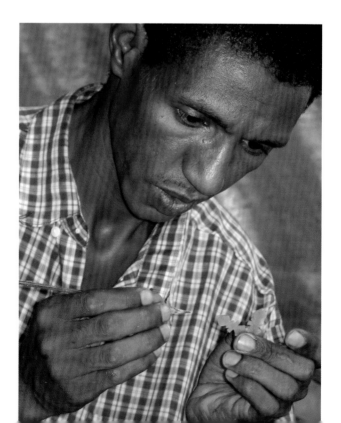

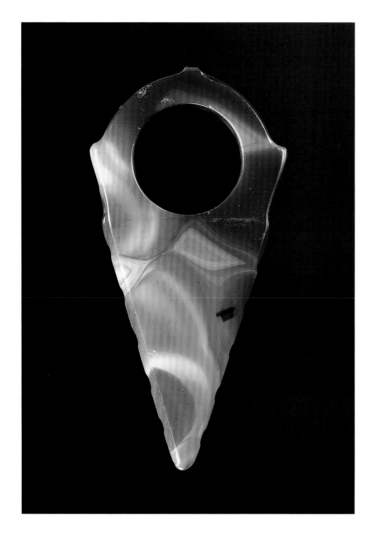

9.10

Pendant (*talhakimt*)

Tuareg
Mali
Agate
6.2 x 3 cm
UCLA Fowler Museum
X88.1463

Agate pendants like this one are strung with crosses and other pendant forms to make elaborate necklaces. Glass, carnelian, and agate beads and pendants were traded from India to East and South Africa as early as 200 CE and continuing to the 1600s. The Islamic bead trade began between 1200 and 1500 CE Many beads used to manufacture Tuareg necklaces are imported. This particular shape of agate pendant was once manufactured in the former Indian state of Cambay and was then supplied to merchants in Nigeria and the Sudan. In the 1900s the trade of agate stones was exploited by German and Czechoslovakian factories and ultimately taken over by the gem industry in Idar-Oberstein, Germany.

The Debate over Origins

The origins of the cross of Agadez[2] (*tenaghalt tan Agadez*)[3] and its stylistic development have been the subject of considerable scholarly speculation and debate for nearly a century. As we shall see below, some argue it is related to the Egyptian ankh, to the Carthaginian goddess Tanit, or to a red-stone pendant called *talhakimt*, which was manufactured in the former Indian state of Cambay (Arkell 1935b, 300-311).

In 1922 the British geographer Francis Rennell Rodd traveled in the Aïr region. In his book *People of the Veil* (1926), he described and presented line drawings of various types of the cross of Agadez (Rodd 1926, 44, 277, 284-85, pls. 36, 37). He later reported that "[t]he Agadez Cross is regarded in Air as being characteristic of themselves, as being the Ornament of *Imajeghan* (nobles), as being *tamzugh* or appertaining to the ruling classes" (Rodd in Arkell 1935a, 306). Rodd suggested that the cross shape was related to Christianity, whereas "the large ring points to some derivation from the Egyptian *Ankh*" (1926, 284-85).

British archaeologist A. J. Arkell posited in 1935 that the cross of Agadez derived from a triangular red-stone pendant known among the Tuareg in Darfur as *talhakimt* (fig. 9.10).[4] Arkell stated with substantial evidence that "[t]here is no doubt that the *t'alhakimt* itself comes from India" (1935a, 301). The worked stone for these pendants was evidently imported to Africa via Indian traders who sold it in Mecca and Medina.[5] Hausa pilgrims from Nigeria then introduced the stone to the western Sudan where the Tuareg obtained it. While the historical evidence for the red-stone *talhakimt* is revealing, Arkell offered no evidence for his assertion that the cross of Agadez was derived from it.

Rodd responded to Arkell in the same article, noting that "the Agadez Cross (*tenaghalt*) was peculiar to Air and was only found among people who had obtained the ornament or borrowed the habit from Air" (Rodd in Arkell 1935a, 304-6). He defended his earlier position, articulated in *People of the Veil*, and repeated his claim that the Agadez cross had its origins in the XII Dynasty Egyptian ankh. He suggested that the protuberances on the *talhakimt* and the excrescences on the cross of Agadez were "vestigial survivors of the upper thickening of the loop of the *Ankh*." He also pointed out that the long neck present in the cross of Agadez was reminiscent of the ankh. Finally, he stated that "The Agadez Cross is mainly a man's ornament though also worn by women" (Rodd in Arkell 1935a, 305).

In 1939 Arkell rekindled the debate with Rodd concerning the stylistic source for the cross of Agadez. At that time he stated erroneously that the Tuareg did not work in stone,[6] then argued that since the sources for *talhakimt* stones and for silver used in the Aïr were regions north of the Sahara, the Egyptian ankh could not be the stylistic basis. Arkell was convinced that there was probably a direct relationship between the red-stone *talhakimt* and the cross of Agadez: "It is just what I should expect, to find that the older *t'alhakimt* is found wherever the Tuareg have resided, (meaning in the northern Tuareg areas of the Hoggar and Agger in Algeria, as well as the Air in Niger) while the more recent *tanaghilt* is confined to the area where it was subsequently invented (Air)" (Arkell 1939, 187).

LOUGHRAN AND SELIGMAN

The hypotheses of Rodd and Arkell aside, another factor may explain the evolution of the cross of Agadez. In 1926 Maurice Reygasse, the director of the Musée du Bardo in Algiers, excavated a large tomb in Abalassa, Al Gerin (Reygasse 1950). The tomb contained the burial remains of Queen Tin Hinan who had lived in the fourth century CE. This find was particularly relevant to the origins of the cross of Agadez because Tin Hinan is believed to have been an ancestress of the Tuareg, and the jewelry found in her tomb had both Roman and Carthaginian characteristics resembling forms the Tuareg use today (Loughran 1996, 266).

In 1954 Raymond Mauny expounded on the historic connection that the Tuareg or their near ancestors had with Carthage. He speculated that the symbolic image of the Carthaginian goddess Tanit, a solar disc with two horns, could have been combined with the Latin cross (fig. 9.11). He further complicated matters by proposing a southern antecedent for the cross of Agadez, possibly a plain triangular pendant known as *zakkat* or a rather complex Hausa cross pendant called *karaga* (Mauny 1954, 71). Using Arkell's distribution argument, Mauny emphasized that the cross of Agadez is worn by Tuareg in southern Niger and not in the Ahaggar to the north. But like many others, he realized the impossibility of definitively resolving the issue and was forced to remark, "We still have no certain knowledge on this subject" (1954, 76).

In an article published in 1977 on the origins of the *talhakimt*, Robert Liu, the editor of *Ornament* magazine and a bead specialist, took up the subject once again. As Arkell had done before him, Liu argued that the origins of the cross of Agadez most probably rest with the *talhakimt* as opposed to the ankh (Liu 1977, 18-22). He based this assertion on stylistic inconsistencies and the lack of intermediate forms in the historical and archaeological records (1977, 20). Liu believed the *talhakimt* had a long-standing history and distribution pattern among the Tuareg and neighboring groups that made the "rapprochement" between the cross of Agadez and the *talhakimt* more plausible.

Rodd's assertion that the cross was once the ornament of the nobles seems reasonable, and other authors such as Dieterlen and Ligers, Göttler, Creyaufmüller, and Arkell have all suggested that this cross form might have symbolized social class and group adherence.[7] It has also been suggested that the cross of Agadez represents a good luck charm or a sexual symbol, as well as a symbol of life (when related to the ankh), of Venus and Mercury, of the four cardinal directions, or of the fertility goddess Tanit, or Astarte, as she was known to the Phoenicians (Mauny 1954, 74). Other symbolism attributed to the cross almost always parallels that of the *talhakimt*. The latter has been considered a fertility symbol because of its red color, and its symbolic representation of the two sexes (Mauny 1954, 73). Of central importance to our historic focus, however, is Mauny's observation that "[w]hether the Cross of Agadez derives from a Mediterranean prototype connoting sexual symbolism or a black African prototype connoting protection, it seems the Tuareg have forgotten the value of the symbol, maybe under the pressure of Islam, and that this ornament only survived out of habit and its undeniable aesthetic value" (1954, 76).

The Cross of Agadez in Contemporary Times

Several scholars conducting research and collecting among the Tuareg in Algeria, Niger, and Mali (Jean Gabus in 1972 and 1978; Nancy Mickelsen from 1974 to 1975; Mark Milburn from 1976 to 1978; Thomas Seligman from 1971 to 2005) have noted that the cross of Agadez was an object intended primarily for males and was given by a father to his son as the boy entered puberty. Dieterlen and Ligers record the words accompanying the ritual presentation of the cross by a father to his son on entering adulthood: "Son, I give you the four directions of the world because we do not know where you will die" (1972, 42). The cross, however, was on occasion worn by women as well.

By the late 1970s, however, the cross of Agadez was almost exclusively worn by women throughout the Tuareg regions. In fact, since Seligman's first research in the Aïr and continuing work throughout the Tuareg regions, he has never observed a man wearing a cross of Agadez. In 1979 the *enad* Saidi Oumba told Seligman that the first cross

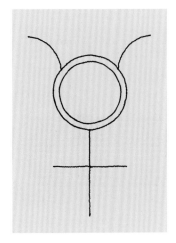

9.11
Drawing demonstrating the possible combination of the solar disk with horns—associated with the Carthaginian goddess Tanit—and the Latin cross, after Mauny (1954).
Illustration by Patrick Fitzgerald.

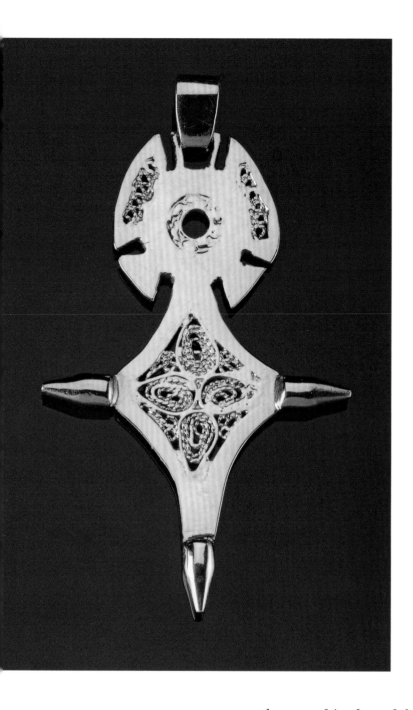

was the cross of Agadez and that the other Tuareg groups created cross designs to suit and proclaim their identity. Agak Mohamed, the master smith at the National Museum of Niamey, made a similar statement to Loughran in 1991.

If the meaning and origins of the cross of Agadez are lost and its gender usage has changed among the Tuareg, what has become of the *tenaghalt?* Creyaufmüller opines, "Generally, many of the pieces retain vestiges of their symbolic meaning, but this symbolism has been increasingly vague over the past decade, as jewelry has become ever more 'Europeanized' with additions such as the loop [referring to a new loop on top of the cross to allow it to hang from a silver chain]" (1984, 39).

The Cross of Agadez as a National and Political Symbol
By virtue of being replicated in gold (fig. 9.12), silver (figs. 9.13, 9.14), and other metals by jewelers in other parts of the world, the cross of Agadez gained increased recognition. La Rahla—Amicale des Sahariens, for example (a group of Europeans headquartered

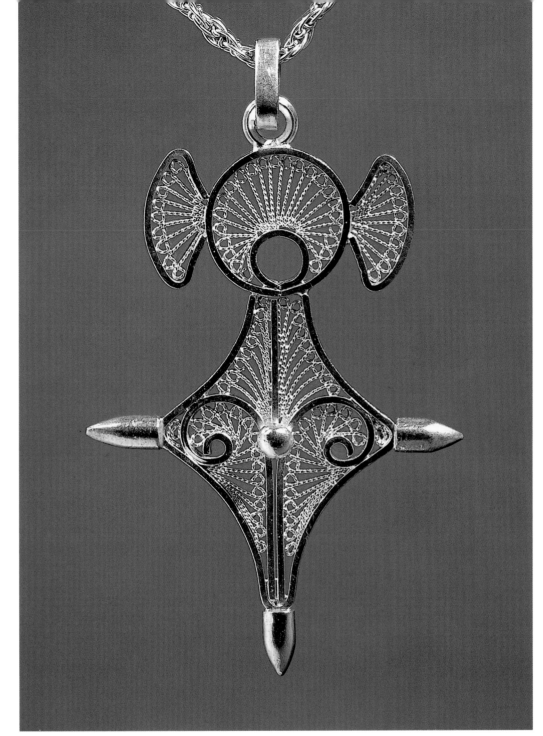

9.12
Cross of Agadez

Darou Samu
Wolof
Dakar, Senegal
Gold
5.4 x 3.2 cm
Private Collection

9.13
**Cross of Agadez with *chi wara*
motifs**

Fulbe
Bamako, Mali
Silver
6.3 x 3.5 x 0.7 cm
UCLA Fowler Museum
X97.17.46

9.14
Filigree cross of Agadez with chain

Fulbe
Bamako, Mali
Silver
Pendant: 7.5 x 4.2 cm
UCLA Fowler Museum
X97.17.45a,b

in Paris who share a strong interest in the Sahara) blended a cross of Agadez with a Tuareg camel saddle to form a symbol for their organization (fig. 9.15). For the French military involved in keeping its colonies under the control in the years preceding independence, the cross of Agadez became the basis for the badge of the 15th Compagnie Saharienne Portée, for the Compagnie Méhariste du Tidikelt—Hoggar, and for the Centre Saharien d'Expérimentations Militaires (CSEM), which tested the French atomic bomb in the Sahara. The United Nations has used the *tenaghalt*, decorated with enamel, as the badge of UN military observers in MINURSO (The United Nations Mission for the Referendum in Western Sahara).[8]

The government of the Republic of Niger uses the cross of Agadez as the centerpiece for the National Order of Niger pendant and for the Order of Academic Palms.[9] The cross also appeared on the cover of the 1989 telephone book for the Republic of Niger, as part of insignia for government projects, on postage stamps (fig. 9.16), and in currency designs (Loughran 1996, figs. 212, 211, 209).

9.15

Key chain and pin

La Rahla—Amicale des Sahariens
Paris, France
Metal
Key chain: 3.5 x 11.4 x 0.3 cm;
Pin: 1.9 x 2.5 x 1.3 cm
Private Collection

9.16

**Postage stamp issued by the
Republic of Niger featuring the
cross of Agadez**

Niger
Paper, ink, glue
2.54 x 1.9 cm
Private Collection

9.17

Top left, *Le monde d' Hermès* (1995,
2: 45) featuring a belt with a cross
of Agadez and assorted other adver-
tisements for Tuareg jewelry.

Photograph by M. Lee Fatherree.

The Cross of Agadez as an African Symbol

The cross of Agadez contines to be used variety of ways; it is adapted to novel forms and is manufactured in new materials. In a Web search conducted in May 2004, Seligman located over one hundred sites offering the cross of Agadez for sale, made by Tuareg and by non-Tuareg alike. In 1998 the Web site of jeweler Michael Babinski opened with an image of a Tuareg-made cross of Agadez. The artist commented on the home page: "People sometimes ask 'where do you get your ideas for jewelry?' I steal them, of course." The site then proceeded to show how Babinski had transformed the cross of Agadez into a great variety of contemporary pendants with jewels, gold, moonstones, and so forth.

Since 1993 Hermès, the famed French couture house, has featured Tuareg leather and jewelry designs in numerous publications advertising its products and has sold silver items produced by the *inadan* of A l'Atelier (see chapter 10 of this volume) in Agadez. The firm's full-color magazine *Le monde d'Hermès* (1995, 2: 45) features a woman's alligator skin belt with a silver buckle in the shape of the cross of Agadez (fig. 9.17).

The cross of Agadez was executed in gold using a filigree technique by Wolof and Malimbe jewelers in the 1950s or 1960s and is now ubiquitous in jewelry stores and markets throughout West and Central Africa, where it is sometimes referred to as the *croix du sud*. From Paris, to Florence, to New York, as well as on the Internet, the cross of Agadez has become increasingly common.[10] In 1996 Loughran noted that "most recently, the manufacture of Agadez crosses has moved across political boundaries: the crosses are now being manufactured by local, 'non-Tuareg' jewelers in Florence, Italy; in Denpasar, Bali; and in Tangiers, Morocco.... The Agadez cross form has passed into the domain of popular culture" (1996, 383). Seligman photographed and purchased two Tuareg style crosses made in Ubud, Bali, in August of 2004 (fig. 9.18a,b). Today, in the world of popular culture, there are a few recognizable designs that seem to instantly say "Africa." These would include the *chi wara* antelope headdress of Mali, the bronze *oba* heads from Benin, Nigeria, the Coptic crosses of Ethiopia, the *kente* cloth of the Asante people of Ghana and Togo, and the cross of Agadez.

The cross of Agadez has certainly not yielded up its secrets or provided a key to its past. Within the corpus of Tuareg jewelry, the cross forms—and that of Agadez in particular—have always held a special appeal and been eagerly sought after. During the French colonial era the crosses (or pendants) worn in certain areas acquired the names of those locales (Creyaufmüller 1983, 60). These were the principal types of crosses or pendants included in early European collections. What remains an enigma is why the cross of Agadez has attracted so much attention as opposed to the *talhakimt* or other pendants. What has made this pendant such an important visual constant over time? Is it the name? The shape? Is it an association with a region that has always drawn seekers of adventure and exotica? In a world burdened with logos, it seems ironic that the cross of Agadez has demonstrated such longevity.

The *inadan* have been pivotal in perpetuating the simplicity and beauty of the cross of Agadez and its tradition, even if many people around the world believe it to originate in Bali or Morocco (Loughran 1996, 383, 387). This symbol and international recognition of it have become increasingly important for the Tuareg as they strive to maintain their identity in the increasingly globalized world.

Ə

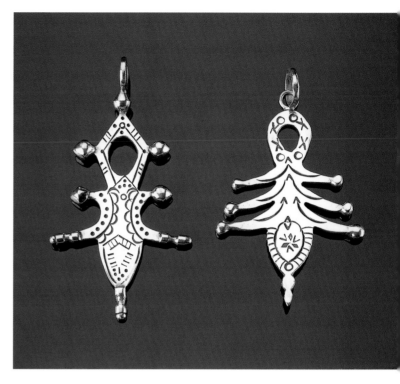

9.18a,b

a. Interpretation of Tuareg cross, 2004
Wayan Sutedja
Ubud, Bali, Indonesia
Silver
5.7 x 3.2 x 0.6 cm
Private Collection

b. Interpretation of Tuareg cross, 2004
Cok Gunk
Ubud, Bali, Indonesia
Silver
5.7 x 3.2 x 0.6 cm
Private Collection

These two crosses were purchased in Ubud, Bali. The fact that the cross of Agadez, as well as other Tuareg cross forms, has become a constant visual motif in African countries is not surprising. Its basic design is now used as a decorative element in items such as teaspoons, letter openers, and so forth. With increased globalization, however, the cross has acquired new nationalities and nomenclatures and has passed into the domain of popular culture. These two cross forms are very similar to Tuareg crosses. Their engraved decorations however, have a distinctly Eastern imprint.

AFRICAN SYMBOLS
IN THE LARGER WORLD

Today many African artists are actively creating new objects, new fashions, new works of art, new music, new architecture, and new cuisine. In short, they are engaged in the modern, global economy and are contributing their aesthetics, distinctive ideas, and creativity. During 2005, which was declared the "Year of Africa" by the European Union, African products, including works of art, were marketed extensively in Europe, and as a consequence many new fusions and collaborations resulted and were promoted.

Given increased exposure and interchange, a key dilemma facing the Tuareg, as well as many other groups of people around the world, is how to benefit from this attention without losing their identity. What will happen as Tuareg lifeways and art continue to be integrated into a vast global industry of cultural commodification? Will all that remains be the well-known form of the cross of Agadez and certain geometric designs of unknown meaning? Or will Tuareg culture and aesthetics remain strong among the Kel Tamasheq as they move into the future?

T.K.S.

J.1a,b (OPPOSITE, TOP)

a. Purse lock
A l'Atelier guild for Hermès
Tuareg
Agadez, Niger
Silver
3.2 x 2.5 cm
Cantor Arts Center
2001.208

b. Purse lock
A l'Atelier guild for Hermès
Tuareg
Agadez, Niger
Silver
2.5 x 2.5 cm
Cantor Arts Center
2001.209

J.2a,b (OPPOSITE, BOTTOM)

a. Bracelet
A l'Atelier guild for Exote,
Alison Mezey, designer
Tuareg
Agadez, Niger
Silver
Diam: 7 cm
Private Collection

b. Ring
A l'Atelier guild for Exote,
Alison Mezey, designer
Tuareg
Agadez, Niger
Silver
Diam: 2.9 cm
Private Collection

J.3 (ABOVE)

Belt buckle set

A l'Atelier guild for Hermès
Tuareg
Agadez, Niger
Silver
Buckle: 5 x 7 x 1.3 cm;
Each ornament: 4.8 x 12.7 cm
Private Collection

J.4
Bracelet

Madi Fode
Tuareg, Kel Ewey
Niamey, Niger
Ebony, silver
Diam: 3.2 cm
UCLA Fowler Museum
X97.17.47

This is a recent bracelet style using
imported ebony overlaid with
engraved silver.

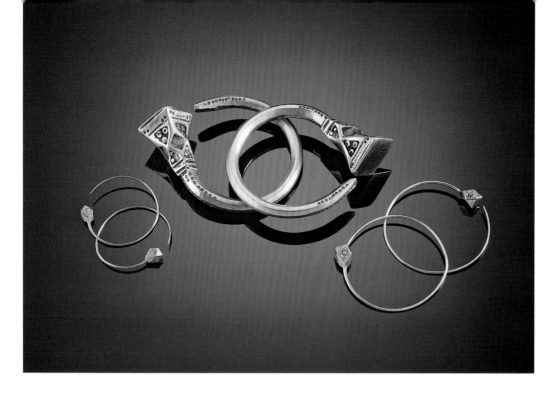

J.5a–c

Earrings (*tizabaten*)

Saidi Oumba
Tuareg, Kel Ewey
Niger
Silver (a & b), gold (c)
Diam. (each) a. 3.8 cm;
b. 6.4 cm; c. 2.9 cm
Private Collection

These earrings are not included in the exhibition and are shown here to illustrate the development of earrings designed for tourists who do not have ear piercings that allow for the large "traditional" earrings to be worn. The smaller pairs in silver and gold are miniature versions of the *tizabaten* worn by Tuareg women.

J.6

Necklace and pendant

Kammo Oumana
Tuareg, Kel Ewey
Niamey, Niger
Silver, stone
L (of necklace and pendant) 30.5 cm;
W (of pendant): 3.8 cm
Private Collection

This new design is based upon the stone *talhakimt* pendant (see fig. 9.10), which is here almost completely covered in silver.

J.7

Scarves with Tuareg motifs

Hermès
Paris, France
Silk
Each: 88.9 x 88.9 cm
Private Collection

The names of these Tuareg-inspired printed designs are *Cuirs du désert* (Desert Leathers), *Cuirs du désert II* (Desert Leathers II); *Parures des sables* (Jewels of the Sands).

J.8a–f

a. Red Handbag (*tissikit*)
Tuareg/French
Agadez/Paris
Leather, Silver
31.8 x 21 x 14 cm
Conservatory of the Hermès Creations, Paris

b. Blue Handbag (*kourboubou*)
Tuareg/French
Agadez/Paris
Leather, silver
15.9 x 23.2 x 6 cm
Conservatory of the Hermès Creations, Paris

c. Cup (*tiffinjart*)
Tuareg/French
Agadez/Paris
Silver
H: 7.3 cm; Diam: 7.3 cm
Conservatory of the Hermès Creations, Paris

d. Belt and buckle
Tuareg/French
Agadez/Paris
Leather, silver
Belt: 92.4 x 3.5 cm;
Buckle: 4.8 x 6 cm
Hermès Paris Creations

e. Bracelet (*iwill*)
Tuareg/French
Agadez/Paris
Leather, silver
Bracelet: 27 x 2.5 cm;
Buckle: 1.6 x 1.6 cm
Hermès Paris Creations

f. Necklace (*houmeissa*)
Tuareg/French
Agadez/Paris
Leather, silver
Cord: 63.5 cm; Pendant: 5 x 6 cm
Hermès Paris Creations

The silver pieces on these Hermès products were made by A l'Atelier in Agadez as specific commissions with precise specifications determined by Hermès. The engraved surface patterns are unique and designed by the *enad* who made the piece. Upon completion the silver pieces were shipped from Agadez to Paris where the finished products were assembled. These products were given names by Hermès derived from Tamasheq and were available for purchase only in Hermès stores.

10

A L'ATELIER

Jean-Yves Brizot

The workshop resonates with a breath that I could imagine nowhere else. It is the breath of the bellows, their hypnotic rhythm infusing the vibration of fire—a heart of molten orange beating the tempo of creation—while the floor shakes as if to keep our free and creative abilities awake. Inspiration is dictated by the heavy, animated breath of this forge, like a living being with the telluric respiration of a giant thaumaturge.

There is magic as well in the invocation to the gods of fire and earth, for whom the blacksmith is our intercessor and our guard against the formidable fury they may unleash. Here the memory of a universal Vulcan that preceded the gods, preceded even the thought of their names, comes alive.

There is, too, the rhythm of hammers on anvils that occasionally fades beneath the chant of voices raised in unison; it breaks off in one place only to strike up anew in another, where the artisans sleep, dreaming of forms yet to come, their busy hands skillful even in dreams. Then there is the apprentice who, dozing beside his master—his body exhausted from leaning over the piece that is to be—suddenly takes flight like a dervish. He becomes a whirlwind rushing across the work space, a laugh that bursts forth and cuts through the fear of those beings to whom he will give birth, confronting the taboo of giving form to the formless, the immaterial—a migratory golem that has escaped the cold, awaiting the new soul he will glean from the heat of the sands tirelessly melted by the fires of the forge.

A Tuareg blacksmith who wishes to give anthropomorphic or zoomorphic form to an object must first receive the express dispensation of the marabouts. Without this, fabricating any likeness of the living is forbidden, and anyone who does so must, from that day on, take full charge of his creation, bearing it with him even into the otherworld of the Muslim paradise. There the representations become incarnate and ascribe to their creator the responsibility for each of their acts, each of their thoughts.

Every imitator of God's work thus becomes an evil demiurge, bringing disorder to his luminous order. And each of the delinquent creatures he has formed becomes responsible for this by a magical extension of the ancient spirit worship that survives to this day and was normalized on contact with Islam, which it in turn has penetrated. This syncretistic trend has merged archaic beliefs with a new faith that respects the dogma as well as its own origins.

And though one may carve, file, and cut as if into flesh, there is a freedom that returns with each object produced, posing ever more forcefully the primordial question of the

10.1
Fire and sparks in a forge.
Photograph by Jean-Yves Brizot, Agadez, Niger, 1999-2000.

relation of man to matter, to creation, and to his gods. The luminous evanescence of that very object that one strives to grasp, which already takes on an entire life of its own, is made of dedicated work, of that time wrested from an all-consuming contemplation, or from those other long hours normally spent at tea or at the pleasant conversation so dear to the Saharans.

The workshop is also the unity of thoughts that, amid the concentration on their shared labor, their intermingled work, suddenly realize that they are no longer alone. Like the rhythm of the hammers on the anvils, these thoughts rise up in a single voice to celebrate the harmony of the unique being, of its art of being, even more than its art of making.

It is that leisurely hum of street noise, in mocking counterpoint to the intense concentration on the creation of forms. It is the garden just outside the door of the workshop, which the wind suddenly animates, rustling through the orange trees and setting birds in flight, disrupting the peace of these idle, restless witnesses, and catching lizards momentarily off guard, distracting them from their normally attentive saurian tranquillity. It is, moreover, this outside and inside, amid the intensity of their confrontation, that make the workshop a place like no other, through which the desire of a shared creation wafts, ceaselessly renewed, as if brought to life. There is, too, the breath of that spirit that embraces all things, the breath that calls it back to that which it once was and once more shall be, in the blaze of its realized present. And finally, it is the spirit magnified, inflated with the idea of its realization, undeniably concrete and proud.

Here the memory of the elders abides and always will. From them comes the heritage of word, gesture, and skill: "Our children are devils," they say, astounded by the knowledge bequeathed to them, a knowledge that the elders themselves had received from their own fathers gradually, through learned initiations, under the very same tents or shelters that harbor this work today. Their children have brilliantly seized on this knowledge to lead it toward a sort of aesthetic ideal, one which they sometimes find themselves thinking—as if with regret—could be in vain.

What a long way they have come from form as a talisman worn to ward off death, to exorcise the evil magic of the other, to that magnified form that they hold up as a mirror of themselves. A mirror that reflects them after they have seen themselves in it, their every gesture incarnate in this matter that they tame and imprison in their skillful snare of subtle and precise movements.

The workshop is, finally, that place where matter develops relations that no matter could degrade. Of course, we, the artisans here, are perpetually happy to share, by the grace of the completed objects, in this matter that we have transformed and which makes of us creators whose sole ambition is to realize all our dreams attached to this matter, all our dreams devoted to time.

Within their community the *inadan* are those who are feared, scoffed at, and mocked, those whom you'll be advised, sometimes even still, not to trust, for they must bear the weight of their skill in transforming matter, in making it other, and suffer the eternal suspicion of being able to do the same with any words or with any person. They also fill the role of a foil or mirror in the complex organization of Tuareg society.

It is they, however, who, in the secrecy of their forge and their fire, faithful to the tradition that makes them a sort of brotherhood of "Saharan alchemists," are the keepers of the secrets and traditions of the whole community. Nothing can be had without them, from tools to weapons, from amulets to everyday objects. Their presence is felt at every moment, trivial or critical, of people's lives, thanks to their numerous objects that fill the needs of all.

No marriage, baptism, or any other rite marking essential life passages takes place without the blacksmiths' mediation between the netherworld—the land of the spirits, of the jinn—and the world of men. They carry out this role with a lightness that is sometimes capricious but always animated, always clairvoyant.

The blacksmiths have their own founding myths to explain the separation of the different guilds to which they belong by virtue of their station, and also their origin, which they link, out of bravado, and perhaps shards of memory, to the highest ancient civilizations. Here they show their creativity, reappropriating language, which their society in its pyramidal structure had confiscated from them, with an inexhaustible inventiveness that makes fun of others but also of themselves.

Perhaps that is the true magic—that universe so near and yet so far, in which the ties formed between man and matter break free of the burden of their supposedly insurmountable difference. It is a light that radiates from the eyes of he who creates, as well as from the object over which it passes, thereby leaving a visible trace of its most mysterious glimmers, the ones most evocative not only to the men but also to the material that surrounds them, from which they have been born...together with the light and the fire.

冒

NOTES TO THE TEXT

Chapter 1 (Seligman)
This is intended as a very general introduction to Tuareg history and social, political, and economic systems that will provide a context for the more in-depth essays that follow, focusing on Tuareg art and artists. For an excellent and detailed description of Tuareg ethnography in English, see Nicolaisen, *Ecology and Culture of the Pastoral Tuareg* (1963) and Nicolaisen and Nicolaisen *The Pastoral Tuareg: Ecology, Culture, and Society* (1997). A larger body of literature exists in French; see especially Bernus. I am indebted to these sources for much of the information in this introduction.

1. See Lhote (1959) for more information on the most-studied and illustrated group of central Saharan rock paintings and petroglyphs.
2. The origin of the word "Tuareg" may have come from the name of the group of people known as the Targa, living in the area of the Sahara known in Arabic as the Fezzan. Some sources think Tuareg is an Arabic word meaning "abandoned of God" or "abandoner of the faith."
3. A "cross cousin" is the child of the mother's brother or the father's sister.

Chapter 2 (Castelli Gattinara)
This essay was translated from the Italian by Kristyne Loughran.

1. The word *amenokal* comes from *am* (to own, the owner) and *akal* (country). It is used to designate the head of a confederation of Tuareg groups. The *amenokal* was chosen from an aristocratic and warrior family. The nomination had to be approved by all the heads of groups. In the past, the *amenokal* had to insure the protection of the confederation and could exercise his authority (which extended to the judiciary) over a specific territory. Every group had to give him an annual tribute including animals or foodstuffs; caravans had to pay a right of passage; and farmers had to yield a percentage of their produce. The French wanted to reduce the power exercised by the *amenokal* by naming some known and accepted chiefs for smaller groups. These chiefs are still in power and also served as go-betweens for the Tuareg and the group officially in power—French until 1960 and African after that.
2. The word *rezzu* is of Arabic origin (from the Maghreb) and alludes to the group of armed men who are making the raid, as well as the raid itself. Saint-Exupéry in *Courrier Sud* (1929, 222) says: "A *rezzu* of three hundred guns arrived secretly from the north, appeared from the east and massacred a caravan." These undertakings do not resemble the Western concept of a raid, even if certain characteristics are similar. A *rezzu* was usually retaliated with a counter-*rezzu*, the group and the camp that were attacked and robbed of their animals organized another expedition against their attackers.
3. The Tuareg use a script that is called Tifinar. According to Prasse (1972, 149), the name derives from the Greek term *phoinikos*, which referred to the Phoenicians; whereas Rinn (1889, 6) interprets it analytically as "that which was sent by God the creator." This script includes twenty-four signs and an indefinite number of composite signs. Its origin is unknown. It shares some letters with the Phoenician alphabet, which in turn are also present in some Libyan inscriptions of the last centuries BCE. Other signs share characteristics of the cuneiform alphabet. The Tuareg use Tifinar to write everything of a transitory and temporary nature such as a love message, an appointment, a letter, a shopping list. Everything that is intended to last—history, tradition, cultural patrimony, norms—is transmitted orally. The Tuareg also often use Tifinar signs as ornamental elements. For example, they might appear as decoration on a travel bag, a camel saddle, or a leather box containing little glasses for tea. Tifinar is also used by smiths in the camp to sign bracelets, pendants, or any piece of silver jewelry.
4. The wars conducted by the Tuareg must not be confused with the *rezzu* (see note 2, above). The first wars were conducted to take over a particular territory, to subordinate other groups, to defend themselves from invasions and from outside attacks. *Rezzia* (pl. of *rezzu*), on the other hand, as we have seen, were ventures organized with youthful spirit, used to demonstrate one's own worth, and, most importantly, to refurbish the group with animals and slaves.
5. Tuareg men wear a large tunic, which reaches to the ground and covers the arms. When they fight, the men hitch up their garments to promote freedom of movement. A long veil (*tagulmust*) is wound around the head many times so that the face is hidden and only the eyes are visible. It is important that a warrior not be easily recognized so that the enemy may not know exactly whom he is fighting.
6. Toubou are nomadic peoples with dark skin whose origins are uncertain but probably include Ethiopian influences. They largely intermarried with Sudanese groups. They live in the Tibesti region in Chad and enter Niger toward the oasis of Kawar where they have often provoked fights with Tuareg groups and caravans.
7. The original Tamasheq transcription of these verses has been lost.
8. Tuareg men and women often dress their hair in long braids.
9. Modibo Keita was the president of Mali and belonged to an ethnic group whose members in the past had been enslaved by the Tuareg.
10. The Ifoghas are an important Tuareg confederation in Mali.
11. This is an aspect of feminine beauty, charm, and appeal.
12. For the Tuareg, a woman must be fat to be beautiful. This is evidence of her husband's wealth.
13. A marabout is a religious man, student of the sacred Islamic scriptures. In the community he functions like a priest.
14. The word "Tenere" means the "desert of only sand."
15. The original Tamasheq transcription of these verses has been lost.
16. "Buzu" and "Bella" are words used by Hausa or Djerma groups to refer to ex-slaves who still work for their masters or are organized in their own camps. This group is completely assimilated into Tuareg groups, and its members follow Tuareg habits, values, and social rules.
17. Agadez is a large oasis town in Niger on the edge of the Tenere.
18. This is the language spoken by the Tuareg. It is a Berber language with probable Phoenician origins (see chapter 1 of this volume).
19. The Sahel (or the shore of the desert), which is inhabited by the Tuareg, has a short rainy season in July and August. These rains, which are few and random, allow the grass to grow and turn an immense expanse of the desert into a pasture.
20. The Fulbe, who are also called the Peul or Wodabe, are nomadic herdsmen and live in continuous migration in the same territories that are inhabited by the Tuareg. There is mutual respect between the two groups and rarely any cause for friction.
21. *Imzad* literally means "hair," and, by extension, the violin (the string of this musical instrument is made of horsehair). It is a monochord violin, made with half of a sun-dried gourd, onto which a very thin skin is attached with wooden nails. In the center there is a sound hole. Then a wooden handle is attached. The *imzad* is only played by women, and its playing is an art form. A mother teaches her daughter to appreciate the profound beauty of a sound that may seem monodic to someone whose hasty ear was educated in the polyphonic culture of the West. There are a series of tones that point to memories that can only be appreciated by those who are familiar with these rhythms. The *imzad* is a noble and elegant instrument. It is played during every prominent occasion, and for men it evokes amorous encounters. (See chapter 5 of this volume.)

Chapter 3 (ag Ewangaye)
This essay was translated from the French by Rose Vekony.

1. The term "Amazigh" (free people) refers to the Tuareg people. The word "Tuareg" has been used and abused by the Western world. It was originally derived from the word "Attuarikk," which was used by Arab historians in the past to refer to us. We are, therefore, known in the West through the lens of Arab literature. We call ourselves Kel Tamasheq (those who speak Tamasheq). We are a nation in all aspects of the term,

strongly identified by our common language and all other characteristics based on liberty and nobility. The term "Amazigh" is used primarily among Kel Tamasheq (or Tuareg) militants in the Tamazagha (Amazigh identity) cause who inhabit the Maghreb and countries of the Sahel. Amazigh is an old term that we are reviving as we battle to recover our identity and the requisite political power for our survival as a people. Our survival is a concern of the entire Maghreb (Morocco, Algeria, Tunisia), the Makrech (Libya), and the three countries of the Sahel (Mali, Niger, and Burkina Faso).

2. This study was largely inspired by (although it occasionally departs from) the works of: Hélène Claudot-Hawad, anthropologist, CNRS (Centre national de la recherche scientifique, France); Hawad, Tuareg philosopher, writer, and calligrapher (France); and Dominique Casajus, researcher, CNRS (France). Since it is intended for the general reader, I have tried to be as succinct as possible. The essay will later be incorporated into a more detailed scholarly study for the good of the Tuareg people, whose history, civilization, and culture are ill served by the sometimes fanciful writings of specialists who make no effort to carry out fully objective research, preferring an approach that deforms the Tuareg in the prism of their own culture. A new generation of Tuareg scholars is emerging. Their mission will be to round out all that has been said or written about us. They are capable of this task, but it will not succeed without the understanding of researchers who are already established and known in this area.

3. At the time of this writing the rate of exchange was approximately five hundred CFAF to one US dollar.

Chapter 4 (Bernus)
This essay was translated from the French by Rose Vekony.

1. The names of Tuareg languages always take the feminine form of the name of the group that speaks them. Hence *enad*, yields *tenet*.

Chapter 5 (Borel)
This essay was translated from the French by Rose Vekony.

1. This poses a dilemma for researchers who hope to identify a melody by humming it for their informants for they can easily provoke laughter and ridicule; and once people no longer take them seriously, they lose credibility.

2. The Cure Salée (lit., salt cure) is a gathering of nomadic peoples after the rains in the grassy plains around In Gall. There the herds eat grasses with a high salt content. The Tuareg and Fulbe peoples hold festivals, feasts, and markets during this period.

Chapter 6 (Rasmussen)

1. The artisans in the multiethnic Saharan town of Agadez, Niger, who make sandals popular among Tuareg are called *mai takalmin* (derived from the Hausa term for these sandals). These artisans are generally not called by the Tamasheq term for Tuareg artisans, *inadan*, and some are not ethnic Tuareg. Rather, these sandal makers are often Agadezian, a group of Songhai origins who today speak Hausa and Tamasheq. They are considered distinct from the Tuareg *inadan*, in local viewpoint, because they do not work with fire and metals at the forge.

2. Nobles and artisans traditionally have practiced a client-patron relationship characterized by mutual rights, obligations, and, ideally, joking relationships. There are vestiges of this relationship in the countryside today, where artisans sing praise songs at weddings and name days celebrated by their noble patrons; help arrange their marriages; and manufacture jewelry, tools, and weapons for them. In return, nobles are supposed to provide artisans with gifts and remuneration of food and cash. These relationships are now under some stress, however, since many nobles are impoverished and can no longer support their attached artisans.

3. "Fashion Blitz in Sahara Desert Goes against the Grain of Niger." *Houston Chronicle*, November 14, 1998.

Chapter 7 (Loughran)
The information in this chapter is based on data that I collected during field research conducted in the Republic of Niger from 1990 to 1991. I would like to acknowledge the support of a Fulbright-Hays Doctoral Dissertation Research Abroad Grant. I wish to thank the informants I worked with while I was in Niger and Thomas Seligman for his comments and suggestions. Most of my field interviews were conducted in French, and the translations are mine.

1. See for example, Arkell (1935a, 1935b), Barth ([1857] 1965), de Zeltner (1914), Duveyrier ([1864] 1973), Eudel (1902), Foley (1930), Palmer (1936), Rodd (1926), and Steinilber-Oberlin (1934).

2. In 1864 Duveyrier described women wearing rings, glass or silver bracelets, and some glass beads (Duveyrier [1864] 1973, 407-8). In the 1930s Dr. Foley, who traveled in the Ahaggar region of Algeria, described the leather amulets men and women wore hanging on braided leather strands. Men also wore stone bracelets on both of their upper arms. He noted, however, that women seemed to wear greater amounts of jewelry than men.

3. For more information on the manufacturing techniques and materials used by *inadan*, see Loughran (1995).

4. Creyaufmüller (1983, 60) has suggested that the naming of crosses after geographical regions most probably began in the colonial era.

5. *Elkiss* (pl., *elkizan*) bracelets are made of solid silver and are considered highly desirable items. The polyhedral end knobs are incised with triangles, squares, and geometric motifs. The word *elkiss* means "wrist."

6. Unless otherwise indicated, all personal communications date to my 1990-1991 stay in Niger. As noted above, most interviews were conducted in French, and the translations are mine.

7. According to Rasmussen, "In Tuareg art the way things move is more important than their physiognomy.... Artistic form needs to be set in motion to be complete" (1994, 91-92).

8. *Aleshu* cloth is a shiny cotton cloth dyed with indigo.

9. Sieber (1972, 12) draws attention to the importance of noise as it relates to the wearing of jewelry: "African attitudes toward the accouterments of rank seem to declare themselves in three views: first, prestige dress must be conspicuous. Second, it may announce itself with sound. Third, it is often additive. Thus prestige may declare itself by a conspicuously visible and audible accumulation of ornament."

10. According to Rodd (1926, 285-86): "No man among the Tuareg will be seen who does not wear one or more arm rings, usually above the elbow and upon either or both arms.... The flat rings seem to be very important, for they are passed on from father to son. They are often mended with riveted brass plates if they happen to have been broken, and sometimes bear inscriptions, for the most part only names, in Tifinar." Nicolas (1950, 117) relates the *iwuki* are used both as adornment and as weapons.

11. An informant, Liliane, also called the head knot *sokolo* (personal communication Niamey).

12. The spelling of the Tamasheq words is taken from Casajus in this instance.

13. Bernus (1981, 141-56) notes that in the case of divorce, the time of isolation is three months and ten days, and the woman's next husband cuts the white cord from her neck.

14. Nicolaisen (1961, 133), notes the Tuareg believe *tehot* stems from jealousy and envy.

15. The word "Bella" is a Songhai term used for autonomous groups of former servile classes (Bernus 2001, 67).

16. See Gouletquer (1992) for the *collier d'Agadez*, which symbolizes the town and its neighborhoods in relation to the sultan's palace. Dieterlen and Ligers (1972) wrote an article on the symbology of a contrasting group of cross shapes and pendants from Mali, and Rodd (1926), Dudot

(1955), Gabus (1982), and many others have discussed the cross types and typologies and origins.

17. *Khomessa* amulets are made of at least five (and up to thirteen) faceted diamond shapes that are attached to one another and then fixed on a leather or silver base.

18. Nicolaisen (1961, 129) reports that shells are generally used as protection against the evil eye and illnesses.

19. Arkell (1935a, 298) notes that "the red color of carnelian has always been responsible for the belief that it possesses the magic property of being good for the blood and so promoting fertility."

20. Kel Esuf means "people of the void, of the ground." These are spirits and are thought to be responsible for unusual occurrences (Nicolas 1950, 242–49).

21. Eudel (1902, 524) also mentions that since the Tuareg are nomads, the Tahegart women buy their jewelry in the oases of In Salah, El-Golea, and Touat. His description includes necklaces, bracelets, earrings, and rings, and he states that when pieces are made of gold, they are usually larger than the silver ones, especially when he refers to earrings, "when they are in gold, the diameter is even larger," and to bracelets, "in gold, it is flat, 4 to 5 cm wide."

    Many authors, when mentioning Tuareg jewelry, make a point of noting that silver is worn by the Tuareg because they are Islamized and because they believe it brings happiness and good fortune to the wearer (Rasmussen 1987, 13; Gabus 1958, 48; Lhote 1984, 160). Silver jewelry traditions are readily related to Berber and nomadic peoples, and to those who live in rural environments. In addition to the classical correlation is the belief that: rural + traditional = silver. This same assertion was made to me quite often in the field and seemed plausible enough, though Camps-Fabrer suggests the preference for silver in Kabylie, Algeria, is due to both the taste and the rural customs known all over Algeria and in Morocco (Camps-Fabrer 1990, 21). Women are said not to like gold jewelry because this material is too similar to brass. I do not believe, however, that the rejection of gold in the rural milieu should be attributed to the impure nature ascribed to this metal by the commentators on the Koran, since urban dwellers prefer gold to silver. Realistically, the reason for the preponderance of silver in a rural milieu is probably because it is less expensive than gold.

22. The *elgettara* beads, illustrated in Balout (1959), are said to have been manufactured in the Sudan, possibly of elephant or hippopotamus teeth, which are considered very precious in the Ahaggar because they are rare.

23. When I was at the Cure Salée, I met a young woman who had divorced a year before and who was constantly changing clothes and jewelry in the hopes of attracting another suitor. One afternoon, as she left the concession we were staying in, I asked her where she was going, and she turned laughing and said: "You do your research. I am going to do my research now" (personal communication, In Gall).

24. The Cure Salée is the French expression for "salt cure." Its purpose is to give mineral salts to the herds. During the Cure Salée people converge on the plains west of Agadez from distant regions, and celebrations are held.

25. One young man in particular changed from one brightly colored damask ensemble to another and finally got my attention when he decided to wash his veil. It dried in ten minutes.

26. Alphadi is a fashion designer who lives and works in Niamey. He created FIMA (Festival international de la mode africaine) to draw attention to African fashion designers and jewelers. The first FIMA event was held near Agadez. It was a big media event, and many European fashion designers attended and presented their own designs.

27. One afternoon Azara took great pains to show me a jewelry catalog. When I visited Ahanti's workshop, his principal request was that I send him jewelry catalogs.

28. For example, the necklaces made of *ezmaman* beads are worn with the heavy polyhedral end-knob bracelets but don't have matching earrings or rings.

29. Ahanti was the favorite goldsmith in Agadez when I was there in 1991.

30. He was trained by his father and manufactured many items such as *negneg* beads, the *ezmaman* necklaces, and little *chatchats*.

31. Gabus (1958, 31) remarks that decorative aspects of Saharan art forms recall illuminated manuscripts because of their precision and elegance.

32. The photographs I am referring to are a photo archive I prepared prior to doing fieldwork. Many of the photographed items are objects that were collected in the early part of the twentieth century and are now in museum collections. The archive also included field photographs from published sources.

Chapter 8 (Seligman)

1. Personal communication from Andi Ouhoulou, translated from Tamasheq, the language of the Tuareg, into French by her oldest son, Salah Saidi, 2001. All translations from the French are mine.

2. The Aïr is the region around the Aïr Mountains in north central Niger, to the north of the major trading center of Agadez.

3. I first briefly met Saidi Oumba and Andi Ouhoulou in 1971 on my initial trip to northern Niger. I returned in 1979 to conduct the first of many extended periods of field research (including stays in 1980, 1981, 1984, 1997, 2000, 2001, and 2004) in the Tuareg regions of Niger, Mali, and Algeria. The role of the *inadan*, including Saidi, Andi, and their extended families in particular, became the center of much of this investigation.

4. Niger, a former French colony, became an independent country in 1960.

5. See Bernus (chapter 4 of this volume) for a broader discussion of the *inadan* within Tuareg social hierarchies. See Nicolaisen (1963) for a complete anthropological description of the Tuareg. Also see Gabus (1971) for more detail on the objects made and used by the Tuareg.

6. Until quite recently the Western perspective on African societies has largely valued the idea of "tradition," while simultaneously valorizing and being repulsed by the "exotic" or "primitive." Hence much twentieth-century literature on the Tuareg paid scant attention to the *inadan*, and those researchers who did (e.g., Gardi 1969) regarded them as makers of inherited object types, design patterns, and techniques of manufacture. Only in the last three decades has there been an attempt to understand the creative aspects of the traditional artisan/artist throughout Africa, and this shift has barely affected the literature on the Tuareg (see Loughran 1996).

7. Go to your favorite computer search engine and type in "Tuareg art" or "Tuareg jewelry" to see this global reach.

8. As will be explained later, male artists (*inadan*) are the ones on the edge of change as they directly engage the global marketplace and often have the capacity to speak several languages (including French, German, and English) and to command most of the financial assets. The women (*tinadan*), in addition to their work with leather, fiber, and hair plaiting, are responsible for the home. Today it is the *inadan* who travel and sell to a wide audience; the *tinadan*, who are socially equal to the men in many aspects (which is somewhat unusual in African cultures), are more limited in commercial interaction and potential.

9. It is common among *inadan* to "brag" about the position, patronage, and creativity of their families. While it is clear that Saidi's family were important *inadan*, there were also other *inadan* families of prominence, such as the Koumama family. As there was always competition for patronage and sales in the towns, telling people of your family's prominence was seen as a good business practice.

10. Marabout is the commonly used Arabic term for an Islamic teacher or holy man.

11. Silver jewelry is a form of portable wealth for the Tuareg who often sell or trade it when necessary or desirable. The droughts of this period created a huge need for money, and many Tuareg sold jewelry, often via the *inadan* of their confederation.

12. Tamasheq is a Berber language spoken in a variety of dialects among the Tuareg of Algeria, Niger, Mali, and Burkina Faso. Hausa is a widely

spoken language of the Hausa people of northern Nigeria and southern Niger. It has now become the major trade language spoken throughout most of Niger and by almost all Tuareg living in Agadez. The "official" language of Niger, however, is French. Interestingly, when I was traveling with Tuareg friends from Agadez they often ceased speaking Hausa among themselves after leaving the town when going into the Aïr or the Tenere Desert and conversed in Tamasheq. The retention of Tamasheq is today an important social and political issue for the Tuareg.

13. Mano Dayak and his French wife, Odile, had opened Temet Voyages in 1970. Mano, from a noble Tuareg family, went on to become one of the most prominent and internationally well-known leaders of the Tuareg. He was instrumental in the organization of the Tuareg rebellion of the 1990s and was mysteriously killed in a plane crash on December 15, 1995, while on his way to negotiate a peace accord with the government of the Republic of Niger.

14. The handle and hilt of a Tuareg sword (*takuba*) is always covered in leather, brass, and copper (and now sometimes silver) to allow the user to hold the sword, which has an iron blade, and not be polluted by this contact. The touch of iron is reserved for the adversary.

15. The Tuareg often refer to any person from North Africa as an "Arab." These "Arabs" are primarily traders or, in a few cases, Islamic scholars or teachers who have come from Libya to teach in Koranic schools.

16. According to Saidi, because he was new at goldwork, he kept the filings left over from the jewelry making as was common with silver. With gold's much greater worth, however, even a gram of filings has considerable value. I suspect, however, that Saidi knew what he was doing and justified it to the Algerian woman, the court, and to me with the analogy to silverwork. Saidi was jailed for a short time, and this caused a serious, if temporary, setback for him, as well as for his family and its reputation.

17. *Forgeron* is a French term for metalworker and is loosely used to refer to the *inadan* who make jewelry and leather. The blue color in the sign was understood to symbolize the "Blue People," or Tuareg.

18. "Hausazation" refers to the transformation of Agadez from a town of fewer than ten thousand in 1975 to over fifty thousand today. Because the city is the major trade and commercial center of northern Niger, many Hausa traders and some fundamentalist Islamic teachers have moved there. This has caused considerable stress on the environment, especially in terms of water supply and pollution. It has also had a negative impact in social terms with the Tuareg feeling constantly "squeezed" by Hausa language and culture, as well as the stricter form of Islam that the Hausa embrace. Some Tuareg also refer to this phenomenon as "Islamization," but in either case, it is a source of considerable concern for many noble Tuareg. The *inadan*, however, generally exploit the new market opportunities created by the enlarging population successfully, so that today many of the most well-to-do Tuareg are *inadan*, while the *imajeren* have in some cases slipped into poverty.

19. It is still very common among the Tuareg, and especially among the *inadan*, to marry cousins or other distant relatives.

20. As others point out in this volume, including Mohamed ag Ewangaye (see chapter 3), while most *inadan* might know the name for a design motif, as Saidi seems to, these motifs do not necessarily relate to any cosmological or spiritual dimension. They may be purely designs adopted from common things seen in the Tuareg world.

21. It is quite common for Tuareg to adopt another name for themselves, which makes it challenging to keep track of who is who. Tuareg custom is for children to be given a first name and to assume their father's first name as their last name. For instance, Saidi Oumba's first son Salah is properly known as Salah Saidi.

22. It has been estimated by a project funded by the government of Luxembourg—which aims to create marketing cooperatives for *inadan* in several Tuareg communities in the Aïr as well as Agadez and Niamey—that there are about fifteen thousand *inadan* working in and around Agadez out of a total population of about sixty thousand.

23. Elhadji Koumama regularly travels to the Bay Area to show and sell work with Elston's assistance, and they are building a joint compound in Agadez where Elston plans on spending more time. They have a Web site <www.tuaregjewelry.com>, which at this writing appears at the top of the page in a Google search for Tuareg jewelry. The Oumba family is not represented on the Web, nor do they have a Western business partner.

24. Bryan Bender, "U.S. Hunting Militants Along Algerian Border," *Boston Globe* (reprinted in *San Francisco Chronicle*, March 11, 2004). There were also news stories from the Associated Press by Todd Pitman and from the Pentagon by Alex Belida (February 25, 2004). See also Jeremy Keenan, "Americans and 'Bad People' in the Sahara-Sahel," *Review of African Political Economy* 31, no. 99 (2004): 130-39.

25. *Le Démocrate* (daily newspaper in Niger), February 19 through 25, 2004.

26. Perhaps the one definitively good piece of news in recent years, especially for rural Tuareg, was the above-average rainfall that occurred in 2003. This was severely reversed, however, in 2005 when the rains failed and locusts descended on the crops causing widespread famine in Niger.

27. I would like to point out that I have had the full understanding and permission of the family members whom I have described in this chapter. I also am fully aware that Saidi and his older sons take great pride in being portrayed in an exhibition and publication, as they hope (or assume) that it will be good for their reputation and hence for business. How this plays out remains to be seen.

Chapter 9 (Loughran and Seligman)

1. See, for example, Mauny (1954), Dudot (1955), Creyaufmüller (1983; 1984), Beltrami (1986), and others.

2. It is often referred to by its French name, *croix d'Agadez*.

3. According to Casajus (1987a, 298), *tenaghalt* means "that which flows, that which is made by fusion." *Tenaghalt tan Agadez* refers specifically to the cross of Agadez.

4. Darfur is in present-day eastern Chad and western Sudan and served as a refuge for some Tuareg who fled the Aïr as a result of the French colonial occupation and the French siege of Agadez in 1917. Thus Arkell's sources among the Tuareg had been displaced for almost a generation, which may have affected their knowledge of Aïr jewelry traditions.

5. The stones now come from German and Czechoslovakian factories.

6. Urvoy (1955) mentions that soft soapstone and slate were worked into amulets for men and others by Tuareg in the Aïr region.

7. Dieterlen and Ligers (1972), Creyaufmüller (1983; 1984), Rodd (1926), Arkell (1935a), and Göttler (personal communication, 1992). It has been suggested that crosses were designated by group names and different types were used by different social classes.

8. <www.manntaylor.com/Agades.html>.

9. <www.emering.com/medals/french/niger>.

10. See for instance <www.la-place-vendome.com>, or search for Tuareg jewelry or cross of Agadez.

Chapter 10 (Brizot)
This essay was translated from the French by Rose Vekony.

REFERENCES CITED

Abiodun, Rowland, Henry J. Drewal, and John Pemberton
1994   *The Yoruba Artist: New Theoretical Perspectives on African Arts.*
Washington, D.C.: Smithsonian Institution.

Abu-Lughod, Lila
2002   "Do Muslim Women Really Need Saving? Anthropological Reflections
on Cultural Relativism and Its Others." *American Anthropologist* 103,
no. 4 (September): 783-90.

Arkell, A. J.
1935a   "Forms of the Talhâkim and the Tanâghilit as Adopted from the
Tuareg by Various West African Tribes." *Journal of the Royal Anthropological Institute* 65: 307-10.
1935b   "Some Tuareg Ornaments and Their Connection with India." *Journal
of the Royal Anthropological Institute* 65: 297-306.
1939   "'T'alhâkimt' and 'Tanâghilt': Some North African Finger-Rings
Illustrating the Connexion of the Tuareg with the 'Ankh' of Ancient
Egypt." *Man* 39 (December): 184-201.

Balout, Lionel
1959   *Touareg Ahaggar.* Vol. 1 of *Collections ethnographiques.* Musée
d'ethnographie et de préhistoire du Bardo. Paris: Arts et Métiers
Graphiques.

Barnes, Ruth, and Joanne Eicher, eds.
1992   *Dress and Gender: Making and Meaning in Cultural Contexts.* New
York: Berg.

Barth, Heinrich
[1857] 1965   *Travels and Discoveries in North and Central Africa: Being a
Journal of an Expedition Undertaken under the Auspices of H.B.M.'s
Government in the Years 1849-1855.* London: F. Cass.
1859   *Travels and Discoveries in North and Central Africa: From the Journal
of an Expedition Undertaken under the Auspices of H.B.M.'s Government in the Years 1849-1855.* Philadelphia: J. W. Bradley.

Bary, Erwin de
1898   *Le dernier rapport d'un Européen sur Ghât et les Touareg de l'Aïr:
Journal de voyage d'Erwin de Bary, 1876-1877.* Translated and
annotated by Henri Schirmer. Paris: Librairie Fischbacher.

Beltrami, Vanni
1986   *La "croce" di Agadès: Simbolismi e paralleli di un tipico gioiello
saheliano.* Rome: Istituto italo-africano.

Benhazera, Maurice
1908   *Six mois chez les Touareg du Ahaggar.* Algiers: Adolphe Jourdan.

Bernus, Edmond
1981   *Touaregs nigériens: Unité culturelle et diversité régionale d'un peuple
pasteur.* Paris: Editions ORSTOM.
1983   "Place et rôle du forgeron dans la société touarègue." In *Métallurgies
africaines: Nouvelles contributions,* edited by Nicole Echard, 237-51.
Mémoires de la Société des Africanistes 9. Paris: Société des Africanistes.
1993   *Touaregs nigériens: Unité culturelle et diversité régionale d'un peuple
pasteur.* 2d ed. Paris: L'Harmattan.
2001   "Germaine Dieterlen et les bijoux touaregs." *Journal des Africanistes*
71, no. 1: 63-68.

Biebuyck, Daniel, and Nelly Van den Abbeele
1984   *The Power of Headdresses: A Cross-Cultural Study of Forms and
Functions.* Brussels: Tendi.

Bonte, Pierre
1976   "Structure de classe et structures sociales chez les Kel Gress." *Revue
de l'Occident musulman et de la Méditerranée,* no. 21: 141-62.

Boucher, Jean-François
1982   *Les insignes sahariens.* Bobigny: SOGICO.

Briggs, Lloyd Cabot
1965   "European Blades in Tuareg Swords and Daggers." *Journal of the
Arms and Armour Society* 5, no. 2 (June): 37-95.

Camps-Fabrer, Henriette
1990   *Bijoux berbères d'Algérie.* Aix-en-Provence: Edisud.

Casajus, Dominique
1987a   "Crafts and Ceremonies: The *Inadan* in Tuareg Society." In *The Other
Nomads: Peripatetic Minorities in Cross-Cultural Perspective,* edited
by Aparna Rao, 291-310. Kölner ethnologische Mitteilungen 8.
Cologne: Böhlau.
1987b   *La tente dans la solitude: La société et les morts chez les Touaregs Kel
Ferwan.* New York: Cambridge University Press; Paris: Editions de
la Maison des sciences de l'homme.
1989   "Sur l'argot des forgerons touaregs." *Awal: Cahiers d'études berbères,*
no. 5.

Castelli Gattinara, Gian Carlo
1992   *I Tuareg attraverso la loro poesia orale.* Rome: Consiglio nazionale
delle ricerche.

Claudot-Hawad, Hélène
1993   *Les Touaregs: Portrait en fragments.* Aix-en-Provence: Edisud.

Clifford, James
1988   *The Predicament of Culture: Twentieth-Century Ethnography, Literature, and Art.* Cambridge, Mass.: Harvard University Press.

Cole, Herbert M.
1982   *Mbari: Art and Life among the Owerri Igbo.* Bloomington: Indiana
University Press.

Creyaufmüller, W.
1983   "Agades Cross Pendants: Structural Components and Their Modifications." Part 1. *Ornament* 7, no. 2: 16-21, 60-61.
1984   "Agades Cross Pendants: Structural Components and Their Modifications." Part 2. *Ornament* 7, no. 3: 37-39.

Dayak, Mano
1992   *Touareg: La tragedie.* Paris: Editions Jean-Claude Lattes.

D'Azevedo, Warren
1973   *The Traditional Artist in African Societies.* Bloomington: Indiana
University Press.

Dieterlen, Germaine, and Ziedonis Ligers
1972   "Contribution à l'étude des bijoux touareg." *Journal de la Société des
Africanistes* 42, no. 1: 29-53.

Drewel, Henry John, and John Pemberton with Rowland Abiodun
1989   *Yoruba: Nine Centuries of African Art and Thought.* New York: Harry
N. Abrams.

Drouin, Jeannine
1982   "Lexique anthropomorphe et métaphorique de la selle de chameau en
touareg." *Production pastorale et société,* no. 11 (autumn): 89-96.

Dudot, B.
1955   "Notes sur la croix d'Agadès." *Notes africaines* 68: 106-8.

Durou, Jean-Marc, and Marc de Gouvenain
1997   *Le grand rêve saharien*. Arles: Actes Sud.

Duveyrier, M. Henri
1864   *Exploration du Sahara: Les Touareg du nord*. Paris: Challamel Aîné.
[1864] 1973   *Les Touareg du nord: Exploration du Sahara*. Paris: Challamel Aîné. Reprint, Nendeln: Kraus.

Echard, Nicole
1992   "A Propos de la métallurgie: Systèmes, technique, organisation sociale et histoire." In Edmond Bernus and Nicole Échard, *La région d'In Gall-Tegidda-n-Tesemt: Programme archéologique d'urgence, 1977-1981*. Études nigériennes 52. Niamey: Institut de recherches en sciences humaines.

Eicher, Joanne, ed.
1995   *Dress and Ethnicity: Change across Space and Time*. Oxford: Berg.

Eudel, Paul
1902   *L'orfèvrerie algérienne et tunisienne*. Algiers: Adolphe Jourdan.

Fischer, Eberhard, and Hans Himmelheber
1984   *The Arts of the Dan in West Africa*. Zurich: Museum Rietberg.

Foley, H.
1930   "Moeurs et médecine des Touaregs de l'Ahaggar." *Archives de l'Institut Pasteur d'Algérie* 8: 165-287.

Foucauld, Charles de
1925   *Poésies touarègues: Dialecte de l'Ahaggar*. Vol. 1. Paris: Ernest Leroux.
1930   *Poésies touarègues: Dialecte de l'Ahaggar*. Vol. 2. Paris: Ernest Leroux.
1940   *Dictionnaire abrégé touareg-français des noms propres: Dialecte de l'Ahaggar*. Paris: Larousse.
1951-52   *Dictionnaire touareg-français: Dialecte de l'Ahaggar*. 4 vols. Paris: Imprimerie nationale.

Foureau, F.
1905   *Documents scientifiques de la Mission saharienne (Mission Foureau-Lamy)*. Paris. Masson.

Frank, Barbara E.
1988   "Mande Leatherworking: A Study of Style, Technology, and Identity." Ph.D. diss., Indiana University.

Gabus, Jean
1958   *Au Sahara: Arts et symboles*. Neuchâtel: La Baconnière.
1971   *Les Touaregs*. Neuchâtel: Musée d'ethnographie.
1982   *Sahara: Bijoux et techniques*. Neuchâtel: La Baconnière.

Galand-Pernet, Paulette
1978   "Images et image de la femme dans les *Poésies touarègues de l'Ahaggar*." *Littérature orale arabo-berbère* 9: 5-52.

Gardi, René
1969   *African Crafts and Craftsmen*. Translated by Sigrid MacCrae. New York: Van Nostrand Reinhold.
1970   *Sahara*. Bern: Kummerly and Frey.

Gast, Marceau
1962   "Mission ethnographique en Ahaggar (mai 1961)." *Bulletin de Liaison saharienne* 13, no. 46: 140-69.

Ghubayd agg-Alawjeli
1975   *Histoire des Kel-Denneg avant l'arrivée des Français*. Edited by Karl-G. Prasse. Copenhagen: Akademisk Forlag.

Goldstein-Gidoni, Ofra
1999   "Komono and the Construction of Gendered and Cultural Identities." *Ethnology* 38, no. 4: 351-71.

Göttler, Gerhard
1989   *Die Tuareg: Kulturelle Einheit und regionale Vielfalt eines Hirtenvolkes*. Cologne: DuMont.

Gouletquer, Pierre
1992   "Bijoux d'Agadez et In Gall." *Journal des Africanistes* 62, no. 2: 115-29.

Houston Chronicle
1998   "Fashion Blitz in Sahara Desert Goes aagainst the Grain of Niger." November 14, A22.

Hureiki, Jacques
2003   *Essai sur les origines des Touaregs: Herméneutique culturelle des Touaregs de la région de Tombouctou*. Paris: Karthala.

Joseph, Nathan
1986   *Uniforms and Nonuniforms: Communication through Clothing*. Westport, Conn.: Greenwood.

Keenan, Jeremy
2004   *The Lesser Gods of the Sahara: Social Change and Contested Terrain amongst the Tuareg of Algeria*. London: Frank Cass.

Kuper, Hilda
1973   "Costume and Identity." *Comparative Studies in Society and History* 15: 348-67.

Lhote, Henri
1955   *Les Touaregs du Hoggar*. 2d ed. Paris: Payot.
1959   *The Search for the Tassili Frescoes: The Story of the Prehistoric Rock-Paintings of the Sahara*. New York: Dutton.
1984   *Les Touaregs du Hoggar*. Paris: Armand Colin.

Liu, R.
1977   "T'alhakimt (Talhatana), a Tuareg Ornament: Its Origins, Derivatives, Copies, and Distribution." *Bead Journal* 3, no. 2: 18-22.

Loughran, Kristyne S.
1995   *Art from the Forge*. Washington D.C.: National Museum of African Art.
1996   "Tuareg Jewelry: Continuity and Change." Ph.D. diss., Indiana University.

Lynch, Annette
1999   *Dress, Gender, and Cultural Change*. New York: Berg.

Lyon, G. F.
1821   *A Narrative of Travels in Northern Africa in the Years 1818, 19, and 20*. London: John Murray.

Mauny, Raymond
1954   "Une énigme non résolue: Origine et symbolique de la croix d'Agadès." *Notes africaines*, no. 63 (July): 70-79.

McNaughton, Patrick
1988   *The Mande Blacksmith: Knowledge, Power, and Art in West Africa*. Bloomington: Indiana University Press.

Mickelsen, Nancy R.
1976   "Tuareg Jewelry." *African Arts* 9, no. 2 (January): 16-19.

Milburn, Mark
1980   "The Rape of the Agadez Cross." *Almogaren* 9/10: 135-54.

Morel, M. H.
1943   "Essai sur l'épée des Touareg de l'Ahaggar (*takouba*)." *Travaux de l'Institut de recherches sahariennes* 2: 121-68.

Murphy, Robert F.
1964   "Social Distance and the Veil." *American Anthropologist* 66: 1257-74.
1967   "Tuareg Kinship." *American Anthropologist* 69: 163-70.

Nicolaisen, Ida, and Johannes Nicolaisen
1997   *The Pastoral Tuareg: Ecology, Culture, and Society.* Carlsberg Foundation's Nomad Research Project. Copenhagen: Rhodos International Science and Art Publishers.

Nicolaisen, Johannes
1961   "Essai sur la religion et la magie touarègues." *Folk* 3: 113-62.
1963   *Ecology and Culture of the Pastoral Tuareg: With Particular Reference to the Tuareg of Ahaggar and Ayr.* Copenhagen: National Museum.

Nicolas, Francis
1939   "Notes sur la société et l'état chez les Twareg du Dinnik (Iullemmeden de l'Est)." *Bulletin de l'Ifan* 1: 579-86.
1950   *Tamesna: Les Ioullemmeden de l'Est, ou Touâreg "Kel Dinnîk," cercle de T'àwa, colonie du Niger.* Paris: Imprimerie nationale.

Palmer, H. R.
1936   "Some Touareg Ornaments." *Man* 36: 167.

Prasse, Karl-G.
1972   *Manuel de grammaire touarègue.* Cophenagen: Editions de l'Université de Copenhague.
2003   *Dictionnaire touareg-français (Niger)=Tamazeq-Tafranist (Niger) alqamus.* Copenhagen: Museum Tusculanum.

Rasmussen, Susan
1987   "The Use and Abuse of 'Natural' Symbols: Jewelry and Gender Typifications in Tuareg Ritual and Cosmology." Paper presented at the thirtieth Annual Meeting of the African Studies Association, November.
1991   "Veiled Self, Transparent Meanings: Tuareg Headdress as Social Expression." *Ethnology* 30, no. 2: 101-17.
1994   "The 'Head Dance,' Contested Self, and Art as a Balancing Act in Tuareg Spirit Possession." *Africa* 64, no. 1: 74-98.
1995   *Spirit Possession and Personhood among the Kel Ewey Tuareg.* Cambridge: Cambridge University Press.
1997a   "Between Ritual, Theater, and Play: Blacksmith Praise at Tuareg Marriage." *Journal of American Folklore* 110: 3-26.
1997b   *The Poetics and Politics of Tuareg Aging: Life Course and Personal Destiny in Niger.* DeKalb: Northern Illinois University Press.
2001   *Healing in Community: Medicine, Contested Terrains, and Cultural Encounters among the Tuareg.* Westport, Conn.: Bergin and Garvey.

Reygasse, Maurice
1950   *Monuments funeraires preislamiques de l'Afrique du Nord.* Paris: Arts et Métiers Graphiques.

Rinn, Louis
1889   *Les origines berbères: Etudes linguistiques et ethnologiques de l'Afrique du Nord.* Paris: Arts et Métiers Graphiques.

Rodd, Francis James Rennell
1926   *People of the Veil.* London: Macmillan.

Saenz, Candelario
1980   "Kinship and Social Organisation of the *Inadan*." Paper presented at the roundtable "*Parenté-touarègue*," CNRS, Gif-sur-Yvette, September.

Saint-Exupéry, Antoine de
1929   *Courrier sud.* Paris: Editions Gallimard.

Sieber, Roy
1972   "The Forgotten Arts of Adornment." *Africa Report* (September-October): 29-35.

Steinilber-Oberlin, E.
1934   *Au coeur du Hoggar mysterieux: Les Touareg tels que je les ai vus.* Paris: Editions Pierre Roger.

Stocking, George W., ed.
1985   *Objects and Others: Essays on Museums and Material Culture.* History of Anthropology 3. Madison: University of Wisconsin Press.

Tamzali, Wassyla
1984   *Abzim: Parures et bijoux des femmes d'Algérie.* Paris: Dessain et Tolra.

Thompson, Robert Farris
1974   *African Art in Motion: Icon and Art in the Collection of Katherine Coryton White.* Berkeley: University of California Press.

Urvoy, Y.
1955   "L'art dans le territoire du Niger." *Etudes nigériennes* 2, no. 7: 68.

Vogel, Susan M.
1997   *Baule: African Art, Western Eyes.* New Haven: Yale University Press.

Walentowitz, Saskia
2002   "Partir sans quitter: Rites et gestes autour des déplacements féminins chez les Ineslimen de l'Azawagh." In *Voyager d'un point de vue nomade*, edited by Hélène Claudot-Hawad, 37-53. Paris: Editions Paris-Méditerranée de l'IREMAM.

Weiner, Annette B., and Jane Schneider, eds.
1989   *Cloth and Human Experience.* Washington, D.C.: Smithsonian Institution.

Zeltner, Frantz de
1914   "Les Touareg du Sud." *Journal of the Royal Anthropological Institute* 44: 351-75.

INDEX

Islamic, 19-22, 25, 59-60, 70-73, *73*, 145-48, 156, 224, 232-33, *233*, 267, 275*n*18
   jewelry's association with, 167
   poetry's treatment of, 40
religious teachers. *See ineslemen*
resistance movement, 27, 62-63, 231, 234
   artisanship influences of, 66
   causation of, 223-24
   clothing influenced by, 153, 154
   music influences of, 131-32
   peace treaties and, 227
   Tuareg fighter in, 65, *65*
rezzu (the raid), 31
ring(s), 169, 202-3
   A l'Atelier guild, *262*, 263
   man's, 206, *206*
   tisek, 175, *175*, 206, *206*
rituals
   adanay (fattening), 149
   coming of age, 83, 146, 147-48, 150-51, 179, 203, 257
   cross of Agadez, 257
   knife, 91
   naming, 185, *185*
   spirit possession, 125-26, 151
   sword, 83, 179, 203
   tagulmust, 146, 150-51
   tende, 48-50, *49*, *85*, 118, *118*, *123*, 123-26, *127*
   women's headdress, 147-48
rock paintings, 19, *20-21*, 54
Rodd, Francis James Rennell, 54, 256
Rosabelor, 188

saddles. *See* camel saddles
Saenz, Candelario, 75
Sahara Desert, Northern Africa, *28-29*
   development of, 214, 223
   history of, 28
Saidi, Al Hassan, 221
   clothing of, 154, *154*
   commercial ventures by, 224-26, 229, 233-36
   demonstrating silverwork, 229, *229*
   international travel by, 225, 229
   jewelry motifs and, *222*, 222-23
Saidi, Atyi, 217, *217*
Saidi, Chemo, 38, *38*, 144, *144*, 216
   in embroidered blouse, 221, *221*
   leatherwork by, 220
Saidi, El Faki, 221
   clothing of, 154, *154*
   commercial ventures by, 233, 235
Saidi, Gonda, 216, 217, *217*, 221
   commercial ventures by, 224-26, 233-34
Saidi, Ousmane (Mania), 221, *225*
   clothing of, 154, *154*
   commercial ventures by, 228-29, 231-36
   cross forms made by, 173, *173*
   gold work by, 231-32
   international travel by, 225, 229
   jewelry motifs and, *222*, 222-23
   necklace made by, 230, *230*
Saidi, Salah, 216, 217, *217*
   amulet made by, 238, *239*
   apprenticeship by, 220-21
   commercial ventures by, 224-26, 231, 233-35

earrings designed by, 189, *189*, 192, *192*
   examining silver jewelry, 221, *221*
   gold work by, 218, *218*, 230, *230*
   jewelry motifs and, *222*, 222-23
   on motorbike, 226, *226*
   workshop poster of, 233, *233*
Saint-Exupéry, Antoine de, 246
Salon International Artisinat de Ouagadougou, 224
salt
   block for, 100, *100*
   caravans yielding, 27, *45*, 45-47, *46*
   ponds of, 47, *47*
salt, pepper shakers and tray, 225, *225*
Samu, Darou, 259
sandals (*tadakat*), 145, *145*
Saudi Arabia, 188. *See also* Arabs
   coins of, 189, 190, 231
scarves, 265, *265*
schools, 152, 156, 221
   funding of, 232
   girls enrolled in, 153
   Koranic, 216, 232
seknes inadan (animal's back), 86
September 11, 2001, 232-33, 234-36
shields (*agher*), 112-13, 113
silversmith(s), 229, *229*
   catalog of designs by, 202, *202*
   difficulties of, 239
   mixing of metals by, 231
   motif designs for, *222*, 222-23
   payment to, 190
   processes used by, 169, 194, 202, *202*
   resource material for, 184-85, 231
   tools of, 220, 231
singing. *See* vocal music
slaves (*iklan*), 22-23. *See also* vassals
   clothing of, 149
   freedom of, 27, 152
   jewelry of, 183
smiths. *See also* inadan
   black, *61*, 77-78
   gold, 189, 190, *218*, 218-20, *230*, 230-32
   leather, 19, 58, *58*, *76*, 76-78, 115, *115*, 217, *217*, 220, *220*, 242-43, *243*
   material resources for, 19, 68, 77-78, 184-85, 220, 231
   silver, 169, 184-85, 190, 194, 202, 220, *222*, 222-23, 229, *229*, 231, 239
   women (*tinadan*), 19, *30*, 31, 77-78, 91, 115, 144, *144*, 213, 220, 241, 274*n*8
   wood, 77-78
soapstone carvings, 68, *68*, 228
spears (*allagh*), 112-13, 113
spirit possession, 125-26, 151
spoons (*tesukalt*), 91, 98, *98*, 99, *99*
Sudan, 142
sugar hammers (*tefedist*), 135, *136-37*, 137
sugar shears (*temoda ton essukor*), 134, 135, *135*, 137, *137*
Sutedja, Wayan, 261
swords (*takuba*)
   classification of, 82
   components of, 84, 91
   dance using, 85, *85*
   origins of, 84
   rituals for, 83, 179, 203
   with sheaths, *74*, 75, 78, *78*, 82-84, *83*, 114, *114*, 131, 179, 203
   symbolism of, 83, 84, 179

learning process for, 120
love songs as, 119-20
mouth play (*belluwel*), 129-30
throat play (*akhaguwwen*), 130
traditional epic, 119

Wadjo, Atenhanana, 254
wallets
    enafad, 158, *159-60*, 161
    enefel n' tan 'tot, 158, *159-60*, 161
    ettabu, 161, *161*
    tarallabt, 161, *161*
weapons. *See also* knife(ves); swords
    daggers, 114-15, *114-15*
    knives, 91, 114, *114*, 248, *248*
    rifles, 131
    shields, *112-13*, 113
    spears, *112-13*, 113
    swords, *74*, 75, 78, *78*, 82-85, *83*, *85*, 91, 114, *114*, 131, 179, 203
weddings
    bridewealth (*taggalt*) and, 182, 206, 207
    dance at, 187, *187*
    dress associated with, 141, *141*, *166*, 167, 179, *179*
    henna decoration for, 167
    jewelry associated with, *166*, 167, 171, 172, *172*, 175, 179, *179*, 182, 200, *200*, 206, *206*, 207, *207*
    organization of, 25
    ornaments (*tisakhsar*) for, 182
    tende at, *123*, 123-24
windscreens, 91, *92*, 93
Wolof and Malimbe jewelers, 261
women. *See also tinadan* (women smiths)
    aesthetic code for, 121
    artisans, 144, *144*
    coming of age rituals for, 147-48
    fashion trends influenced by, 188
    homemaking roles of, 91
    ideal traits of, 25, 149, 158
    jewelry's generational transitions in, 179-82
    music performance by, 117-19, 121-30
    poetry references to, 36-41, 44
    pricing disparities and, 220, 241, 274n8
    religious restriction of, 146
    saddles for, *80*, 80-81
woodworkers, 77-78
World Bank, 154

Yahaya, Aboubacar (Adi), 207

CONTRIBUTORS

Edmond Bernus (1929-2004) was the emeritus director of research at the Institut de recherche pour le développement (IRD, formerly ORSTOM). Commencing his research in Africa in 1954, he focused upon Guinea and, somewhat later, Côte d'Ivoire. His study of the Tuareg of Niger, however, initially undertaken in 1965, remained a consuming passion for the remainder of his life. Bernus was the author of numerous scholarly publications on the pastoral Tuareg, notably *Touaregs nigériens: Unité culturelle et diversité régionale d'un peuple pasteur* (1981). He contributed as well to many publications about the Sahara and the Tuareg aimed at a more general audience.

François Borel is adjunct curator at the Musée d'ethnographie, Neuchâtel, Switzerland, where he is in charge of the musical instrument collections, the African Sahel collections, and the sound archives. In addition he teaches ethnomusicology at the Institut d'ethnologie at the Université de Neuchâtel. His research focus is the music of Niger and particularly that of the Tuareg.

Jean-Yves Brizot is an adventure tour guide in Algeria, Libya, and Niger. In the mid-1990s he began a jewelry guild with several Tuareg *inadan* in Agadez, Niger. Called "A l'Atelier," the guild produced high-quality silver jewelry for Hermès, Paris, and for American designer Alison Mezey.

Gian Carlo Castelli Gattinara is professor emeritus of cultural anthropology at the Università "G. d'Annunzio," Chieti, Italy. He has conducted extensive fieldwork focusing on the structure and philosophy of nomadic societies in Afghanistan, Syria, Tunisia, Mauritania, Lesotho, and Niger and has published extensively on each of these regions. His volume *I Tuareg* (The Tuareg) was published in 1992.

Mohamed ag Ewangaye comes from a Tuareg *inadan* family and lived a nomadic existence until he was fourteen. In 1989, while still in his early twenties, he experienced firsthand the turmoil engendered by the negotiated reintegration of the Tuareg into the mainstream of economic and political life in Niger. In response to the disaster that ensued in 1990, Ewangaye became a political activist, along with Mano Dayak, Rhissa ag Boula, and others. Having had the benefit of a university education, Ewangaye decided that it was his ancestral right and responsibility to correct the writings of outsiders on the Tuareg and to explain their true story to the world. He has therefore coupled his formal instruction with his traditional Tuareg education to help his people rewrite their history and engage in the global debate among cultures and civilizations.

Kristyne Loughran completed her doctorate in art history in 1996 at the University of Indiana at Bloomington. She conducted eighteen months of field research in Niamey, Niger, during which she focused on Tuareg jewelry manufacture and style. She has published several articles on jewelry and fashion in Africa and continues to carry out research on the Tuareg.

Susan Rasmussen is a professor of anthropology at the University of Houston in Texas. She first became acquainted with the Tuareg as a Peace Corps volunteer in Agadez, Niger, in 1974 and has continued to conduct extensive fieldwork in this area. Although much of her research relates to dress, she has also closely examined the healing rituals practiced by Tuareg women. Her publications include a number of articles and three books on Tuareg culture in Niger and Mali and the Tuareg Diaspora in Europe and America.

Thomas K. Seligman is the John & Jill Freidenrich Director of the Cantor Arts Center at Stanford University. After completing work as a Peace Corps volunteer in Liberia in 1971, he began conducting research among the *inadan* of the Kel Ewey in Agadez, Niger, working most closely with the Oumba and Ouhoulou families. He has curated numerous exhibitions, authored several articles and catalogs, and continues to do field research in Niger and Mali.